CENTURY

THE ROMAN EMPIRE'S INCREDIBLE
FIRST HUNDRED YEARS

*The story of the people of the first-century Roman
Empire who created the western world's religious,
cultural and political foundations.*

Warren Steck

◆ FriesenPress

Suite 300 - 990 Fort St
Victoria, BC, V8V 3K2
Canada

www.friesenpress.com

ISBN
978-1-5255-2904-7 (Hardcover)
978-1-5255-2905-4 (Paperback)
978-1-5255-2906-1 (eBook)

1. History, Historiography

Distributed to the trade by The Ingram Book Company

Table of Contents

Preface

This is the story of the first century, written as a "documentary novel" based on ancient records that have come down to us from that time. The background of the story is factual, researched history of people who really existed and of events that really happened. The foreground stories -- of the remarkable Herodian family and of the earliest days of Christianity -- are also mostly fact, but in part speculation and in smaller part fiction, all woven around that background. Thus, CENTURY is essentially non-fiction with an overlay of speculation, story-telling and fictional elements. All but four of the characters in this book are real, historical individuals.

Quotations from ancient sources come from the *New English Bible New Testament* translation (1961) or from J. B. Phillips' *The New Testament in Modern English* (1960); with minor phrasing amendments, from the old William Whiston translation (1737) of the *Complete Works of Flavius Josephus*; from the J. C. Yardley translation (2008) of Cornelius Tacitus' *Annals* and the Church & Brodribb edition (1999) of Tacitus' *Histories*; from the Wordsworth edition (1997) of Suetonius' *Lives of the Twelve Caesars*; from the still-standard 1897 translations of the Anti-Nicene Fathers series; and from the abridged translation (1989) of Eusebius' *The History of the Church* by G. A. Williamson and Andrew Louth. These and other sources are detailed in the Bibliography.

I am indebted to the University of Victoria (Canada) and the University of Saskatchewan for generous library research privileges; to David Ford, Prof. Eric Sager, Dr. Richard Buryan and The Rev. John Macquarrie for useful and thought-provoking discussions; to Prof. Anthony Barrett (University of British Columbia) for detailed chronological information on imperial men and women; to the staff at FriesenPress for much-needed guidance and skill in moving the book through the publication process;

and to my wife Jean Gordon whose patience and forbearance over the years of CENTURY's creation have been truly remarkable.

Warren Steck
Victoria, Canada
May 2018

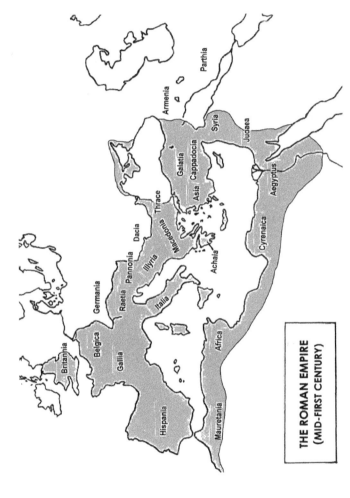

Map of the Roman Empire in the first century AD

I

EMPIRE

FROM REPUBLIC TO EMPIRE

On the first day of January in the 754th Roman year since the founding of the City, the emperor Caesar Augustus, with the priests of the Colleges and the two new Consuls, all accompanied by twelve lictors and a body of German guardsmen, ceremonially closed the great bronze doors of the ancient Temple of Janus in central Rome. That act signified peace throughout the empire, a rare condition. Augustus and his retinue were quite unaware that the day would come to be known to later ages as the first day of the First Century. All that Augustus was keenly aware of was the pain.

Augustus was no longer young. At 66, he was an old man by the standards of the times. As he climbed the steps of the temple he felt the customary pain in his knees, and every night his back ached. The first day of the year was especially trying as it brought much ceremonial: the Janus Temple rites; the renewal of the military oaths to the emperor as Commander-in-Chief; the greeting of the new Consuls at the Senate House; and then supper with eminent guests. He longed for evening when he could fling off his heavy woollen toga – the formal wear of the Romans – enjoy a warm bath and a massage, read the day's despatches -- and sleep. His body-servant Eumenides (he was actually a slave) knew his master's every aching point and every weary muscle. As Augustus relaxed under the massage, he murmured, "Why do people want to be kings or princes or commanders? Do they realize what unrelenting, thankless, killing work it is?" Augustus knew it well. He had been emperor for thirty years and would survive the grind for another fourteen. His health had never been good but the doctors kept him going – and by force of will he kept himself going.

He had not come to the emperorship easily, for that office had no predecessors – he himself had created the imperial institution and was the first occupant of what would soon become known as "the throne of the Caesars". The emperor was born in 62 BC as Caesar Octavianus; Caesar was the family name. His great-uncle was Caius Julius Caesar -- the Julius Caesar of fame who conquered Gaul in the 50s BC and ruled Rome as dictator from 49 to 44 BC, when he was assassinated in the Senate House on the Ides of March. The elder Caesar had adopted young Octavianus as his son and made him his heir. To universal surprise, in 44 BC the teenager boldly claimed that inheritance and vowed revenge on his adoptive father's killers. What followed were thirteen years of large-scale civil war which degenerated into a free-for-all struggle for control of the empire. First, Caesar's assassins Cassius and Brutus were eliminated in a big battle at Pharsalus in northern Greece. Then Octavianus and the son of old General Pompey fell out and fought, and at last in 31 BC the grand alliance of Octavianus' erstwhile partner General Mark Antony and Queen Cleopatra of Egypt was destroyed in a great sea-battle off Actium in Greece. The General and his Egyptian Queen both committed suicide. By 30 BC only Octavianus was left. He not only received his family inheritance, he received the uncontested control of the whole vast Roman state. Over the years which followed he founded the Roman empire and gently buried the five-hundred-year-old Roman republic.

Octavianus was 33 when he officially became the Head of State in 27 BC, by assent of the Roman Senate and People. He took new titles "Princeps" ("First Citizen") and "Augustus" but he carefully avoided the title "Imperator" – commander -- with its new sense of "Emperor", and also the old Roman office of "Dictator". He laid down a firm foundation; Octavianus was the first of a 1500-year-long line of Roman and Byzantine Emperors, and was the man who skilfully, quietly guided the Roman state's transition from the ancient, broken-down Roman Republic to the brassy new Roman Empire.

The Republic was already ancient in Augustus' time. According to Roman tradition, the city of Rome had been founded in 753 BC and for a time it was ruled by Etruscan kings. Those kings were overthrown in 509 BC and an aristocratic Republic was inaugurated, governed by a pair of chief executives (the Consuls) and a council of elders called the Senate. From such humble beginnings, this city-state grew in the next quarter-millennium to control all of central Italy; and it kept on expanding. One by one the neighbouring tribes, then the whole Etruscan confederacy, and finally the far-flung Carthaginian empire were conquered by the militaristic Romans. By the first century BC this expansion had created a huge new empire. In Augustus' time near the end of that century, the Roman-ruled lands already stretched from the North Sea southward to the Sahara Desert, and from Portugal east to the Red Sea and the Arabian Desert, encompassing perhaps seventy million inhabitants. These inhabitants possessed diverse cultures and civilizations, for until the Roman conquests they had lived in independent kingdoms. Italy was the Roman homeland, but even there, folk memories remained alive of the many different peoples who had lived there independently alongside the Romans before they lived under the Romans. There were Gauls in the Po Valley, Etruscans to the north of Rome, Samnites, Sabines, Latins, Oscans, Greeks in the south of the peninsula, and even remnants of Carthaginian settlements on Sicily. But to the Romans of the empire, Italy was long unified and was "home". The south of France and all of Spain and Portugal came under Roman rule in the 100s BC. Western North Africa, parts of the Balkans and Turkey were also conquered then. France, Belgium and parts of Germany were all conquered by Julius Caesar in the 50s BC; while Syria, Palestine, Egypt and parts of North Africa were forcibly brought into the empire by Gnaeus Pompey in the

60s BC, turning the whole Mediterranean into a "Roman lake". Soon the Black Sea and Red Sea too were dominated by Rome. In 30 BC Egypt fell to the Romans.

So, Rome was an empire in its operations well before it became a monarchical empire in theory. Caesar Augustus officially presided over it from 27 BC to AD 14. His phenomenal career was marked by brilliant strategic moves, utter ruthlessness, brazen hypocrisy (mixed with powerful principles), military ability, political genius, unexpectedly long life, and the luck of the gods. He was well-remembered as the great Founder and even as a god by later Romans, and his hard-won "Roman Peace" lasted – though with significant interruptions – for almost three centuries.

The first century AD had immediate roots in the first century BC. In 100 BC, Alexander the Great had been dead for over two hundred years and his vast empire in the east, stretching from Greece all the way to Afghanistan and India, had been fought over and divided up among the several generals who were his successors. That had created a vast multi-state Greek-culture area in the Middle East. In the western part of the Mediterranean, the Roman Republic, under the rule of its Senate, was well on its way to forging its own empire based on the conquest of states around its existing territories in Italy. In 202 BC the Romans scored a hard-fought victory over Hannibal and the Carthaginian empire, centred in present-day Tunisia. That twenty-year war was the making of Rome – and the making of Roman militarism. Somewhat like the British Empire of the nineteenth century, the Roman realm seemed to invite – or create -- opportunities for its own further expansion. The expansion did not unfold in any deeply premeditated way or according to any overall plan. It happened mostly through chance and through the unlovely qualities of aggressiveness and greed of the militaristic old Republic. For the Romans were militarists, and long remained so. One after another, the peoples of North Africa, western Europe and the Greek kingdoms of the eastern Mediterranean fell prey to Roman might driven by Roman politics, an increasingly dysfunctional Senate, Roman cupidity and the Romans' inability to tolerate rivals.

The Roman Republic around 509 BC was just a small town with farms round-about; one could walk easily in a morning from its territories to those of neighbouring little statelets. But little Rome even then could not get along with its neighbours. One after another, those neighbours fought with Rome – and lost. By 250 BC Rome ruled most of Italy, its neighbours having been absorbed into the fabric of "joint communities" in which the defeated peoples gained Roman status. Rome's greatest rival was beyond Italy: the Carthaginian empire, based across the Mediterranean Sea on the North African coast. After two colossal wars Carthage finally went down to defeat in 202 BC. But it was a near thing. So, for good measure, the Romans provoked a third war and totally erased the city of Carthage in 146 BC. The Romans by then had possession of parts of Spain which had long been part of the Carthaginian empire, and they had solidified their grip on all the main islands of the western Mediterranean: Sicily, Sardinia, Corsica and the Balearics.

The empire kept expanding by naked conquest. The pivotal year was 146 BC -- the year that Carthage was obliterated and Roman armies marched east to "liberate" Greece and to begin picking off the surrounding Hellenistic kingdoms. Those eastern kingdoms were the remains of Alexander the Great's empire. Alexander's successors were never able to put his empire back together, but they did manage to spawn numerous mutually hostile kingdoms which enjoyed considerable power and glory: Hellenistic Egypt; the Seleucid Empire of Syria originally extending east to India; a few small Greek-Macedonian kingdoms in the Balkans; and a cluster of small but wealthy kingdoms in Asia Minor (the western part of present-day Turkey). Rome managed to take over all of these states. Asia Minor (Turkey) was next added piecemeal; it was the turn of Syria and Palestine in the 60s BC when General Gnaeus Pompey marched his armies through the eastern Mediterranean lands. The Romans proved militarily invincible on all fronts. Their empire coalesced around the Mediterranean Sea. The Romans considered it their "Inner Sea" and used it as the maritime connector which bound the empire together.

But conquest did not bring immediate peace or prosperity, for the Roman leaders fell out among themselves so that the half-century from 82 to 30 BC saw off-again, on-again civil war among senatorial factions and Roman warlords: Marius, Sulla, Julius Caesar, Lepidus, Brutus, Cassius, Pompey and his son, Crassus, Mark Antony, Octavianus, and others. The contenders fought for no less than total one-man control of the powerful and now-wealthy Roman state.

In practice the Roman Republic was governed by a Senate comprising the most important citizens. The Roman "logo" was an eagle with the letters SPQR -- meaning "Senatus Populusque Romanus": the Roman Senate and People. The Republic still had, as of old, as its leading officers a pair of elected **Consuls** who served annual terms as king-like joint "chief magistrates". There were large numbers of other public offices too, all typically thought of as magistracies. The **tribunes'** main job – basically – was to defend the lower classes from the depredations of the powerful; the tribunes' persons were sacrosanct and they could veto legislation. There were many **quaestors** involved in lawmaking, public administration and finance. Quaestors were lower-level magistrates who nonetheless wielded a lot of power. **Aediles** were the next level up; they managed public works and public events; and a bewildering array of other business. **Praetors** wielded even more power. They originally had managed or audited the public purse. Their duties became more extensive and prestigious by the first century AD, and re-focused on the administration of justice. These various **magistrates** not only heard legal cases but could in some circumstances propound new laws. **Lictors** carried the axe-and-rods symbols of public power in front of officials. Lower officials got only one lictor or none at all; higher officials got more, and the Consuls and later the emperors had twelve. Two state **censors** oversaw census-taking and judicial reviews. A handful of ongoing Committees (or Assemblies) had existed for hundreds of years. The Comitia Curiata was the oldest such group. To it had been added over the centuries a Comitia Plebis representing the common people, and a tribal Comitia Centuriata. The Senate under the republic, and increasingly the emperor in the times of the empire, could appoint representatives with such titles as **prefect, procurator, legate, propraetor** and so forth, to oversee certain regions of the empire or to exercise specified functions. Each title had its own nuanced meaning as to powers delegated. The state was concerned, indeed obsessed, with laws, much as modern states are. However, enforcement was haphazard, amateurish and usually in response to complaints. In the courts, officers such as the **evocatus** (bailiff) brought prisoners to the trial, there to be defended by an amateur **advocatus** (defense lawyer) before a **magistratus** (judge) who was likely also an amateur in law. And there were a great many other judicial offices, each with its title. Besides all these civil officials – mostly drawn from rich senatorial families during the Republic -- were great generals (**imperatores, legati**) commanding the active military forces. These were almost always drawn from the younger senatorial class, the appointments being part of a career system (the **cursus honorum**) by which senators filled a series of posts of ever-increasing responsibility and honour. Command of an army sometimes capped an already illustrious career; but often bright young sons of senators were put in charge of armies. This implies a dynamic move-about career of increasing honour and influence. A young senator might begin as an aedile or a tribune, and over the years gain experience in most of the state offices, ending up in the top job of Consul – or as an army commander or a provincial governor overseas. At the beginning of the first century, the title "imperator" (Commander-in-Chief; "Emperor") at last became the sole prerogative of one man, and the consulate became more and more an honorary one-year appointment. Indeed, the busy men who were chosen as Consuls generally served only for a few weeks and then the workload was taken over by a "suffect Consul" for the remainder of the year.

Curiously, there was nothing in the system which we would recognize as a bureaucracy. In fact the untidy governance system of ancient republican Rome, designed for a small city-state, was not efficient, and so for times of real crisis, the old Republic had evolved an office of **dictator**, in which post one man could be mandated to rule by decree for six months.

But after massive use, overuse and abuse during the wars of the first century BC, that office disappeared in the empire, being superseded by the ever-growing powers of the emperors.

Although the Roman military organization was highly effective, the political Republic as a whole was a ramshackle affair, run by-guess and by-gosh by a closed-shop club of rich old families who dominated the Senate. The Senate did not actually rule the empire, but it was an indispensable element in the government of the realm. One had to be a millionaire to qualify for the senatorial class; good family connections also mattered. Then you might be appointed to the Senate. This ancient institution – the name Senate connotes Elders -- had worked tolerably well when Rome was just a city-state but as the imperial realm grew, the limitations of a parochial Rome-based Senate became all too clear. The Senate was a club of amateurs, largely inexperienced at ruling foreigners, and much more interested in serving its own members than in serving subjects or the as-yet shadowy concept of "the state". Moreover, the Senate proved morally wanting and hopelessly Rome-centred. The Senate itself as an institution grew too large to manage, and too many of its members lacked the training and competence (not to say the probity, honesty and drive) to govern a large state. As the Roman territories expanded and the vast booty of conquests flowed into Rome, the Senate was enlarged eventually to 1000, and membership in the Senate became a ticket to immense wealth and influence, to be gained by fair means or – more often -- otherwise. It still didn't work. In the early empire its membership was pared back to just 300 men (and no women). Worse still, the Consuls and Senate lacked a proper supporting bureaucracy of the kind essential for managing any empire. Senators sent abroad as provincial governors were expected to use a mixture of local talent, local elites and a small core of auxiliary troops to carry out their missions. That never worked very well. Last but by no means least, most Roman senators in the period before Augustus were ruthlessly venal. The first century BC saw the rise of massive corruption as the wealth of a plundered world flowed into Roman pockets. Power and wealth were everyone's aim, and few limits were set on the means of obtaining them. This condition became even more prevalent in the first century AD, when murder, frame-ups, bribery, treachery, assassination, denunciations, blackmail, blatant law-breaking and brute force became the tools of the trade for everyone in power -- or wanting to be in power. The imperial households were hotbeds of scheming, skulduggery and deal-making. Even the emperors, who had already reached the pinnacle of the system, were not above initiating frame-ups to profit by confiscations of great estates.

The Roman conquests of the late second century BC and the deplorable economic condition of most ordinary people of the late Republic generated an internal crisis in 120 BC.

The issue was land reform. The rich had cornered most of Italy's land. The farming population and in particular the Italian veterans of the wars wanted land of their own to farm, a traditional reward of veterans. When the brother senators Gaius and Tiberius Gracchus proposed sweeping reforms to landholding, they were soon put out of the way by their landowning colleagues – by murder. The Senate split into irreconcilable factions, and in the 80s BC the military weighed in. Blood was spilled. Revenge followed inexorably. The resulting civil wars lasted for fifty years and destroyed the Republic. The warlords, whose military activities were closely geared to their own attainment of unlimited power, were merciless. Julius Caesar was the one exception.

The legacy of the prolonged orgy of violence was disruption of the whole Mediterranean world – its politics, its economy and its cultures. The sacking of great cities such as Carthage, Corinth, Jerusalem and Alexandria, and the subjugation of whole nations threw millions of people upon the slave markets and triggered flights and emigrations almost everywhere. Entire countries were plundered by the Romans or went up in smoke through the crushing costs of continuous, large-scale warfare. In 63 BC Rome's General Pompey marched his armies through the whole eastern Mediterranean, stopping just long enough at Jerusalem to despoil that city and violate its ancient Temple. But Pompey ultimately met his match in Julius Caesar (his former ally) and was brought down and murdered in Egypt. At mid-century in 49 BC, Julius Caesar marched his armies south from just-conquered Gaul into Italy and, crossing the Rubicon River which was the southern limit of his legal authority, he effectively declared war on the Roman Senate itself. He won that war handily and became Dictator. Caesar carried out no massacres (to everyone's surprise) and planned far-reaching reforms, but he only had time to implement the first few of those – changes to land-holding and a thorough-going reform of the calendar. Many senators believed that Caesar intended never to relinquish his dictatorship and that he was scheming to be crowned as a king. So, in the Senate House on 15 March 44 BC, Caesar was murdered by a cabal of zealous young Senators, and the Roman world which had paused for a few years in its strife returned to the battlefields. Young Octavianus eventually came out on top and became Caesar Augustus.

Augustus was utterly ruthless but a consummately shrewd politician, a moderately competent strategist and a skilful re-organizer. Apart from his ruthlessness, he was a devious "George Washington" figure of the Roman Empire and was well-remembered – remaining first in the hearts of his countrymen despite his numerous missteps. He did not seek his main power through the discredited office of Dictator. Instead he accumulated power piecemeal by taking on, one after another, all the major offices of the state and army. His style was not confrontation but rather co-optation. He took great care not to flaunt his power; he wore no crown and had no throne. Instead, he projected the image of being just another senator who happened to be "first among equals". Hence his title of "Princeps" meaning First Citizen. His own spacious house served as his "palace", and he created no "court". In theory and in his rhetoric, Augustus maintained the Roman Republic, but in fact he quietly and very deliberately brought in a new monarchical system. The days of rule by the corrupt, dis-united Senate were gone forever, although the Senate itself was remarkably slow to grasp that reality. Make-believe went on for a further two hundred years. The Senate never showed itself an able body for managing the empire. Prudent Augustus did not press the matter to a conclusion but continued to pretend that the senators were the backbone of the state and that he himself was merely the chief senator. And the senators pretended to believe it, reveling in the sunshine of Augustus' friendship and eager to serve the Princeps – and to be rewarded by him with high positions, titles, glory and wealth.

Augustus and the Senate divided the rule of the empire. Most inner parts of the empire remained theoretically under the control of the Senate. These peaceful "senatorial provinces" had as their governors senators chosen (sometimes by lot) by the Senate, who went out to the provinces as officials responsible to the Senate. The taxes which those procurators and governors collected went into a state fund over which the Senate had control. However, some provinces – generally "problem" frontier provinces such as Egypt, Syria and Germany -- were assigned to the emperor as his territories to govern. Because they were "problem" areas, they had legions stationed in them, and those legions were under the authority of the emperor. Indeed, as Commander-in-Chief, the emperor was in charge of all imperial military forces. Thus, the emperors held the ultimate power cards. For those parts of the empire assigned to his direct rule, an emperor would send out governors called either legates or sometimes prefects or procurators, who reported in any case directly to him. Such governors were often not senators but members of the somewhat less prestigious "knights" class (**equites**). The taxes raised in these imperial provinces went straight into the emperor's own account, called the **fiscus**, for the emperor to spend. That was how it began, but by the mid-first century the powers of appointment and both tax funds had fallen effectively under the emperor's control.

AN IRON KING

During the years when Caesar Octavianus was fighting for his life and destiny in the civil wars, the states of the eastern Mediterranean were in upheaval. In 39 BC an ethnic Edomite adventurer named Herod got the Romans' approval and support to take care of the problem area of Palestine. Herod's father had been the effective ruler of the area on Rome's behalf, but as he died when the Parthian Empire made a military grab for his little kingdom, Herod fled west, begged General Mark Antony for help, and returned home as a Roman-sanctioned king with Roman legionaries who soon routed the Parthians. Then came a shock. The "liberated" people of Jerusalem wouldn't let Herod into the city – they didn't want him for their king. He was a "foreigner" – at worst an Arab and at best an Edomite. The Israelites wanted an ethnic Israelite as a ruler. Herod, never a gentle man, immediately laid siege to the city and took it by force. He ordered a fearful massacre of its inhabitants. This very bad start to his reign earned him no Jewish friends. But Herod didn't care, for his main friends were instead the Romans – although nominally he claimed to be of the Jewish faith. Nominally. It was a thin fiction, for he lived the life of a pagan potentate for all of his thirty-four years on the throne.

Herod surmounted many challenges by remaining a staunch friend of Rome. Early in his reign his patron General Mark Antony was defeated by Caesar Octavianus, necessitating a delicate political about-face from Herod. Yet he managed it nicely and remained a firm friend of Caesar Augustus. Despite his bad press from Jews and Christians alike, Herod was an effective ruler. He became a great builder. He built whole cities such as Caesarea Maritima and Sebaste; great fortresses such as Machaerus, Masada and Herodium in the south, and he re-built in great splendour the Temple of Yahweh at Jerusalem – "Solomon's Temple". All this building cost enormous amounts of money, obtained by heavy royal taxation – which fell on top of the Romans' taxes and which caused furious resentment among Herod's subjects.

Few people liked Herod, not even his own family members. He was an iron king and ruled despotically with an iron hand. We would term him a "strongman". He suffered from deep paranoia and an increasing inability to manage anger – not ideal qualities in a despotic king. He was perennially suspicious of everyone, especially members of his own family.

His kingdom comprised Judaea, Samaria, Galilee, Peraea (Trans-Jordan) and Idumaea (his native country); his subjects were mostly Jewish but included very significant numbers of pagan Greeks.

Herod was married ten times and sired a great many sons and daughters. At times he had two or even three wives concurrently. By his first wife Doris he produced a son Antipater; by his passionately loved second wife Mariamme he had two sons Alexander and Aristobulus; by a second Mariamme came a boy Herod-Philip ("Herod II"); by his Samaritan wife Malthake he sired Herod Antipas the future "tetrarch" and Herod Archelaus the future "ethnarch". By a Jerusalemite woman named Cleopatra he fathered another Philip ("Philip the tetrarch"). There were also daughters Salampsio, Mariamme and Cypros.

Besides all his wives and progeny, Herod had a number of siblings. They all lived in fear of the king, and with good reason – he had his own uncle Joseph and his sister Salome's husband Costabar executed for suspected disloyalty, and Herod's brother Phasael only escaped execution by dying at home first. Herod's sister Salome – not the Salome of the "seven veils", but rather her aunt – was another tough character very like the king, and the only one of the family who would berate and criticize Herod to his face. He put up with this because he felt his sister was consistently loyal and truthful to him. She was in fact a great intriguer and a constant trouble-maker, but she survived and was even given a generous inheritance when the old king died in 4 BC. She then became the very wealthy ruler of several Palestinian cities and their surrounding areas: Jamnia, Ashdod and Ashkelon on the coast, and big farm properties around Jericho. Yes, old Salome was a greedy schemer, who contrived the deaths of several family members. Framing Herod's much-loved wife the first Mariamme, Salome induced Herod to execute her. She also worked on Mariamme's sons Alexander and Aristobulus and got them executed in 7 BC. Mariamme's detestable mother was then done away with. Was Salome positioning herself to succeed Herod? If so, it didn't happen, even though in Herod's final days of life he decided – on Salome's advice – to kill his suspect eldest son Antipater. The way to the throne was opening.

Herod wrote six Wills, each time changing the succession and the bequests. Upon Herod's death these Wills required innumerable conferences and negotiations as each would-be heir sought the best deal for himself. The Roman emperor was involved in untangling the Wills and in settling the succession. In the end the Romans dictated the succession, breaking up the kingdom. Herod's four remaining sons did quite well out of it. Herod-Philip (Herod II) was given immense private wealth but set aside politically; he moved to Rome with his wife Herodias and their daughter Salome. Herod Archelaus became "ethnarch" of Judaea, Samaria and Idumaea, with a promise of a future kingship if he did well. (He didn't.) Herod Antipas became "tetrarch" of Galilee and Peraea; the other Philip became "tetrarch" of territories on the east side of the Jordan River. It was all a sharp rebuke for Salome.

Salome was married three times, first to her uncle Joseph. Though Roman law held marriages to aunts, uncles, nieces and first cousins to be incestuous and illegal, Jewish law allowed many such pairings (including niece-uncle but not aunt-nephew marriages). The Herodians were enthusiastic inbreeders; it eventually wiped out the clan. Salome and Joseph produced no children. With her second husband Costabar (from Idumaea) she produced a daughter Berenike and a son Antipater. Costobar was later executed by Herod the Great for disloyalty and plotting. Finally, in her later years, there was a childless marriage to Alexas Helcias, a commander of Herod's armed forces.

When the seventy-five-year-old Salome died in AD 10 there was a big surprise: she willed her territories and most of her wealth not to her two children Antipater and Berenike, but to her friend and confidante the empress Livia Augusta, the wife of Caesar Augustus. Salome's family line's wealth was thereby greatly diminished, leaving Antipater and his wife Cypros II (a daughter of old Herod) very well-off but by no means opulently rich. Salome's posterity immediately became a "cadet" non-ruling branch of the Herodians, yet that branch was to produce in the next two generations one figure of world importance and two of historic significance.

—

The peace of the year AD 1 did not last long. Caesar Augustus for long had clung to plans to conquer all of Germany. But Germany proved a tough nut. When the first century opened, yet another Roman invasion of "free Germany" was about to get underway. It was well planned and amply resourced. In the summer of AD 9, three legions – 20,000 soldiers – crossed the Rhine River near the present Dutch-German border and proceeded northeast. The aim was to advance the imperial frontier in Germany from the Rhine River to the Elbe. The legions' general, Quinctilius Varus, was experienced and possessed a good record of military successes. He was however known as a merciless soldier. Their guide through the German forests was a Roman knight named Arminius who claimed to be an ethnic German turned Roman. There were many such people. But in fact, Arminius was heart-and-soul a German (his real name was Hermann) and was secretly the over-chieftain of the tribes of the area. He was not leading the Roman legions to victory but into a well-prepared ambush. The legions were strung out in single file along a narrow forest track between a huge bog and the primeval forest, near the Weser River. Hidden in the forest were nearly 25,000 well-armed Germans.

The ambush was stunningly successful. The 20,000 Roman soldiers were slaughtered to a man. Varus fell on his own sword in the best tradition of defeated generals. When the news reached Augustus in Rome he collapsed. At one stroke of misfortune one-eighth of the entire Roman military had vanished. The imperial dream of northern conquest was dashed, and the German frontier was left unguarded. On the German side there was celebration, and an immediate counter-invasion of the empire to liberate the already-occupied parts of Germany. Augustus ordered his best general, Tiberius, to Germany to try to retrieve the situation.

Tiberius successfully defended the pre-existing boundaries of Roman Germany through the next two years, but he realized that any attempt to re-invade free Germany would be futile. Germanic peoples remained as

Rome's threatening northern neighbours for four hundred years before finally – in the 400s – taking over permanently the whole western half of the empire. Augustus, over seventy years old in AD 9, next over-reacted, deciding to place eight legions permanently near the German frontier, a huge concentration of troops which would in itself cause plenty of problems for Rome later in the century.

Rome had many supposed "enemies". North of the Danube frontier lived Sarmatians and Dacians, two large and related tribes, along with a string of smaller tribal populations. Usually these neighbours were placid but when under capable, ambitious rulers they could cause major trouble for Rome. The first century should have been a relatively quiet time, but the Romans persisted in their dreams of extending their empire north of the Danube. After mid-century the Dacians found a leader who could resist those incursions vigorously. Following many minor eruptions, a slow-paced showdown began in the 80s and continued for forty years.

Rome feared the Parthians to the east, and the Parthians feared the Romans. That Persian-dominated empire was big, militarily strong, but politically disunited, fractious and in perpetual uproar due to never-ending rebellions and plots by its regional kings. The King-of-Kings was in theory the overlord in a feudal regime, but he spent most of his energies bringing restive or rebellious feudal under-kings to heel. The eastern edge of Roman territories was always in danger of a sudden invasion by Parthians, but they seldom showed much staying power. They had invaded Roman Syria in 38 BC and tried again in AD 20, but with no lasting results. The Parthians admired the Romans for their stable government, their glorious emperors, their conspicuous wealth, and their tough, disciplined armies. The two empires maintained a love-hate relationship throughout the first century – a sort of ongoing Cold War which now and then flared up into hot war. Armenia, a Parthian sub-kingdom which periodically became a Roman sub-kingdom, was the cause of incessant friction. Neither empire was ever able to deliver a knock-out blow to the other, though in general the Romans held the upper hand. Armenia – situated between the Black Sea and the Caspian Sea -- was a perennial bone of contention.

On the south, all was quiet. The imperial lands in Africa were protected by the Sahara Desert and, south of Egypt, by friendly Sudanese states of Nubia and – later on -- Axum. Such rebellions as did occur were at the western end of north Africa, in present-day Morocco, where ethnic Berbers resisted the Roman advance for centuries.

Augustus distributed twenty-eight Roman legions around the frontiers to safeguard the empire against its neighbours. The German, Danubian and Parthian fronts got two-thirds of all the legions, with the German front along the Rhine River remaining most important in the minds of first-century Romans. The frontier legions kept the "barbarian" neighbours out of the imperial lands and, as far as was possible, on good terms with the empire. That was the strategy. But it was mixed up with Rome's mania for conquest as well as defence, and so it was a strategy fraught with problems. If all was quiet on the frontiers, idle legionary troops easily became bored and restive. Since terms of enlistment in the Roman armies were harsh, mutiny was never far from the surface. If the officers took steps to maintain strict discipline they might only add to the dissatisfaction of the rank and file, and if they relaxed discipline they increased the tendency of the troops to be self-willed and obstreperous. Every legion had its malcontents and trouble-makers. Even fighting between legions occurred from time to time, and no decade passed in the first century without some legion mutinying or proclaiming a "new emperor" from its own ranks. Then the treason had to be suppressed by strong persuasion or, more often, by external force. Through the first century AD, the armed forces became arbiters of political power, and that role remained entrenched for centuries to come.

Old Herod's death in March of 4 BC and the confusion over the succession were the signals for uprisings all throughout his kingdom. While the old king's sons squabbled about who would get what powers and territory and money, long-suppressed Jewish resentment burst forth as mobs formed "armies" which sought to liberate Israel from the Herodians.

The rebellions were serious enough to require Roman armies to put them down. At the rebel-held city of Sepphoris in Galilee the Romans resorted to siege and storming, with consequent massacre and fire. The city was razed to the ground and its inhabitants sold into slavery. Judaeans referred to the troubles as "Varus' War" after the Roman General Quinctilius Varus – he who a dozen years later would meet his end in the German debacle -- who led the military suppression of the Judean rebels. Augustus decided that Herod's trouble-ridden kingdom would have to be broken up. Each of Herod's sons could rule a piece, but none would possess it all.

THE FIRST EMPERORS: AUGUSTUS AND TIBERIUS

Augustus created and controlled his new imperial system for over forty years with masterful skill. Few of his successors manifested comparable abilities. Augustus himself, it must be admitted, did not provide very well for many future circumstances. His golden reputation is belied by the many strategic mistakes of his reign. The empire had no Constitution, no rules for succession, no structured bureaucracy. Augustus decided arbitrarily, for reasons unclear then and still unclear now, to institute dynastic succession and to keep the rulership within his own tightly-knit family. There were no Roman precedents for an imperial system, and Augustus enunciated no theory of how it should work. He initially presented himself as just a senator who happened to be first among equals. The Senate over time invested him with the powers of almost all the recognized offices of state, and those investitures were the legal basis of his rule. When old Augustus settled on Tiberius as his successor, he had the Senate invest him with one power after another to smooth his way. Subsequent Julio-Claudian emperors of the first century sought and got the same packages of powers from the Senate upon accession, but they were never fully viewed as "successors" in the dynastic sense of having a birthright to those powers. The Senate clung to the belief that it had the right – and maybe the duty – to select emperors. In fact the army soon became the determining factor in choosing new emperors. The emperors so chosen increasingly made themselves into absolute monarchs, wore gorgeous attire and sat on real thrones in sumptuous palaces. And they often misbehaved in quite spectacular fashion, some even aspiring to be living gods.

The empire-wide peace following the victory of Caesar Augustus gave the early first century AD a character wholly different from that of the violent preceding century. Indeed, the events of the long-lasting Roman Peace set the stage for all of subsequent Western history right down to our own day. Especially in the nineteenth century the Roman triad of 'Peace, Power and Possession of an empire' exerted strong fascination on all the great European powers of the day, which saw themselves as empire-building heirs of the Romans. The fashion of public buildings that looked Roman persisted into the mid-twentieth century. But when Augustus took power, no one could foresee that his peace would be of long duration or have such deep impact. Long-lasting peace came as a slowly-unfolding surprise to the Roman world.

Caesar Augustus had literally to invent the empire. He decided from the outset that his rule would be a monarchy reserved for his family. He belonged to the Julian clan of Gaius Julius Caesar, which was intermarried with the Claudian clan. Both these clans were very ancient and very prestigious and would have described themselves as "of the ruling class" if not "the ruling class" of Rome. From the very beginning, the rule of the empire was made very much a family affair and it long remained so; emperors of the closely-related Julian and Claudian families presided over it for exactly one hundred years, from 31 BC to AD 68. It was a tightly closed family shop. That is rather puzzling because Augustus' own progeny numbered just a single daughter, Julia, from his previous marriage. The rest of his "sons" were acquired by adoption. Wayward Julia – a great disappointment to her father – married general Marcus Agrippa (Augustus' first designated successor) and produced two sons Lucius and Gaius who were the first of the adoptees and were designated successors. Born as Augustus' grandsons, they became his sons through adoption after old Agrippa died unexpectedly. Augustus himself had moved from being Julius Caesar's great-nephew to being his son by adoption. Adoption in the Roman tradition implied no weaker relationship than a natural one, and five of the first-century emperors – Augustus, Tiberius, Claudius, Domitian and Nerva -- adopted relatives as their "sons" and designated successors.

At the beginning of Augustus' reign, the succession was not a great issue, for the emperor was young. Augustus faced two more pressing issues at the outset of his rule. One was the out-of-control militarization of the Roman state; the other was the severe economic and cultural disorder wrought by the long civil wars. He dealt with both issues squarely and very effectively, but not very wisely. First, Augustus demobilized most of the armed forces, which initially had numbered about 700,000 men. The 175,000 who remained in service were re-structured into new forces including 28 legions of six or seven thousand men each, whose loyalty was no longer to be to individual commanders but to the state and especially to the emperor as Commander-in-Chief. These legions and an equal number of regional auxiliaries were distributed throughout the fringes of the empire as defence forces and policing forces (the Romans never developed separate police forces). Legions were sent to the frontiers. The huge savings realized from this wholesale demobilization were re-invested partly in the new legions, and partly on cultural and religious initiatives. Yet 350,000 soldiers were more than the empire really needed or could afford, and inactivity on the far frontiers was recognized as a danger – it gave the soldiers time to think about themselves and their beefs. The remedies were to maintain very strict discipline, to keep the troops busy with daily work, and to fight limited aggressive wars now and then. There were "controlled" wars in Egypt (AD 19), North Africa (AD 21 and 30), the Balkans (6-9, 14, 33, 69 and 85-87), Britain (43-46), Germany (7-9, 14-15, 24, 68-72) and Armenia (51-53 and 60-63). Lots of other skirmishes and "bandit suppression" actions took place too, and riots large and small were put down with troops. A major insurrection in Alexandria in AD 38 was suppressed by the Egyptian legions with enormous loss of life. Sometimes it went horribly wrong, as in the German rout of Quinctilius Varus in AD 9. In AD 66 an uncontrolled Roman-Judaean war erupted and in 69 there was a year-long, bloody uncontrolled civil war in Italy.

The empire tended to enforce its peace by terror – responding to uprisings by letting loose the troops to massacre and destroy more or less indiscriminately. Most such actions were small-scale, localized and brief. However, every city had its mob and sometimes things got out of hand. The Alexandrian rising of 38, the British insurrection of 60-61, and the Roman-Judaean War of 66-71 were in no sense controlled exercises; even less was the civil war of the year 69.

Disorder was recognized as a problem in Augustus' reign. In some regions the Romans left local rulers in place to keep things quiet. This was how the Herod dynasty came to power in Palestine. Augustus personally came to dislike Herod, but the old ogre did keep the peace, and was a consistent friend of Rome. So he remained in place, as did his sons, all through the reigns of Augustus and Tiberius. Indeed, Herodians remained in power here and there in the East all through the first century. Such local rulers varied in value but were generally useful in difficult places. No one in that age had a clear grasp of economic process. Augustus spent vast sums – mostly the windfall from looting Egypt – on building and re-building civic infrastructure throughout Italy. The original King Herod too spent huge sums on building. But their successors couldn't keep up the pace, and the towns and cities of the empire soon came to prefer fun facilities – baths, theaters, racetracks -- over dull temples, harbour works, aqueducts and administrative buildings.

In the empire's vigorous first century the various provinces and client kingdoms were mostly still separate societies, often formerly independent kingdoms. Most retained their own languages and customs. Sometimes their kings and administrative structures were left in place, as with King Herod in Palestine. For most subjects, Rome was far away. The Romans were much more interested in tax collection than in cultural Romanization. However, Romanization did slowly take place, more thoroughly in the west than in the east. In the western half of the empire – present-day Portugal, Spain, France, Belgium, south Germany, Switzerland, Austria, Italy, Illyria, Tunisia, Algeria and Morocco – Rome remained the "central" city and Latin became the language of everyday life and business. The eastern half of the empire – today's Greece, Macedonia, Bulgaria, Turkey, Syria, Palestine, Lebanon, Jordan, Armenia, Libya and Egypt – already possessed high Greek-derived cultures, several great cities of its own (Alexandria, Antioch, Corinth, Ephesus, Cyrene and Jerusalem) and used Greek as the everyday language. Greek never did get displaced, and eventually in the sixth century it became the official language of all "Romans". The first century was the toughest hurdle for the imperial Romans. In the first century they invented as they went along, challenges were daunting, and many mistakes were made. But if the first century was dynamic at the top, the life of its ordinary people changed little over the hundred years. The second century was by general consent the zenith of the empire, the third century a time of desperate troubles, and the fourth a period of transformation -- into a grim bureaucratic and totalitarian Christian state.

Rome taxed all its subject peoples, at least outside Italy. If imperial taxation levels didn't go down, at least they didn't rise dramatically in the first century. That rise came later, along with galloping inflation. Two kinds of tax existed. Tax on land applied to all land irrespective of who owned it; in theory every landowner paid. And there was a head tax applicable to every free person. Roman citizens sometimes paid a reduced rate, or none at all, and the great and very wealthy had a knack – as in every society – for avoiding taxes, sometimes paying nothing. By modern standards tax rates seem modest – maybe 10% of annual incomes -- but those taxes impacted on a population which was much poorer than in most modern states. Moreover, taxation was not graduated – taxes in theory hit rich and poor alike although the poor were much less able to bear them. There was no graded income tax such as we know today, and few inheritance taxes. In addition to the taxes imposed by the Romans, there would usually be local taxation by client kings, princes or municipalities. Head taxes pre-dominated everywhere, along with transfer taxes on goods. Tax avoidance and tax evasion were rampant, and as always the rich were much more successful than the poor at evasion. The job of tax collection was initially farmed out to private enterprise, whose collectors over-charged so as to realize a handsome profit for themselves. Squeeze was part of the system, as were graft, bribery and cheating by tax collectors and taxpayers. Moreover the local and imperial governments provided virtually no counter-balancing social services. Tax money was spent on the military, on public works and on the follies and fancies of the imperial court. Where there were local rulers, as in Palestine, they levied taxes too, for use in their territories. Herod and his successors were a second level of burden on the people of Palestine, but at least the taxes they collected were spent in Palestine.

Augustus distinguished carefully between state funds (the "aerarium" revenues under the control of the Senate) and his own private tax-derived revenues (the "fiscus") as emperor. The emperors' revenues were immense, for they included all the tax income from entire designated imperial provinces of the empire – for example Egypt, Gaul and Syria. The rest of the provinces were in theory governed by the Senate as separate "senatorial" provinces. It was too neat. It didn't take long for state funds and private funds to become thoroughly mixed up and to fall under the effective control of the emperors. Augustus set up a flawed system and his successors were not careful. Fifty years after Augustus' death Nero had his hands deep in both pockets.

The Julio-Claudian dynasty was very much a "Cosa Nostra" affair. The first emperor, Augustus, went to fantastic lengths to ensure that his family – termed the August Family -- kept the dynastic succession and all the power, but he was very unlucky in that effort. He disliked his scandalous daughter Julia from his first marriage; but he and his second wife Livia produced no children. His adopted sons Lucius and Gaius -- Julia's children, adopted by Augustus and designated as successors – died natural deaths one after the other, in 4 BC and AD 2. Their real father, the earlier-designated successor Marcus Agrippa, was also dead.

Suddenly the succession was in crisis. Finally the elderly emperor in desperation adopted his step-son Tiberius – the military hero from his own wife Livia's first marriage -- as his son and successor, even though Tiberius himself was no longer young. On Augustus' death at age 80 in AD 14, the succession went to Tiberius, though not without troubles.

"What's this succession business?" wondered many senators. Just because Augustus was their "first citizen" it didn't follow that he should have the right to name a successor – surely that was the Senate's right. Augustus disagreed but had never bothered to inform the Senate of his game. And so it remained a perceived Senatorial right, and became passionately perceived, never forgotten by the senators but seldom exercised in imperial times. For Augustus conferred powers little by little on Tiberius so that eventually he became a sort of co-emperor with Augustus himself. It was then almost impossible for the Senate to refuse to let Tiberius exercise the powers with which it had already invested him. Yet from the very first succession in AD 14 this matter rankled the Senate. Not until AD 96 would the senators' day come to freely choose a new emperor. Thus the successful, incorruptible and grouchy old Stoic general Tiberius became the successor of Augustus.

But what a general he was! He had expanded the empire in the Balkans during AD 6-8 by conquering Pannonia (=Hungary), and then the very next year he had taken over command in Germany to retrieve the catastrophic defeat of Varus and to prevent an even greater debacle there. His troops loved him. Tiberius' reward in the year 12 was to be named imperial successor and to be formally adopted as Augustus' son. Just two years later, in 14, he duly became the second Roman emperor.

And the Senate grumbled on for years. Tiberius had not been their choice. They didn't like the old curmudgeon – a Stoic by belief. But they ratified his powers anyway, unhappy but without a clear alternative. More surprising, the legionary rank and file grumbled, and a few legions in the Balkans and Germany came to mutiny. The legionaries had no problem with Tiberius; their problems were with the harsh terms of service which Augustus had forced upon them. The mutinous legions felt that now was the moment to strike for redress and better terms. Tiberius sent one of his adopted sons (Drusus Sr) to the Balkans and the other (Germanicus) to Germany to confront the rebellious legions there and to try to reach a peaceful resolution of their problems. Success was achieved, but just barely. In fact the resolution achieved by Germanicus involved both a large pay-out of money to the troops and execution of some dissident ringleaders. The relationship between the August Family and its armies rested on such a thin edge.

Tiberius was a competent and at times thoughtful man with a superb military record, but with limited experience in offices of state. He had virtually no aptitude for the job of emperor. Some people adored him, but not many in Rome itself. He lacked the "touch" and the slippery charisma of Augustus and he was widely seen as a hard, unemotional, over-principled old curmudgeon. He was a Stoic by philosophy and was uptight by nature, a hard man indeed though not a bad one. Aged 56 when he took over the empire, he was also widely considered too old and too old-fashioned for the job. Tiberius came from one of the oldest Roman families, from the cream of the old Republican aristocracy, and he remained always overly conscious of his sterling origins and reluctant to give his trust to "new men" or to people of other classes. In return, he did not get their trust. His moral principles were unassailable, but with them came rigidity, inflexibility, demanding standards and an aloofness that put people off. He came across as a snob, even as a hypocrite. Moreover, his ethics were those of an earlier time, a time which had largely vanished during Augustus' long tenure as Princeps. Above all Tiberius was a dreadful communicator. Somehow, he always presented his worst face to the world, and seemed always to put his wrong foot forward. Yet he was a capable leader, in his way. It was Tiberius who had provided strong and essential support for Augustus during the last failing years of the latter's reign.

Under Tiberius a number of areas of authority quietly moved from the Senate's purview to the emperor's. This was not a pre-meditated plot to weaken the Senate but rather a recognition that the Senate was inherently weak, class-biased and not very able at managing the great new business of empire – as the recent creation of the office of *Princeps* had demonstrated. Unfortunately, the Senate viewed the changes as pre-meditated and hostile actions. No love was lost between the Senate and the emperor. The senators had not wanted Tiberius and he knew that. The emperor treated some of the most trenchant outspoken criticisms by senators as treason, and the critics paid the price. Tiberius' reputation as a tyrant arose from a long string of treason trials. First some devious senator would denounce another; there would be a trial and the man charged tended to get convicted – and executed.

Tiberius tried to solve root problems – always a dangerous course for any leader. Also, he had the temperament of the military General which he was. He strove for greater administrative efficiency by creating a tiny court bureaucracy of "assistants" around himself. That was the way it worked in the Army. This was not well-received by the Senate, for he used talented slaves or freedmen as his assistants, men of no social standing. Senators didn't like to mix and do business with such "inferiors". Or, Tiberius resorted to old family friends. Initially it was a very small team indeed, just part of his regular household, yet under Tiberius the first instances of "ministerial favorites" and extra-legal actions by them appeared. Tiberius signally failed to implement checks and restraints on his household officials, who literally got away with murder. The trend to employment of non-senatorial personnel in the emperor's household – the emerging "court" – in itself angered the Senators. The Senate excoriated these imperial court upstarts; they were mostly social nobodies, and in senatorial histories like those of Tacitus and Suetonius they all come down to us as villains. As do also their ministerial personnel.

Tiberius' first "prime minister" Aelius Seianus really was a villain who aspired to the throne, and he was eventually executed. Seianus, whose intelligence and efficiency were not in question, was the son of Seius Strabo, one of the Praetorian Prefects. Seianus himself was a knight -- brilliant, energetic, amiable and well-connected. Tiberius engaged Seianus in AD 22, found his services very satisfactory indeed – the man was a born manager -- and so the emperor kept on increasing his powers step by step until around 29 the thought occurred to the Senate that Seianus was being groomed as Tiberius' successor. In response to Tiberius' "court", and in opposition to the anti-Senate tendencies of this presumed new successor, the senatorial class opposed Tiberius, and he took it as another attack on himself and his position as Head of State – sedition or treason. On the dubious evidence of informers and spies, Seianus – ostensibly on behalf of the emperor -- began charging opponents with treason and having them executed. Compliant courts, the back-room manoeuvres of unrestrained officials – especially Seianus himself -- and self-seeking denouncers (they got a share of the confiscations which generally accompanied condemnations) made convictions easy to get. Then in 26 Tiberius made the huge error of leaving hateful Rome to live on the beautiful isle of Capri near Naples. Seianus effectively took over at Rome. In 31, after nine years in his ministerial post, and possessing such immense amounts of power as to suggest that he would certainly be the next to occupy the throne, Seianus was suddenly denounced by Tiberius himself, arrested, condemned and executed. Many of his cronies were also done away with. The knight who replaced him, Naevius Macro, was an even worse scoundrel, but he survived into the next reign by restraining his ambitions. Tiberius had left Rome in 26 and he never returned to residence there. He lived out his remaining dozen years on Capri south of Rome. Seianus, then Macro, essentially took over the reins in Rome. Tiberius' reign ended in a wash of blood and bad feelings at Rome.

Yet things came off well in the empire as a whole during Tiberius' reign. Away from the capital, people were unaware of court scandals and senatorial machinations. Who cared if senator So-and-So was executed? Except in the first decade, the economy was buoyant, still reaping the benefits of peace. Minor risings and upheavals occurred from time to time, but major disasters were avoided and the work of Augustus was consolidated. In some directions the penny-pinching Tiberius caused needless difficulties. Where Augustus had sponsored extensive new building in Italy, especially in the capital – "he found it in brick and left it in marble" -- Tiberius built almost nothing except a couple of aqueducts, to the chagrin of the building industry.

Having quite correctly discerned that the ancient annual voting on the Field of Mars had become a sham, just an excuse for a holiday, Tiberius abruptly ended the process. Everyone was angered; their votes had been stolen. Worse, their holiday had been stolen. The emperor should have foreseen those reactions. And so it went year after year. By 26 Tiberius himself – he was approaching seventy -- was exhausted and exasperated, and he harkened to the welcome words of his courtier Seianus inviting him to rule from pleasant Capri instead of from oppressive Rome. Tiberius moved to Capri – a major blunder that left Seianus as the vital communications link. Yet after Seianus' fall the emperor would still not return to Rome. Who would be Tiberius' successor? No one knew, and the emperor wouldn't say. Until AD 19 it had been obvious to all that Tiberius' popular adopted son Drusus Germanicus was the right man, and the successor they wanted. The son of Tiberius' brother, Germanicus was a dashing and ever-victorious general, a man who "showed well", and he was married to a remarkable woman named Vipsania Agrippina who was a granddaughter of Augustus and a much-respected political personality in her own right. Then in AD 19 Germanicus died in Syria in murky circumstances and the question of the succession became bedeviled by the presence of several potential claimants. Germanicus and Agrippina had four young sons, but Tiberius himself soon no longer had a living son, for his Drusus had died in 23 AD. There were collateral relatives with reasonable succession claims too. And there was Agrippina Sr. herself. Her father General Agrippa had been Augustus' first choice as his successor, but had died in 12 BC. Agrippina Sr's marriage to General Germanicus produced four sons and three daughters, and the sons at least were all potential occupants of the throne.

During the 20s, the villainous Seianus successively liquidated Agrippina Sr. and all but one of her sons, and when in 23 Tiberius' adopted son Drusus died a natural death, it began to look like Augustus' dilemma repeating itself. Who would succeed? In his final years, old

Tiberius foolishly willed the empire jointly to Germanicus' only surviving and youngest son Gaius Caligula and Tiberius' none-too-bright grandson Tiberius Gemellus. But his wishes were completely ignored after his death.

After Tiberius' twenty-three years on the throne, people were weary of the old man. He was a strict and honest administrator but no manager, and a fatally poor communicator. He bored everybody, and they bored him. Tiberius chose his subordinates poorly and managed them poorly. In 19 AD he sent off the unsuitable senator Cnaeus Calpurnius Piso to be the governor of Syria (considered the most important province), then when trouble resulted he sent off his charismatic nephew General Germanicus to be a sort of "super-governor" of the same area. Germanicus and Piso opposed each other to the brink of civil war, whereupon Tiberius replaced Piso with a more tractable Governor. But Piso wouldn't accept that replacement and stayed on in Syria where he struggled on acrimoniously. The strange behaviour of both Piso and Tiberius remains to this day inexplicable. Most unfortunately, at that point Germanicus fell ill and died in Syria, and gossip throughout the empire cried "poison !" It was very widely assumed that Piso had poisoned the heir to the throne. It was untrue, but in the circumstances a very believable slander. Against his greatest reluctance Piso was induced to return to Rome where he promptly committed suicide after being reviled by everyone. Tiberius who had appointed him declined to support his case in any way.

In AD 26 Tiberius sent the inexperienced knight Pontius Pilate to Judaea as Prefect, and he lasted there for ten full years despite his rather poor performance. In Tiberius' final years the court was in a continual uproar of rumour and gossip. At Rome especially, informers denounced some important person almost every month, and many – innocent or guilty – were executed as a result. The rumour mill was kept busy whispering of the supposed immorality and cruelty of the emperor on Capri, but in fact he passed most of his time there grinding away at administrative work. The final years of the reign were chaotic. There was no mourning upon Tiberius' death in 37, shortly before his eightieth birthday; instead there was jubilation in the streets of Rome. The old monster was finally gone. Gossip was sure that he too had been poisoned, or suffocated... or whatever... by his successor. In a world without newspapers, rumour and gossip ran wild and conspiracy theories abounded. And as well, celebrity poisonings really did occur from time to time.

There were enthusiastic hopes for the next reign. Nobody paid any attention to Tiberius' plan of joint emperors. Ascending the throne was **Gaius Caesar** ("Caligula", ruled 37-41) the youngest and only surviving son of the late and wildly popular General Germanicus. Just twenty-five years old on his accession, good-looking, with impeccable family credentials (he was Augustus' great-grandson through his mother Agrippina), Gaius seemed everything that Tiberius wasn't. This time the Senate was enthusiastic. But the senators were in for disappointment. Poor Tiberius Gemellus was put to death promptly – that was the first sign.

II
LIFE IN THE FIRST CENTURY

THE POOR

Seventy million people lived within the Roman empire in the first century. They represented many cultures and ethnic nationalities, and they were divided sharply into social and economic classes. Quality of life depended somewhat on where you lived and greatly on your gender, but much more still on your class and financial circumstances. Perhaps 90% of the population was poor or just barely middle class; the remaining 10% was reasonably well-off and very influential, forming a tiny elite monied class. There was no dominant "middle class" as in most modern states. The wealthy elites controlled every aspect of life for everyone, mostly for their own benefit, and the rest of the population toiled and tried with might and main to subsist and somehow rise out of poverty into a better class. As kings and emperors and other "elite" members of society lived their pleasant lives, the vast masses toiled at their work, trying to make ends meet and to pay their taxes.

The state, being a tool of the rich and well-born, looked after its supporters well and dealt with its Italian poor after a fashion. The rest of the empire was largely left to its own devices of life and culture. Government took a strictly hands-off attitude to business; private enterprise was almost completely unfettered and unregulated. There were, for instance, no restrictions on working conditions, or on prices or wages; no "warranties" or vendor licensing; almost no import-export duties. **Caveat emptor** ("Buyer, beware") was a Roman proverb. Much of the business practice of the empire would qualify as fraud or corruption in our twenty-first century society. Since the Roman empire had no income taxes, it not surprisingly had some very rich people alongside its huge mass of very poor people. The poor were effectively in competition with slaves for menial jobs. The tiny middle class never grew large or influential even though some individuals gained or lost large amounts of money and moved across class lines. Wealth tended to concentrate in Rome and other big cities, where the smart-set rich liked to live. To a large extent the people of Italy – the old Romans themselves -- were scarcely taxed at all. Italy was instead a beneficiary of the taxes paid by others, elsewhere. These others were openly termed "subject peoples". The subject peoples paid two kinds of tax to Rome. A head tax fell on every person irrespective of their ability to pay. Property taxes fell unevenly on those who owned property. In addition, people might be taxed by a regional prince or king whom Rome had left in place to mind an area. Municipalities might also impose taxes on their inhabitants. The result was to skim off most of the "surplus" of poor people and to keep everyone down.

Agriculture was the mainstay of the empire. Manufacturing played a secondary role in the imperial economy. Everything from clothing to tools to construction materials to war gear to ships to containers to metal goods was manufactured by hand in vast quantities. Most of these everyday goods were produced locally everywhere, and most were used locally. In addition, each region of the empire produced certain specialty goods: Italy and Gaul excelled in ceramics, Spain in metal goods, Greece and Anatolia in statuary and other luxury items, and so forth. These goods could be sold throughout the empire and exported to regions beyond. Egypt, Sicily and North Africa produced grain crops that fed the empire. The coming of the Roman empire facilitated the movement and marketing of specialties through the whole realm, and thus stimulated business activity and specialization. Ship transport then as now was cheap but slow. Shipwrecks occurred but were not so very frequent. Transport by cart or wagon on the network of Roman highways was more expensive and also slow. Those facts favoured water transport via the Mediterranean or the great rivers of the hinterland regions.

There was no central bank in the empire, nor any modern-type banks at all. Everyday business transactions were carried out in cash, and even some large-scale mobile operations (such as a legion) might rely on strongboxes full of gold and silver coins which traveled with the operation to meet payroll needs. Sensibly, the empire took great care to ensure that its soldiery got paid on time. Letters of credit existed but there was always a risk that they would not (or could not) be honoured. Loans might not be repaid. Capital invested in businesses could be lost if the business failed, or if a cargo ship sank, or if a warehouse burned down; and these were not unknown events. In this kind of high-risk environment, profit margins tended to be very high on traded products. An entrepreneur who succeeded in getting his shipload of luxury items to the market made a quick fortune.

The cash-and-carry business trade required a huge amount of coinage. There was no paper money. In a world without news media, however, coins were a medium for getting government propaganda disseminated to the people of the empire. Coins usually showed the face of the reigning emperor and bore some slogan. Immense numbers of first-century coins have survived to the present day.

The economy ran on the labour and sweat of poor but free people, and of slaves. Well-to-do people didn't perform manual labour. Their lives were passed in leisure and in local political affairs; they constituted a land-owning revenue-receiving gentry class. They would often hold official appointments in the local or imperial administration and would become public people. Their "output" was in large part influence. Everyone else worked. The poor worked hard; children were put to work very early. The slaves worked hardest of all.

—

Even most Italians were poor. Unemployment was rife because free workers often could not compete with slaves. In Rome itself, some 40% of the population was made up of slaves. To avoid outright starvation – which had been occurring even in the capital as late as the reign of Tiberius (AD 14-37) -- a free grain dole was instituted in Rome, paid for out of general tax revenues. A few other cities followed suit. The burden of taxation everywhere fell mainly on the poor outside of Italy; it was much-resented. The taxation of Rome's "subjects" went to produce free grain and amenities for Italy, support for the armies, buildings, and money for the court.

The empire was first and foremost a place of towns and cities. The population of the realm was concentrated in the east in those towns and cities rather than in the countryside. Rome was by far the largest city, with over a million inhabitants. It was the world's largest city in the first century. In the East, Alexandria and Antioch were metropolises with at least 300,000 people each. Other notable cities included Jerusalem, Damascus, Ephesus, Carthage, Corinth, Philippi, Athens, Cyrene, Neapolis (Naples), Mediolanum (Milan), Massilia (Marseille), Lugdunum (Lyons) and Corduba (Cordova). In the early first century the great cities often resembled the chaotically laid out centres of the Middle Ages which were to follow, but by the end of the third century civic improvements had been introduced by the Romans' flair for rational layouts, straight streets, water supply systems, sewer systems, and limits on the height of buildings. Both Rome and Constantinople even got street lighting around AD 350. Regular garbage collection followed not much later. Sounds modern, but rank poverty was always present everywhere, inflation was continuous, and taxes kept rising. The first century was both the best and the worst time to live in a big Roman city. Rich and poor lived together in the cities. The rich had great mansions and spacious gardens, the poor usually resided in multi-story apartment blocks. Construction practices for these were questionable, and safety was not a concern. Fires were deadly but at least ensured that urban re-building occurred frequently. Rome suffered major first-century fires in AD 24, 59, 64, 69, 72 and 80. There were no reliable systems of fire insurance and no effective fire departments. City Watch para-military groups (**vigiles**) were however used as firefighters and informal police in Rome. Sanitation benefitted from the Romans' attention to aqueducts and municipal sewer systems, but street cleaning was not a priority. Neither was professional policing. There were no hospitals, no playgrounds and little public green space.

The population of the empire was young, for fewer people lived to advanced ages then. The empire was in this respect very much a third-world place, with high child mortality and thus short average lifespans. It was to a surprising degree a world run by teenagers and men in their 20s and 30s. Nero was a teenager at his accession. The famous Herodian Queen Berenike had been divorced twice by age sixteen. Adulthood arrived early for everybody – at twelve or fourteen in legal terms. Though the Romans like the Greeks celebrated youth, there was no recognition of "adolescence"; people moved abruptly from childhood to adulthood. Males would enter the workforce around age 12 and by that time would be unschooled but work-trained and sexually experienced. Typically, girls married at 12-15, raised families, and died in their 40s or 50s, being already grandparents. Vast numbers of people of all ages were mowed down by infections and diseases, periodic epidemics, or accidents. Sickness and suffering were endemic, and wealth was no protection. Before the second century, smallpox, measles and diphtheria were unknown in Europe; also unknown was syphilis. On the other hand, some diseases rare in the modern world were all-too-familiar in the first century: leprosy, typhoid and plague, for instance. Many in the lower reaches of society succumbed to sheer overwork, malnutrition and despair. Some starved to death. Suicide was common as a way out from the overwhelming troubles of life. But it had always been so and did not seem abnormal.

For poor people there was no schooling – work began in childhood and ended only at death. There were certainly no free public schools.

Only the rich could "retire", and even then without any earned pensions. They had to rely on accumulated wealth or ongoing income from their assets. Leisure – for those who had any -- was mostly provided by the many holidays of imperial paganism; almost half the days of the Roman year were designated as holy festival days of some kind. Slaves got far fewer holidays, but not none.

Not surprisingly in view of its demographics, the empire was a very sexually active society, and one without effective means of contraception or much respect for celibacy and chastity. It was considered normal in antiquity – except among Jews, Christians and Isis-worshippers – for men to obtain sexual release with pre-pubescent boys, or with slaves or either sex. Unwanted babies – legitimate or illegitimate newborns which simply could not be provided for – were very frequently abandoned to die of exposure. To this practice too, Jews and Christians and Isis-worshippers were implacably opposed. Women often died in ways connected with childbirth. Men tended to be somewhat older than women at marriage, but they too died at what we would consider early ages. A man who reached fifty was thought to have lived to a good age, and those who made it past sixty were admired for that achievement. The wealthy and privileged being better-fed, better-housed and better cared for lived somewhat longer, but there was no recognized class of "the elderly" in the modern sense. Augustus and Tiberius, the first two emperors, lived to near 80, and Claudius made it to 75, but Caligula and Nero were scarcely 30 at death. Death ensured that marriages – even happy loving ones – rarely lasted beyond fifteen or twenty years. But divorce was very easy for both pagans and Jews, and was probably commoner in the first century than in any century before or after. Only the Christians set their face against it.

Thus, a man or woman might go through two or three or more marriages over a lifetime, and not necessarily because spouses had passed away. Divorce being rampant, marital fidelity was much praised in pagan society -- because of its rarity. Adultery was rampant too. Emperor Claudius was married five times, Nero five (including twice to males), Caligula four, and Augustus and Tiberius twice each. Only the Flavian emperors Vespasian and Domitian stayed with one wife through thick and thin -- but the Flavian family was laced with Christians, and that may have exerted an effect. The Samaritan woman with whom Jesus chatted at the town well had had five past husbands plus a current "partner". King Herod was married to ten wives. Homosexuality in the empire was so common as to be unremarkable and was accepted – in fact embraced -- except by a few religions including, once again, Judaism, Christianity and Isis-worship. In theory, macho Roman men were supposed to penetrate younger male partners but not be penetrated. In practice, just about anything went on, as several spectacular Roman court cases revealed. Sex with slaves was universal, but male sex with younger boys – free or bond -- was particularly common and in some quarters was even considered beneficial to the boys. Lesbian relationships must have been common too but were not much talked about in the Romans' literature. St Paul railed against gay and lesbian behaviour. First-century Christianity injected new notes of religious chastity and sexual fidelity between partners which resonated with many pagan Romans and Greeks who were unhappy with their own sex-drenched, debauched societies. The first century, not the later empire, saw the peak of Roman sexual "decadence".

Apart from the cities, ancient agriculture was a place of the poor. That agriculture was inefficient and non-mechanized and lacked well-developed crop varieties. Levelled fields would be plowed in the spring, using oxen or horses and a shallow-set wooden plow board or a metal plowshare that turned the soil over but did not accomplish much more than that. Animal manure might be worked into the soil, then crop seed would be broadcast on the field. Certain crops such as peas and beans and other garden species would be planted in rows, as we still do today. Crop production required a great input of labour which on larger farms was provided mostly by slaves. When the crop was ready to be harvested, masses of people would take sickles or knives into the fields to reap by hand. Cereal crops might be stooked or left loose to dry in the field before being taken to a threshing floor where (again by hand, laboriously) the edible seed would be separated from the straw and the chaff. Crop failures triggered famines.

The empire saw a good deal of economic rationalization of agriculture. The Herodian rulers right from Herod the Great were attentive to improving their regions' agriculture. The tetrarch Philip turned his little principality from poor to prosperous in that way. Grain production became a specialty of Egypt, Sicily, Africa and Gaul. Olive oil production, initially centred in Italy and Greece, was extended to Spain. By modern standards, a disproportionate amount of land – especially in Italy -- was given over to production of grapes for wine-making. The ancient world had no distilled liquors like whiskey, vodka, rum and so forth, and beer was popular only in the northern parts of the empire. "Civilized" people drank wine – usually diluted with equal parts of water. Most wine was of poor quality but cheap. The best wines from southern Italy were much sought after but expensive. The town of Pompeii owed much of its prosperity to the fine wines of its region.

Given peace, people traveled more, though the poor could not afford to travel widely. All the Herodian rulers sent their children from Palestine to be educated in Rome; many other notables must have done the same. The poor never had such educational opportunities. Jews from all over traveled to Jerusalem for great Temple festivals; pagan pilgrims journeyed to great shrines such as the Temple of Diana at Ephesus or to one or other of the Oracles; and innumerable "tourists" went to see Rome or Alexandria just for the fun of it.

After Augustus, not just armies moved incessantly across the empire. Merchants, businessmen and imperial bureaucrats traveled the length and breadth of the realm. Even a certain amount of tourism developed. Legionaries in large numbers visited far parts of the empire, generally on foot but without the necessity of fighting bloody battles. Young legionaries had time to dictate letters home, and their letters would be carried over land or sea by the imperial postal service or by army couriers. There was a good deal of travel into the empire by outsiders – including northern Germans, black Africans, Arabs, Buddhists and Hindus from India, and Parthians. A few Buddhist missionaries were active in the eastern fringes of the empire, presumably winning some converts. Religions and cults native to the eastern Mediterranean began to extend their reach westward across the empire, however most of these cults never became significant in the west until later, more troubled centuries. The trend to religious syncretism – the merging of gods -- had begun after Alexander the Great's imperial adventures, and it accelerated in the first century AD. Many social experiments – political, religious, intellectual, cultural and commercial -- were going on in the first century, even among the poor.

Taxes were collected from citizens and non-citizens by ruthless methods, and there might be local and other taxes to pay apart from the imperial assessments. There were few social services from the state – most tax money went for infrastructure, the military and the imperial court -- so every individual relied upon personal wealth, the safety net of family and friends, clubs and associations, patrons, and the favour of the gods to stay financially and socially afloat. Many did not manage to stay afloat.

In the uncertainties of life, poor people looked for protectors: friends, family, patrons and the gods. The custom of patronage began as a Roman one and slowly spread through the whole realm. It resembled a mini-feudal system. Wealthy, powerful men ("patrons") would have lesser people as "clients". These clients were expected to support the patron in his undertakings, to vote for him in elections, to assist him at need, to honour his household, and to steer him into any "best business opportunities" that might arise. In return, a patron was expected to help his clients find or move up in jobs, to give them gifts, to invite them to occasional meals, and to extend protection to them from the numerous predators of the empire – including the state itself. This last was important. A good patron would favour his clients, buy from their shops, assist them through times of crisis, and encourage their continued fidelity. Great and illustrious patrons might have among their many clients men of considerable standing. Every morning, clients began their day by calling on their patron to pay their respects. Clients would arrive at their patron's house early in the morning. "Good morning, magistrate Lucianus, sir" or

"Good morning, your excellency Cornelius Aemilius" would elicit such a reply as "Good morning, Petronius Septimius, my friend." The patron might spend only that moment with a client of low importance, reserving his conversation time for men of greater social standing. Petronius might be given a cup of warm wine and some bread to dip in olive oil, as a token breakfast. Petronius would chat then with other clients – he would see them every day and hence would know them – and then thank and bid goodbye to his patron.

On lower levels patronage was informal, even nominal, for when patrons were lesser folk who could do less for their clients, the clients too were less influential and could do less for their patrons. For that and other reasons, the poor often looked for added protection from their cult organizations or from fraternal societies. The early Christian communities offered their members emergency food, burial services, companionship and resource-sharing. A bishop or presbyter took the place of a patron. Yes, these were Mafia-like systems where patrons were godfathers, but they were not criminal systems, rather sensible mutual-help arrangements.

In the first century, the realm so recently assembled by force was still an assorted lot of provinces, client princedoms and principalities with their own histories and languages and a wide spectrum of religious, ethnic and cultural life. Their common factor was being losers to the Romans. The victorious Romans looked down on all losers, though not equally. Love and respect for one's neighbours were not expected and usually not present. Even among the subjects, Greeks and Semites didn't get along well -- to say the least. The folks in the Balkans didn't like the folks from North Africa. People from Spain had little empathy for their neighbours in Gaul and even less for those in Germany. Everybody wanted to be thought better than the barbarian Germanic tribes yet even the Romans had a sneaking admiration for the Germans as uncorrupted "noble savages" -- who after all had defeated Roman armies on several first-century occasions. And everyone looked down on the powerless, hapless native Egyptians.

Marcus Scaevus Ascanius, a free citizen, operated a small pottery factory in Pompeii. Ascanius – he's imaginary -- was a typical small Italian business owner, renting his factory space at the very edge of the city, and there employing – besides himself, his wife and their two sons – a freedman and three slaves. Ascanius was far from rich, but he was in the "middle class" such as it was. From local clay and water, he manufactured wheel-thrown plates and bowls of various sizes, functional dinnerware. The fresh items were air-dried and then kiln-fired at a low temperature. His wares were certainly not luxury goods, just everyday kitchen and serving items, and Ascanius was more concerned with fast production than with hard finishes, aesthetic beauty or long durability. He sometimes made somewhat better pieces to order, and sold his stock pieces mostly through a shop in western Pompeii. Ascanius always made ends meet. As a free Italian he paid no taxes. His business was steady, year-round and he himself was regarded as honest, affable and competent at his trade. He was thrifty. His family could dress respectably though not richly – there were no silks in his wife's wardrobe. They ate enough to be healthy but none of the family was likely to have obesity problems. Their dwelling space over the shop was unshared with others; not spacious but at least not really cramped. One room of it was used as warehousing space, another as an "office" where accounts and orders were kept, and where the sons slept. The slaves were quartered below and functioned as night guards. Ascanius came as close to being "middle class" as the empire could manifest.

He had a patron: his landlord Lucius Aulus Persennius. Aulus was a well-off capitalist of the equestrian class who owned a good deal of property in Pompeii. Each morning at dawn, all of Aulus' forty or so clients would be at the house paying respects, sharing news, and perhaps enjoying a cup of wine. The more important clients would be taken into the centre of Persennius' house, and the less important would gather in the atrium or the garden. The patron briefly greeted each man (there would not likely be any women present). Then the work day began.

It was quite different in faraway Upper Germany. **Val Osterius** worked as a woodcutter and woodworker not far from a frontier legionary camp. He was a free man, a German, but neither well-off nor a Roman citizen. There was always a market for wood: firewood was needed through the northern winter, logs for construction and roofing, wood for rustic furniture pieces, and planks for wagons and flooring. But Val's work was hard and the returns were not great. Most of Val's wood business was connected with the camp, and of necessity he sometimes did odd-job repair work for the soldiers. His big concession to the Romans was to keep his own hair cut rather short – in a fashion we could accept in the twenty-first century but which was still longish by first-century standards. He lived in the forest in a tiny hamlet of Germans, and his first language was German. He had no slaves; he was his own slave and his wife and children were his assistants. He had no patron.

The people of the hamlet were not Roman citizens and did not live in a full money economy. They grew their own food and hunted, they made their own clothing and footwear, and they bartered. Some of the men had left the settlement and joined auxiliary Roman armed forces. In a later age they could become full legionaries. Coins obtained from the Romans provided Val just enough for occasional luxuries such as knives, a new axe, a metal cooking pot and body ornaments. Val and his family were not so much poor as living largely in a traditional, pre-money economy where no one was rich. They were poverty-stricken but didn't feel it acutely because it was the historic norm. Indeed, times had never been better! At least there was now peace and order in their little world. There were many in the empire in similar circumstances.

—

In the many-layered Roman society the **liberti** ("freedmen") occupied an imprecise position – they were all former slaves who had been freed.

Upon being freed, an ex-slave became a freedman (or freedwoman) and sometimes even a Roman citizen. As citizens, people commanded further respect according to their position in society. Then as now, respect for professionals was almost always greater than respect for ordinary workers. However, the Roman masters of the empire were intensely class conscious, and that consciousness was contagious. It never cut any social ice to be the offspring of slaves – even though you yourself had become a rich freedman. Full respectability took two or three generations to develop, and inevitably involved social connections as well as money. But freedmen were often highly intelligent, were educated in some skill and were strongly motivated to rise in the ranks. The imperial bureaucracy was full of freedmen, often ex-slaves of the emperor himself, freed specifically to be appointed as "freedmen" to some titled office at the court. Under Augustus and more so Tiberius, many "ministers" of the court were freedmen. Freedmen started poor but often made their way upwards.

THE UPPER CLASSES

Apart from the super-wealthy elites, Roman **citizens** were in theory at the top of the imperial heap. In the first century they made up around 10% of the empire's population and were concentrated in Italy. They possessed legal and political privileges not available to other residents of the empire, but they were not necessarily rich or powerful. A citizen could not be crucified for any crime; he had to be tried properly, and if found guilty of a capital offense he would be "politely" beheaded. Until found guilty of an offense, a citizen could not even be beaten or flogged or tortured – standard treatments for non-citizen suspects. Where the non-citizen St. Peter ended up on a cross, the citizen St. Saul (Paul) ended up beheaded. Of course, it was death either way, but beheading was seen as much more honorable, and it was certainly quicker and less painful.

Citizenship didn't automatically make you rich. Financially, most citizens either paid reduced levels of tax or – especially in Italy -- none at all. They had many other perks relating to free food issues, travel rights, rights to general respect from others, exemption from having to billet soldiers, and a degree of protection from bullying by the military. It paid dividends to be a citizen in the first century. That's why many wealthy people paid out big amounts to buy citizenship. Those benefits gradually faded away in the next century as more and more people acquired citizenship, until by 212 AD all free people of the empire were made taxable citizens. But the legal quirks of the Romans were many. No ethnic Egyptian could ever become a citizen. Yet many freed slaves received citizenship automatically upon emancipation.

The Roman state conferred citizenship on its important friends. Old King Herod, a rough diamond as an individual, was given Roman citizenship, along with his whole family. All the Herodians were citizens by birth. Many Gaulish chieftains, Greeks and Spaniards got citizenship by gift. Citizens were not all equal by any means. The most distinguished (it's amazing how well that correlated with the richest) might be addressed as "illustrious" or "famous" or even "noble sir". Letters to such people would begin "Your illustriousness…" or "Your excellency…" because of their jobs or social standing. The wealthiest citizens of sterling lineage could expect to become Senators while those without famous ancestors, although with money galore, might first be officially designated as Equestrians or "knights" (**equites**) -- though that customary English translation doesn't property capture the significance of the title[1]. Any man wearing the gold ring of the Equestrian Order was marked as a "rich big-shot" to be treated well. Jesus' brother James complained about such preferential treatment in first-century churches:

> *Suppose two visitors come to your place of worship, one well-dressed with a gold ring, and the other a poor man in shabby clothes. Would you pay special attention to the rich man, saying,*

---

1 The term **eques** (plural **equites**) originally identified someone wealthy enough to maintain and train a cavalry horse.

*"Please take a good seat", while telling the poor man "You can
stand where you are"? Such inconsistency shows that you are
judging by false standards. [James 2: 2-4]*

Wealthy citizens were in fact few and were visibly distinguished from
the ordinary lot. There were income qualifications for entry into all the
privileged classes. The equestrians (or "knights") were a big economic
cut above the average free person. The qualifications for becoming a
knight were citizenship, social graces and assets above 400,000 sesterces;
that's roughly equivalent to a half-million dollars in 2018 currency. The
spectacular rise of the knights as a business class was a phenomenon
of the booming first century AD. Business people first strove to make
enough to qualify for entry into the equestrian class. Then, entry into the
senatorial class become the next generation's goal. Even greater wealth
was required for entry into that senatorial class: 800,000 sesterces (about
$1 million) was the bare minimum, and in addition candidates for that
class were expected to be citizens "of good family" and to be educated
and well-connected. The emperor himself vetted the appointments.
The senatorial class in Augustus' day comprised a thousand rich Italian
individuals (which Augustus halved), and there may not have been a
great many more equestrians. However, by 100 AD the equestrians were
counted in tens of thousands, and they – even when provincials -- were
fast colonizing the senatorial class. The senators were still limited in
numbers by the will of the emperor, so the admission of wealthy cultured
provincials little by little made the Senate much less "Italian" and much
more cosmopolitan. That came about also because the emperors, having
acquired the power to name people as senators, used that power to begin
bringing in favoured individuals from all over the empire. The emperor
Claudius, himself of most ancient Roman stock, scandalized the old-stock
senators by appointing a few ethnic Gallic citizens to their ranks.

So, the first century saw a meteoric rise of equestrians as a class, from
insignificance to a powerful position in society. Because the first century
also saw a steady decline in the prestige and influence of senators, it is not

surprising that senators of ancient Roman lineage looked down disapprovingly at mere equestrian "upstarts". By century's end, distinguished and wealthy leaders from outside Italy – Gauls, Germans, Spaniards, Africans and Greeks – perhaps local nobility or even descendants of slaves – had made their way into both the equestrian and the senatorial ranks.

There were aristocrats outside Rome's immediate orbit. The most enduring of these were the Herodians of Palestine. Despite Herod the Great's homicidal tendencies within his family, several sons survived to succeed the old king on his death in 4 BC. Herod Archelaus became the ruler of Judaea for ten disappointing years before being sent into forced retirement in Provence by Caesar Augustus. Archelaus' brother Herod Antipas was more astute, more fortunate and more effective. He ruled Galilee and adjacent areas for 43 years before also being booted into retirement, in Aquitaine, by emperor Caligula. Antipas' half-brother Philip ruled east of the Jordan mildly and very successfully for 38 years, right up to his death.

The Herodians were a colourful bunch. Nominally Jewish, most lived in pagan splendour and indulged themselves with building, conspicuous show, clawing their way upwards, and rendering active services to Rome. Some were pious Jews. They all had talent. Their incestuous sexual antics were well-known and were practiced throughout the entire family. They often married uncles, nieces and cousins. The husband of Queen Helena of Adiabene was her full brother. No one seemed to mind. However, while these marriages were incestuous in Roman law, many were not so in Jewish law. For example, around AD 27, the fifty-two-year-old Herod Antipas developed the urge to marry his niece Herodias -- who was also the charming wife of his brother Herod II (Herod-Philip) -- and he did so. The bride, Herodias, herself a grand-daughter of Herod the Great, was perfectly agreeable to this switch of brothers in her bed, for she was irritated by her do-nothing apolitical husband. But a certain Jewish prophet named John the Baptizer was outraged at this act because Herod II – Antipas' brother – was still alive, and the couple had produced a child. John's rigid sense of righteousness outraged, he denounced the marriage publicly and loudly. Antipas promptly arrested John, kept him in prison (but, oddly, visited him regularly) and at length was tricked into executing him. Execution was not Antipas' original intent. But Herodias had a thirteen-year-old daughter Salome -- from her marriage to Herod II -- who danced at a royal birthday party and wangled "any favour" from Uncle Antipas.

"Any favour at all, my child – even half my kingdom" intoned the somewhat tipsy Herod, using the traditional formulaic idiom.

"Mother, what shall I ask for?" Salome whispered to Herodias.

"Ask for the head of John the Baptizer", her mother replied softly. "In a bowl."

The girl hesitated. "Go ahead" prompted Herodias insistently. "Go on; ask now".

Salome approached Herod Antipas. "I would like to have John the Baptizer's head, in a bowl."

Antipas was shocked into sobriety, realizing that he had been tricked, but he felt that his word of honour was at issue. He first begged Salome to choose something else, and when she persisted, he finally gave a guard the necessary order. Fifteen minutes later the freshly-severed head was brought in, in a large shallow bowl. Thus Herodias took her revenge on John for his denunciation of her marriage. A thoroughly superstitious man, Antipas remained uneasy for a very long time afterwards. John continued to haunt his thoughts and his dreams, and he suspected that Jesus of Nazareth was John the Baptizer returned to life. Antipas wanted to meet Jesus. Some years later, he would.

—

At the very top of society, fueled by astronomical revenues from taxes and from those parts of the empire assigned to them as their "personal estate", the tax-free emperors and their courtiers grew more and more powerful, eventually becoming, by the end of the first century, the one and only motor of the state. They represented the state and its imperial power. Yet the empire as a concept slowly continued to mature, and along the way, it developed a more inclusive sense of itself. It was putting down roots! The biggest change during the first century was one of self-perception: in Caesar Augustus' day the Romans viewed their Italy as top dog and the rest of the empire as their property. The imperial subjects realized very well how things stood. By Trajan's reign at century's end, Rome and the rest of the empire were entering into a partnership and becoming a "commonwealth".

Popularly, the Roman emperors have often been portrayed as villainous, lazy, stupid, idle, debauched, luxury-loving softies. The reality was quite different, as the emperors themselves knew. With the possible exception of Claudius and Vitellius, all the first-century emperors were physically fit. They all led strenuously active lives, were intelligent and well-educated, and worked extremely hard. Augustus was right: the job of emperor was a soul-destroying grind of ceaseless effort in a mostly poisonous environment. The emperors were able but overworked managers. Their prestigious position was mostly thankless hard labour, never easing, always stressful and dangerous, sometimes fatal. Still, as they all knew, everyone wanted to be the glorious emperor, to have the power, to reside in luxury in the palace, to be seen and adored in glorious ceremonials, and to live among the gods. The Roman emperor was the ultimate celebrity, whose image was displayed prominently throughout the whole empire.

*[Jesus] said, "Show me a silver coin. Whose head does it show,
and whose inscription? They replied, "Caesar's". "Very good", he
continued, "Then pay Caesar what is due to Caesar, and pay God
what is due to God". [Luke 20: 24-25]*

THE ARMY

The Roman Army had existed from the earliest times. It originally was
a citizen army, mostly farmers called up to fight short-term summer
wars between seed-time and harvest. For obscure reasons it became, by
the time of Hannibal's invasion around 220 BC, a superbly disciplined,
trained and equipped force, formidable on any battlefield. And the
Romans became addicted to war. During the second and first centuries
BC the Army grew larger and even tougher. That's when the empire was
acquired by force. When Augustus triumphed in the civil wars in 31 BC
he acquired command of a professional standing army like no other. It
numbered 700,000 men. In the peace which followed, Augustus first
reduced the army to under 300,000 organized in 32 legions, and Tiberius
further stabilized the Army at about 200,000 organized in 28 legions.

The Roman army was arguably the most important institution of
the empire. From beginning to end, the military was the principal force
in the empire, without whose support no emperor could survive. The
armies defended and policed the empire. The army was the institution
most vital to the emperors – and also most feared by them, for at times
armies mutinied or raised up new emperors of their own choosing. In
the crumbling old Republic, soldiers had looked not to the state, the
Senate or the Consuls for their orders, their pay and their rewards in
the field; they looked to their commanding General. He was expected
to look after "his" troops, which thus amounted to a private army. First
emperor Augustus, who knew first-hand all about this pernicious system,
strove mightily to eradicate it and to make the emperor (himself, at the
time) the real Commander-in-Chief to whom every soldier of every

legion would direct loyalty and obedience, and from whom every soldier could expect his pay and rewards. To promote this change, Augustus appointed rather young, non-senatorial legates as limited-term generals for the individual armies – men without the clout to lead an army against the emperor. Augustus made other changes too, partly for efficiency and partly to prevent renegades from ever gaining control over an army. For Augustus, having earlier been just such a renegade, feared the army. Fatally, Augustus decided to station his legions on distant frontiers, where they would not threaten the emperor in Rome. It was an expedient but bad strategy which seemed sensible at the opening of the first century. But nothing worked, then or later. The army remained a wild card and was soon making and un-making emperors.

Caesar Augustus placed the Roman legions around the periphery of the empire in territories which – along with their legions – were under his direct control, as "imperial provinces". The quiet central parts of the empire which remained under the administrative control of the Senate had almost no legions stationed in them. Recent history had shown Augustus that Roman Germany needed large legionary resources to defend it against the Free Germany beyond: so Roman Germany got almost a quarter of all the empire's legions. Gaul had three legions. Britain received two legions in AD 43 when it was conquered. Syria which faced the Parthian Empire was assigned three legions, and Egypt was given two. Spain started out with three legions but that number was soon reduced to just one. The regions along the Danube River were defended by four legions, and single legions were stationed in relatively peaceful North Africa, the southern Balkans and Anatolia. These numbers kept changing, but the fact of the military being located at frontiers rather than through-out the empire meant that the Roman armies became defensive forces. Unless there was an invasion, legions basically sat tight and waited… bored… for something to do.

Thus the military might of the Empire remained under the close control of the emperors, yet was not very visible to the central empire. In addition to those frontier legionary forces, various sub-kings, regional potentates and local rulers could be counted on to provide auxiliary troops. Those auxiliary forces tended to be kept in the internal parts of the empire. By mid-century, the emperors were in command of vast amounts of money and vast, often restive armed forces. The rapid decline in the power of the Senate during the first century is not surprising in retrospect, but at the time it was much resented by the senators. They too were bored.

—

The Roman legions like all armed forces comprised a complex hierarchy of military officials of which the **centurion** is probably most familiar to modern ears. The army organization was constantly evolving. A first-century centurion commanded about 80-90 soldiers. A full legion numbered about 6000-7000 men, including a few horsemen and non-combatants, and there were sixty centurions in each legion. The legion itself was notionally divided into ten battalion units (cohorts) of about 600-700 men each. The rank and file soldiers were rather poorly paid, but the officers were generously remunerated. Centurions were all graded from the most senior to the most junior, and promotion within each legion was avidly sought. A promotion might involve a move to another legion in the area, or even to one far away. But as centurions generally served for life, the army was their career no matter where they served. Promotion was by merit, and they traveled wherever they were sent. Centurions were the lowest level of "officers" but operationally one of the most important, for on them army discipline ultimately depended.

Much sought after was the post of **military tribune**, of which there were usually six in each legion, again graded. Military tribunes and legates were political appointments and ever remained so, yet in the absence of the legate general, the senior tribune was expected to take over. That was remarkable because the legate legionary commanders and the military tribunes were often young senators working their way up to a provincial governorship, or ex-consuls who had served their term in that office and then had gone on to the next step on the staircase of honours -- a high military command. Both leading officers were to some extent amateurs. The lead military tribune wore a distinctive uniform with a wide purple stripe and served directly under the legion's commanding legate (**legatus**) – the head or General of the legion after the word **imperator** had become the sole prerogative of the emperors. As representatives in the field for Rome, these young legates often took on diplomatic roles as **proconsuls** or local governors, as imperial representatives. In fact both the office of legate and the office of military tribune became political plum appointments as the empire wore on. The English word "governor" covers a whole handful of Latin terms for similar civil imperial functions: legatus, proconsul, procurator, prefect and propraetor.

The auxiliaries supplied by Rome's client rulers were not negligible forces – there were 150,000 to 200,000 of them -- and in a pinch, they would be put at the service of the Roman overlords. Otherwise they formed policing forces in their locales. The Herodian rulers had little mercenary armies for this.

Life in the army was hard. Recruits came from the poor. The training and work assignments were very demanding, and discipline was fierce. Pay for ordinary legionaries was low though not impossibly so but in combat there were usually opportunities for plunder; soldiers eagerly sought such opportunities. Each soldier was supplied with standardized arms including a short sword, a long dagger, a pair of throwing javelins, a shield, and rudimentary armour. On the march, a soldier would also carry cooking utensils, bedding, bits of dis-assembled siege gear, and so forth; a soldier's load was around 25 kg (60 lb). A great deal of time was devoted to training and manoeuvres since in real battle tactics had to be carried out smoothly and without questions or mistakes. That training in addition kept the troops busy and mitigated boredom.

In olden days, the term of military service had been sixteen years. In Augustus' era the men served for twenty, sometimes twenty-five years, and were then retired with a cash settlement and a land grant -- if they survived that long. Caesar Augustus had extreme difficulty financing the army once the booty from the conquest of Egypt dried up. That was why the legions had to be kept down in numbers, and why the emperor imposed the much-resented twenty- to twenty-five-year terms of service. Cautious Augustus consistently overestimated the empire's needs for defence, and kept too many men under arms for too long. In fairness however, we must recognize that he also dreamt of new conquests and needed armies for offence as well as defence. Only at the very end of his long reign did he realize that the empire would have to be stabilized at about its current size. The age of big conquests was over.

The hardness of army life made the army less and less attractive to young Italians. At the start of the first century soldiers mostly came from Italy; it was still a citizen army. By century's end most troops were non-Italian. Germans began to find their way into the army during the first century and proved themselves excellent soldiers.

Although army discipline was tight, there were innumerable mutinies, revolts of legions, and insubordination was a constant feature of the armies. The incitements were exactly those complaints of most other sections of imperial society: "We're not paid enough"; "The boss is too hard on us"; "Our term of service is too long"; "We hate it out here on the godforsaken frontier". But unlike other sections of society, the armies carried power in their hands and could – if push came to shove – pursue their demands by force. Every emperor without exception faced military mutinies and rebellions. The emperors couldn't survive without the armies, but sometimes they didn't survive because of them.

Most emperors feared the armies with good reason and tried to protect themselves from their own legions. Augustus set up a German bodyguard for himself. That didn't last. Tiberius created a special force of supposedly ultra-loyal troops in a personal "Praetorian Guard". These 8,000 crack troops were stationed right in Rome to guard the emperor and his family. The pay was excellent and the quartering and treatment were also good. The Guard was usually under the control of two Praetorian Prefects appointed by the emperor. Alas, these elite Guards and their Prefects proved even more dangerous and troublesome than the frontier armies. Very soon they began to make and un-make emperors themselves.

There was a Roman Navy of sorts, but it was very small. It was not within the roster of legions but was rather an auxiliary force with its own Prefects. There was a naval base at Misenum near Naples, and later on a second base near Ravenna on the Adriatic Sea. Later still, a squadron was kept in the English Channel to link the mainland with by-then Roman Britain. There was a small squadron at Alexandria too. The Navy never became important, for by nature the Romans preferred to rely on land forces.

SLAVERY

The reality of mass slavery was everywhere on display. Slaves made up at least a tenth of the empire's population in the first century – that's around 7,000,000 slaves. They were particularly numerous in Italy. Nearly half the population of Rome was slaves. But slavery had always existed – it was certainly not an invention of the Romans – and it was considered a normal part of every society. At the bottom of society, slaves did a wide variety of work. Slaves were mainly generated by wars, as prisoners of war or (more often) as enslaved non-combatants. In the first century most slaves in the empire were from the East, and a disproportionately large number ended up in Italy. The Roman-Jewish war of AD 66-71 produced at least 100,000 new slaves.

Crushed at the very lowest level of society were many unskilled slaves (perhaps a quarter of the slave population) with no human rights whatsoever. They were simply machines to be worked. Their owners could beat them, or work them to death, or exploit them sexually (that was standard practice), and an owner could summarily dispose of them when they were too old or infirm to work. Slaves were deliberately worked to death in the mines or on the galleys – those destinations were dreaded as court-imposed sentences. But work on the great farming estates was also pitilessly hard. All those things were considered normal, for the early empire was a brutal place in which to be an underdog of any kind. At best, slaves were skilled servants with some education and interesting professional-type duties. At worst they were unfortunates sent – men, women and children too -- to be worked to death underground in the mines, on the galleys, or on industrial production lines. The lot of uneducated slaves on the huge farms was perhaps worst of all because of the great numbers involved and because landlords and farm managers habitually squeezed the last drop out of their properties, including their slaves.

Slaves had no legal rights whatsoever – legally they were just chattel goods -- and any mutiny by slaves was always put down with appalling brutality. For example, Roman law specified that if a household slave murdered a member of the master's family, all the slaves in that household would be crucified. That could involve hundreds of people. That punishment was carried out time and again. We will hear later of a celebrated case in AD 61.

When slaves became too sick or too old to work, they were sold off or simply abandoned to die. Occasionally they were freed but still they were incapable of supporting themselves. Upon death the bodies were sometimes disposed of in large common pits outside the city walls or on waste ground. The City of Rome had two such disposal sites, each of which received dozens of cadavers each day. There were no monuments for such indigent slaves, nor any grave markers. "*Some there are who have no memorial.*"

All that said, it was not unknown for slaves to be employed in households where they were treated with consideration – even as fellow human beings with feelings. It did not happen often. Many of the imperial court slaves were among such fortunates, for the emperor being limitlessly rich had no need to squeeze his slaves – he just wanted reliable skilled services. He even gave his court slaves a small monthly allowance, and of course the aristocracy then adopted that practice. Such fortunate slaves upon death might even be decently buried by their owners or friends. And they might at some point be freed. Many owners considered it meritorious to free at least some of their slaves, either during their own lifetime or in their Wills. Imperial household slaves were the most likely to be freed, and that route provided many of the administrative officials of the Julio-Claudian emperors. Because eminent class-conscious Romans disliked doing business with imperial slaves, the emperors simply freed their slave-officials and made them citizens with official duties. Every slave dreamt of being freed. Everything depended on the luck of the draw of an owner, and on fickle Fortune. For the vast majority of slaves there was no luck or Fortune, just a life of unending drudgery and abuse. Verbal abuse, social abuse, sexual abuse and casual physical abuse.

Yet in the empire, many highly skilled professional services were normally performed by slaves. A rich family's doctor would typically be a slave; so might accountants, managers, scribes, architects and artisans. Such people were valuable and in general were treated as valuable – only they couldn't resign! Most of the empire's slaves came from the northern and eastern parts of the empire, and most spent their servitude in Italy. Greeks made up the majority of highly-skilled slaves.

A master could free a slave by a legal process called manumission. Slaves sometimes could win their freedom by completing a large number of years of service; that was true of imperial slaves in military service. Once in a long while freedom could be bought for cash – the slave effectively bought himself and then freed himself. A freed slave became a "freedman" or "freedwoman", free but still without much social status. These freedmen almost always remained attached to their former owner in a tight patron-client relationship. The patron would use an ex-slave's services and would provide basic social protection and leverage; the freedman became a client of his former master.

By quirks of Roman law, in certain circumstances freed slaves might automatically become Roman citizens upon manumission. Thus, over centuries, the number of slaves declined, and the number of free people – taxpayers -- kept expanding. That, however, did not change the socio-economic need of freed slaves for employers and protectors.

The children of slaves were slaves – that was one means by which an owner could replenish his supply of slaves. But the post-manumission children of freedmen were free, sometimes with citizenship, even if a shadow of social stigma remained on all children of ex-slaves. The next generation wiped that stigma away: the children of new citizens-by-birth were free without taint. Their next challenge was to claw their way higher on the social scale in the class-ridden Roman society. Rising up the social scale depended ultimately on accumulating wealth and influence, for money and lineage were everything in Roman eyes. Thus a freed slave would try to become wealthy and then, ironically, could buy his own herd of slaves.

III
PROPHETS, PREACHERS
AND PRAYERS

MAKING FRIENDS WITH THE GODS

In the first century, every state, every principality, even every little settlement, had its own divinities which somehow had gained acceptance and which commanded beliefs, rites and sacrifices. The early Roman empire was a religious mosaic of immense complexity. The "great religions" of the first-century empire were the cults of classical Greco-Roman paganism; Judaism; the cult of Isis; and the Great Mother cult. Beyond the empire, to the east, were the Zoroastrians of Parthia. In the west were Celtic pantheons. But there were very many lesser faiths too. All were based on superstition, fear, and the desire for divine protection; and all had their peculiar rites.

Religion throughout the empire was in rapid change in the first century. This change was facilitated by three factors. First, the Roman Peace which began in 31 BC under Augustus allowed far greater mobility of ideas across the imperial territory. Second and related to that, there was everywhere a tendency to religious borrowings or mergers as worshippers in every cult tried to subsume or equate other gods to their own. The Romans' own stodgy religion, essentially a matter of state and patriotism, in AD 14 began adding deceased emperors to its already large roster of gods. The late Augustus became a god then by vote of the Senate in that year. There was a certain trend to "shopping for religions" and, hand in hand with that, secular philosophical schools were actively putting themselves forward as alternatives to traditional beliefs. Third, tensions and fractiousness peculiar to Judaism were making that empire-wide religion uncontrollably dynamic. Monotheism was on the march. Already in the early first century, Judaism was a religion of international importance and renown. The century would produce Christianity as a "new Judaism" and would transform the old Judaism into another "new Judaism".

—

In Antiquity, almost everyone was profoundly superstitious and lived in fear of gods – or of God – and of various spirits and invisible forces. It went hand in hand with the ignorance and credulity of the time. For in the ancient world most people were unlearned and illiterate. Even the educated and well-read were steeped in superstition, for the world was poorly understood. Whatever happened was ascribed to the gods. And much could happen. Fear of injury, of sickness, of ill-fortune, of evil spirits, of demonic attack and of magic drove everyone to seek to propitiate the ever-present powers that could work harm, and to beseech still greater powers to give protection against the malevolence of the visible and unseen worlds. Modern people can scarcely grasp how pervasive superstition was in the first century. Everyone – pagans, Jews, Christians, agnostics and atheists – acknowledged the existence of spirits, demons and other mysterious forces of nature. Everyone believed in magic. To be cursed by someone was no laughing matter. Everyone accepted as possible much which we now consider impossible. The gods could if they chose turn you into a tree, or a swan, or a rock; it had happened before. The first-century writer Ovid wrote a whole book about such transformations. Rampant superstition, credulity and the tenuous nature of everyday life fuelled all the religions of the first century.

Worship of gods was manifested in three ways. First, one had to acknowledge the gods by their names, and try to communicate with them. That communication often involved people of the community who possessed special interlocutor skills – priests or shamans. Second, one had to carry out duties of obedience to the perceived will of the gods. This involved attendance at communal worship and participation in set rituals. Third, and very important, one had to placate the gods by gifts and sacrifices. These gifts might be agricultural produce, an animal, or precious goods for the god's shrines and their priests. In times of great crisis – such as a plague or famine – the sacrifice of some member of the community might be made.

The Romans and the Greeks had broadly similar Indo-European pantheons which were quite easily synthesized. But many peoples of the empire had religions which were strange to the Romans, and which in some cases the Romans disliked intensely. The human-sacrifice rituals of the Druids offended the Romans, and the horrifying rites of the Carthaginian goddess Tanit, in which infants were burned as sacrifices, were so offensive that the Romans suppressed them altogether. The Romans were not at all squeamish, but human sacrifice was beyond the limit of their religious toleration. Nor were the Romans keen on the bloody processions of the Syrian Cybele the Great Mother, during which her young priests would in ecstasy whip, lacerate and even castrate themselves.

Only the Jews had evolved a mature monotheism. In their original pantheon of gods, one male god (called El, later Yahweh) had long ago achieved primacy and other gods were demoted to the status of assistants: angels, archangels, cherubim and seraphim. Satan was demoted from god-status to become a rebel angel and thus the prime force of evil -- Yahweh's rebellious servant. That was brought off with considerable intellectual difficulty and Satan retained, even in the first century, the popular image of an independent Evil One working against God yet somehow under his control. The Zoroastrian religion asserted a frankly dual system of two divine Powers of good and evil. More surprisingly, in the first century, some Judaic thought still did envision an all-powerful, eternal God accompanied by other god-like entities, in particular by an eternal entity Wisdom, and perhaps also by an eternal Holy Spirit. Monotheism had been attained, but just barely.

It was a moot point among monotheists whether the gods of the pagans actually existed under the control of God, or whether they were entirely figments of pagan imagination. Opinion was long divided but most monotheists allowed that pagan deities were real, albeit charlatans. All religions faced questions about how their own pantheons were organized. Of course, it was vital to know exactly who held what powers. No use praying for rain to the god of war. Almost always, befriending the gods involved performing certain rituals which were thought to please the divine powers. This was true of all pagan cults as well as the monotheistic Jewish worship. Temples were the acknowledged homes of the gods and the sites of many rituals.

Most polytheistic religions were drifting in the direction of monotheism by the first century. Their gods, goddesses, spirits and demons were all being shuffled in status so that some principal divinity tended to be promoted over all others. For example, the ancient Syrian goddess Cybele (=Artemis) tamed her divine associates early on and rose to the top of the power ladder as the Great Mother. Isis similarly came to overshadow Osiris and Horus and was the focus of the Isis cult of the first century. Originating in Persia, the god Mithras entered the Roman empire virtually as a sole deity. Even the Romans' own religion acknowledged that some divinities were more powerful than others. At the top of the Roman heap were Jupiter Capitolinus, his consort Juno, and Minerva. But many other deities retained primacy within their own spheres: Neptune was supreme in the sea, Vulcan in the deep earth, Apollo in the arts, Diana in the wild forests, and so forth. However, there was no consensus – apart from father Jupiter -- as to who was ultimately one's best bet for protection and aid, and so pagans continued to approach many gods and demi-gods just to be on the safe side. Apart from the gods of the whole community, Romans also honoured family gods called the Lars and Penates, deities of one's own particular family. The Israelites had similar household gods in the time of the patriarch Jacob around 1700 BC.

Religion and the Roman state were not separated in the first-century empire. Indeed, no state of that time was separated from religion; the very idea of a secular-sacred divide was absent. The worship of the Roman gods was held to be a requirement for the empire's receiving the protection and help of those celestial powers. Thus, their worship was an important civic duty of every Roman and of every resident of the empire. It was a mark of patriotism; and the emperor led the religious parade. The Romans were nowhere more conservative and primitivistic than in matters of religious rituals. There, the Romans' inclination to legalism and their full-blown superstition came together. Public rites were celebrated frequently and punctiliously. In imperial Rome, on average, every other day was a religious holiday with its set rituals. If a presiding priest should by chance omit or mis-pronounce a single word of the liturgy, the entire rite had to be repeated from the very beginning. It sometimes happened. The liturgies were written out and assiduously practiced for good reason: some were so ancient that their language could no longer be understood. Because no mistakes on the part of the priest would be tolerated by the gods, an expert official **auditor** ("listener") attended every ritual to ensure that no mispronunciation slipped by. The health of the state might be compromised by mistakes. It would be a fair judgment that the Roman system of ritual was fossilized by the first century and elicited scant emotional response. It offered no personal benefits such as "salvation" or "righteousness" or "forgiveness". It survived because it was traditional, state-driven, state-funded and closely connected in the minds of worshippers with patriotism and good citizenship, as well as with the strong desire for divine protection of the community and the empire.

A religious revolution began in the first-century deification of emperors. When Augustus died in 14, the admiring Roman Senate voted to make him a god. Although this seems extremely presumptuous to twenty-first-century minds, it was an aspect of that tight politico-religious bond that characterized the Roman state and people. That the shade of Augustus had actually been seen rising up into the skies was attested by well-rewarded witnesses. Augustus was declared a god by a vote. Moreover, the next emperor (Tiberius) ensured that Augustus got temples throughout the empire and that those temples were properly staffed with priests and others in the same way as were the temples of the traditional deities. But when Tiberius in his turn passed on, the Senate did nothing to deify him. The senators had never liked Tiberius. You didn't become a god if the senators didn't like you. Nor did the Senate deify the third emperor, Gaius Caligula. The Senate loathed him. It was not until old Claudius died in 54 that the next deification was voted, entailing another batch of temples and priests. The Senate passed on Nero, Galba, Otho and Vitellius, then in AD 79 deified Vespasian. The emperor Titus followed (by a narrow vote) in 81, but Domitian had no chance of being deified as he had a notably abrasive relationship with the Senate. No more political gods were created in the first century apart from the unworthy but Senate-friendly Nerva in 98.

The Romans themselves were not entirely comfortable with the deification of emperors. According to the historian Tacitus, the Senate had to cite a miracle as evidence in support of its deifications. The standard evidence was testimony that the departed emperor's spirit had actually been seen ascending to heaven. "Witnesses" to these ascensions incurred ridicule, made worse by the large gratuities – usually a million sesterces – that they earned from their testimony. Tacitus' report stops just short of open sarcasm. Deification after death soon led to anticipatory deification in life, and some living Roman emperors sought to become quasi-divine rulers. This happened as early as Caligula, the third emperor, who flaunted his self-proclaimed divinity and enthusiastically encouraged his own worship. He scolded the Jewish Temple for making sacrifices only on his behalf: "Not just <u>for</u> me, I want sacrifices <u>to</u> me". Predictably, Caligula and the Jews did not get on well.

Judaism, thanks to historic accidents, was formally recognized as a "legal religion" in the empire, and Jews had important legal privileges available to no other group. The main historic accident was the independent

Jewish state's decision back in 165 BC to seek the active friendship of the Romans. It brought long-term benefits as well as unlooked-for conquest by the Romans. In the deal, the Romans exempted Jews from the requirement to sacrifice to pagan gods (including, in imperial times, the deified emperors). Also, Jews were not liable to serve in the army. In truth, the Romans didn't want troops who would fight and work only six days out of seven, and who needed special diets. Julius Caesar entrenched these privileges and others in a formal treaty in return for Judaean support in his political-military struggles in the eastern Mediterranean in the mid-first century BC. The Judaeans delivered fully on the deal, and later Roman leaders periodically re-confirmed the privileges.

Christianity began its life in the 30s as a new messianic Jewish sect, and for decades almost all Christians were considered simply as Jews who believed that Jesus of Nazareth was their long-awaited Messiah, and who were therefore entitled to the same legal privileges that other Jews enjoyed. But that situation didn't last. Jews and Christians fell out at once over whether Jesus was or was not the Messiah of Israel. Not much later was added the contentious extra issue of gentile converts to Christianity who did not undertake the full requirements of Judaism. By degrees and almost by chance, Christianity became perceived as different from the rest of Judaism and therefore as an illegal religion – a **superstitio** to use the Roman term. Although the earliest Christians were Jews and enjoyed the legal privileges of Jews, those Jews who rejected Jesus as the Messiah soon made it clear to the Roman authorities that the Christians "weren't real Jews" and shouldn't have the status of Jews. And so the Christians eventually lost that legal status. Nonetheless, Christianity managed over less than three hundred years to grow from nothing to take over the empire. During that time it grew somewhat away from its Judaic roots and became a gentile-dominated religion. After the late first century, Christianity never again enjoyed the legal privileges of Judaism, and in fact it became increasingly opposed to Judaism. The feeling was mutual.

While Christianity established itself slowly but continuously, mainstream Judaism by comparison began strong in Augustus' time but suffered massive reverses during the course of the first and second centuries. Those reverses, as we will see later, engendered a new kind of Judaism that has survived ever since.

Contrary to much modern belief, Greco-Roman paganism proved immensely resilient to all challenges. It was not decaying, nor "on the ropes" in the first century. For hundreds of years after Christianity became the official religion of the state in the 300s, pagan practices continued as a sub-culture, especially in rural areas. Indeed, the Latin word **paganus** originally meant simply a country dweller. Vestiges of old paganism remain with us even today in the Easter bunny, Halloween ghosts, decorated Christmas trees, mistletoe, maypoles, Mid-summer's Day open-air celebrations, the veneration of Mary, horoscopes, astrology, lucky/unlucky numbers and so forth. People still exclaim "By Jove" without thinking about the origin of that oath.

The ancients had some odd notions. Around the earth revolved, each day, the moon, the sun and the stars (including five "wandering stars" which we now call planets). It was a cozy little universe, with the stars embedded in a solid dome up in the sky at no great distance. Occasionally a piece of a "star" would fall to earth. The age of the earth was thought to be three or four thousand years, and those numbers found expression in Hebrew dating and in many creation mythologies. Beneath the earth's surface lay a dark, foreboding Underworld full of dead souls. Everybody knew that. There were, here and there, actual openings in the ground thought to connect our world with that Underworld. In such a universe, innumerable beings – visible and invisible -- were moving to and fro working good or ill: good cherubim, seraphim, angels, archangels (all from the heavens above); spirits and sprites; but also wicked devils, goblins, demons, evil spirits, ghosts, ogres and monsters from below. Stories and myths abounded. The good beings were believed to be controlled or controllable by great gods or even by one God, and the "bad" beings – so it was believed – were the agents of malevolent gods or of an Evil One. Almost everyone in those times believed in the material existence of these supernatural beings and in their nearness and malign power. Sacrifices of animals, of harvests, and even of one's own children, might appease the gods and keep their favour. In addition, people relied on charms, talismans, tokens, prayers, spells, incantations and out-and-out magic and witchcraft as defences from evil beings and their destructive powers.

Credence in wonder-workers was strong and universal. Jesus of Nazareth was seen as such a figure; that's why crowds followed him around. However, the pagans had wonder-workers aplenty too. There was the famous Apollonius, for instance. Even the emperor Vespasian worked miraculous healings on occasion. Needless to add that charlatans and frauds also operated in vast numbers.

A general belief in antiquity was that the world had begun with a golden age and had gone downhill ever since. The golden age was followed by a silver age; that in turn was followed by an age of bronze, and at last came an age of iron – the age of the first century. It was a despairing philosophy of anti-progress not unlike what unexpectedly emerged in the late twentieth century. Things go from good to bad and from bad to worse. And all around them, that is what the ancients could see; their pessimism was well justified. The good old days of Saturn's rule were gone forever. Yet the first century produced other views. The Epicureans thought that the world would continue forever, and that there were no gods to fear (or at least that the gods were so distant from mortals that they could not affect men's fates) or to beseech. Man was thus his own master, and Nature was his home, not just his cupboard to loot. To pagans and monotheists alike, the Epicureans were despicable atheists. Although most ancient religions envisioned a cyclical world which renewed, decayed and was renewed again, the Jews and even more so the Christians believed that history is linear, leading upwards to a final God-ordained messianic golden end-age. The only significant difference between the Jews and the Christians in this regard was timing. Christians believed that Jesus the Messiah had already appeared and initiated the arriving golden age. Jews held that the Messiah was yet to appear. And so it stands today.

As we have seen, deified emperors really were treated as gods, and they were expected after death to continue watching from the heavens over the Roman state. What was actually to be venerated was the "genius" or "soul" or spirit of the man. That worship might involve little more than dropping a few flakes of incense into a little marketplace flame burning in front of a statue of the deified man. Or there might be festival rituals complete with sacrifices of bulls or sheep. Either way, worshippers were not expected to go into raptures of ecstasy.

Emperor-worship became a sore point with Christians and Jews alike. Even though Judaism was legally exempted from worshipping the pagan gods, it was politically difficult not to honour the emperor in some visible way. So even the Jerusalem Temple dutifully sacrificed two lambs and a bull each day for the health of the emperor; and the pagan emperors regularly supplied the sacrificial animals and donated generously to the upkeep of the Temple. There was a clear understanding between the Jews and Romans that the former would not be required to worship the pagan gods -- including the emperors. Christians never enjoyed any such understanding or exemptions, and in time they became extremely prickly about emperor-worship. Until the last decade of the first century there was some feeling of accommodation under which a Christian could still offer the pinch of incense at the emperor's statue in each town, without any sense of offending God or betraying Jesus Christ. Beginning in the reign of Domitian, attitudes changed, partly because that emperor claimed divinity in his lifetime. Some Christians then saw the little pinch of incense as worship of an idol, a false god, and they tried to avoid offering it. By the second century that attitude had stiffened and Christians of fanatical faith chose appalling tortures and hideous deaths over any symbolic action that might smack of pagan emperor-worship. The second century, not the first, began the age of martyrs.

The common thread of all religion was protection. The first-century vigour of paganism was due in large measure to the first emperor. Augustus aimed to re-invigorate the traditional Roman paganism of his time and to make religion one of the cornerstones of the empire. And he succeeded. He insisted on stricter public religious observances and called for better private moral behaviour than had previously been manifested. He built new temples, he restored priesthoods and he personally oversaw many rites and observances. Probably, his own faith in the gods of Rome was real. They had brought Rome to ascendency over all others, they had raised up Augustus himself, against all odds, to the pinnacle of power, and they would – he prayed – continue to prosper the empire and his own August Family.

But this pagan worship system was not rooted in any deep moral or ethical beliefs. It didn't touch hearts. Paganism was largely a patriotic duty and a matter of ritual. While the gods were called upon to protect the state, they also were petitioned by ordinary individuals. The empire was full of sick and suffering people because the ancients were largely ignorant on medical matters. Against misfortune, illness and the assault of demonic forces, individuals in ancient times very often placed themselves personally under the special protection of some god or goddess, to whom they gave special fealty and faithful ritual service. In addition, through religious cults or associations, one's co-religionists could provide material support, fellowship and extra prayers in times of trouble or need. This remains a feature of many religions.

At life's end comes death. In paganism most burials used a stone sarcophagus or a small tomb chamber. Whatever the means of disposal of the remains, the significant dead were memorialized by a plaque or monument. In general, anyone could claim a body for the purpose of giving it a decent burial. For example, a Pharisee called Joseph of Arimathea claimed Jesus' body from Pontius Pilate. St. Peter's crucified corpse was claimed by the Christian Pudens family; St. Saul's body was taken and buried by Graecina Pomponia and her friends. Nero's old lover Claudia Acte claimed his body and oversaw its proper and dignified burial, for she still loved him.

Some people died at sea, some fell in battle, and not a few simply disappeared. Those left alive to mourn might take comfort in a belief that the departed were in the care of the gods, or of God. Yet, surprisingly, all religions of the time – including even Judaism and nascent Christianity – were notably unsure about the certainty and quality of "life after death". The pagans lacked a strong belief in afterlife, and most supposed that the immaterial souls of the departed found their way only to eternal imprisonment in Hades beneath the ground. Among Jewish sects, the Sadducees denied any afterlife. But some people – Greeks and many Jews -- spoke hopefully of the "soul" being imperishable and receiving a just reward for a meritorious life. So, prayers to the gods (or God) were regularly made for the dead, and their memory was kept alive. Somewhere, their souls were still around… and the gods were still in charge of them.

The cult of Isis originated in Egypt. Originally it was about Isis' husband the pre-dynastic God-King Osiris, and their son Horus who became the next divine King. By the first century the cult had become a mystery religion and Isis had evolved into a salvation goddess in whose service many people – especially women – found joy and happiness in life. Isis was, apart from the cult of Yahweh, the major cult of antiquity which promised personal salvation to individuals. The goddess's flower-strewn, music-filled processions were frequent events in the cities of the empire, even in Rome itself. The goddess accepted flowers as her preferred sacrifice but rejected blood sacrifices. Among the notable devotees of Isis was the emperor Domitian. The worshippers of Isis – male and female alike -- were subject to an initiation rite but were not barred from worshipping other deities as well. Yet many followers – especially women -- chose Isis as their only deity and personal protectress. Her rituals featured singing and displays of colours (flowers, fabrics, lights), and especially the full moon was associated with her rites. Isis was the model for the later cult of the Virgin Mary.

PALESTINE UNDER THE HERODIANS

The most successful and rigorous religion of the empire in the years 1-65 was arguably Judaism, which had its centre and its holy places in Palestine.

Ancient Jews believed that their ancestor Abraham had entered into an eternal covenant with God under which God would provide protection to Abraham's descendants forever and would grant them a Promised Land (Canaan, roughly modern Palestine) as a home. On the human side, the covenant was to be kept by fidelity to the one God and by male circumcision, which ever after remained essential signs of belonging within the covenant. Later in Jewish history, around the sixth century BC, adherence to the law code of Moses became another requirement for life in the covenant.

The long history of the Jews was a chequered one. After a lengthy exile in Egypt (1700-1400 BC) Israelite descendants of Abraham returned to Palestine under Moses, Aaron and Joshua to conquer or re-occupy land which they understood had been promised to them by God himself. In time, that conquest engendered an Israelite kingdom of considerable glory under King Saul, King David and King Solomon (1050-950 BC). The kingdom then split back into its original two parts. Israel in the north, the larger and more prosperous part, was conquered by the Assyrians in the 700s BC, and the Babylonians conquered the smaller southern kingdom of Judah, with its capital Jerusalem, a hundred and fifty years later. On both occasions there were mass deportations of the inhabitants to Mesopotamia. Both Israel and Judah subsequently passed into the hands of the Persians in the early 500s BC and were in part rehabilitated. The two states next passed to the conquering pagan Greeks under Alexander the Great in 330 BC.

Long subjection to religiously and ethnically alien rulers fanned the flames of religious and ethnic nationalism among the Israelite people of Palestine, so that the period 300 to 60 BC was a time of radicalization, revolts and nationalistic wars against the pagan rulers. During that long period, there developed a cultural divide between those Jews (the so-called "Hebrews") who adhered strictly to traditional Yahwist religion and culture, and those (the so-called "Hellenists") who followed the ancestral religion in the main but allowed themselves some elements of Greek culture. In the last phase of the wars between the Seleucid Greeks and the Judaeans, the strict Jews appealed to the Romans for help. The desired help was immediately forthcoming and effective, to be sure, but the engagement of Rome led ultimately to Palestine's outright conquest by the Romans in 63 BC.

Herod the Great nominally adhered to Judaism as a religion but he was neither religious nor ethnically Israelite. He was very much a Hellenist and in many respects a pagan. Under Roman supervision, he ruled the territories of Judaea, Israel, Samaria, Peraea, Galilee and Transjordan which formed a cohesive geographical block not totally unlike the ancient kingdom of King David. Herod was a full-fledged tyrant, a superb politician, a great builder, a staunch friend of the Romans, and a thoroughly hated man. Married ten times, he spawned the extensive and ruinously in-bred family called the Herodians.

The Herodians tended to be long-lived; Herod the Great reigned from 38 BC to 4 BC. His three surviving sons Herod Antipas, Herod Archelaus and Herod Philip respectively became, after old Herod's death, rulers of Galilee, Samaria-Judaea and the trans-Jordan north country. They too reigned for almost forty years, except for Herod Archelaus who was such an utter failure as a ruler that in AD 6 Augustus "retired" him to southern France. For the next 35 years, Judaea was governed directly by Prefects sent out from Rome, of whom the longest-serving and best known was Pontius Pilate (26-36). In Galilee and adjoining areas, the astute Herod Antipas became the Romans' on-site ruler for 42 years, and his mild-mannered brother Philip ruled the area east of the Jordan for 38 years. Such lengthy reigns speak something of these Herodians' competence and survival skills. These long reigns by capable rulers ensured stability for more than a whole generation.

In the first century BC the Judaic religion gained ground greatly, thanks to four factors. First, it clarified its beliefs and practices via a scholarly working-through of its tenets which culminated at this period. Second, the tenets of Judaism became much more widely known and understood thanks to the translation of the Hebrew Bible into Greek, the common language of the eastern Mediterranean. Also, the religion embarked on modest evangelical activities to attract new converts. Third, the people of Israel proved very fecund during this period, so that the leading eastern cities of the time – especially Antioch and Alexandria -- came to have large Jewish populations. Fourth, and undoubtedly most visible of all, was old King Herod's lavish rebuilding of the Jerusalem Temple as a worthy successor to Solomon's Temple. First-century Judaism centred on the Jerusalem Temple, where the ancient rituals were carried on continuously, every day, by batteries of priests and chief priests under the authority of a High Priest and a Temple Captain. The lower strata of priests served for a month each year but those priests might otherwise reside anywhere in Israel. The high-level priests were permanent Temple staff and resided in Jerusalem itself. The chief priests and High Priest alone had access to the innermost parts of the Temple. The centre of it all was the Holy of Holies, a completely empty cubic chamber where at one time the Ark of the Covenant had resided.

The Jerusalem Temple was no ordinary shrine. It was certainly the largest religious building in the Roman empire and probably the largest building in the world at that time. It not only served as a house of worship, but effectively embodied both the Judaean state and its religion. The Temple High Priests wielded great authority over Jews throughout the empire and over all residents of Judaea, both Jewish and gentile. The Temple comprised a number of courtyards around a central Sanctuary. The first area that a visitor would encounter was the vast Court of the Gentiles, into which even pagans could come. It was walled but not roofed, being an essentially outdoor court. Strictly speaking it was not a Temple court at all, and therefore anyone could enter. A great deal of commercial business took place there. Roman coins and other secular currencies had to be exchanged for shekels which alone could be used in the interior Temple rituals. Animals were sold there in vast numbers for sacrificing. The second courtyard was the Court of Israel, divided into a Court of Men into which only Jewish men could go; and a smaller Court of Women. Next, the Court of the Priests contained the main altar. Sacrifices of animals to the God of the Jews took place on a massive scale at the Temple. The Temple was always full of the sound of terrified and dying animals, and the stench of blood. Rivers of blood flowed into huge drains and down into the depths of the earth below the Temple. Apart from regular thanksgiving and propitiation sacrifices were sacrifices of atonement for special events, and a host of smaller-scale ritual sacrifices prescribed in the Mosaic Law. The penalty for gentile intrusion into the inner courts of the Temple was death. That penalty was posted conspicuously in multi-lingual inscriptions around the entry to the Court of Israel. Next came the Sanctuary, the first roofed-over indoor part, reserved for priests. Finally, at the centre of all, magnificently curtained off, was the Holy of Holies, the very heart of the Temple.

Over the Temple, the Herodian rulers exercised a vague protective role. Herodian kings came to appoint the High Priests, and they increasingly identified themselves with Temple Judaism. But the Herodians were not always pious and with one exception they never won the hearts of the Jews. They remained outsiders and foreigners who were known to be in league with the Romans.

The Jews celebrated many festivals of which the principal ones were Pesach (Passover), Pentecost (Weeks), Purim (Booths) and Yom Kippur (Atonement). It was customary and expected that Jews from wherever would make an effort to come to Jerusalem for Passover in spring, Pentecost in summer and Yom Kippur -- with Booths following – in the autumn. During these great festivals the population of Jerusalem typically tripled as hundreds of thousands of Jews from near and far arrived. The great festivals were both religiously charged and charged too with ethnic and nationalistic fervor. Disorders were so common that the Prefect of Judaea brought troops from Caesarea up to Jerusalem at each festival, to keep order if required. The Herodians too usually showed up at the festivals, even though their adhesion to Judaism was often questionable.

Jews who lived outside Jerusalem normally worshipped in a local synagogue each Friday evening at the beginning of Sabbath. This was universally true of Jews outside Judaea, but even Jerusalem possessed scores of synagogues. Anyone – Jewish or not – could attend synagogue to hear the service and the lessons. Many sympathetic ex-pagans availed themselves of that opportunity. It seems that most synagogue services throughout the empire were conducted partly or entirely in Greek.

The Judaism of the first century was in dynamic change and had lots of philosophical variety. It was a religion of sects each of which professed quite different schedules of beliefs. The sharpening of those sectarian beliefs into mutual intolerance was notable between AD 20 and 65. Many ordinary Jews believed that a Messiah ("redeemer") was about to appear, a warrior-leader who would lead them to predominance over the pagan world and to national independence. This expectation sharpened during the first half of the century as Judaism became stronger, more aggressive, more fanatical, more internalized and more self-assured of coming victory. Many would-be Messiahs rose and fell over the years. The hope of deliverance waxed strong because Roman rule and Greek culture were unpopular with most Jews. Yet some Jews found certain elements of Greek culture distinctly attractive. The dynamism, the relative freedom from petty constraints, the varied philosophies, the sense of internationalism, and the sheer material wealth of the Hellenistic Greeks induced many Jews to "Hellenize" – that is, to adopt to greater or lesser extents Hellenic lifestyles even while holding to most if not all of the religious beliefs of Judaism.

Lax Hellenists were widely scorned and disliked by rigorous Jews, more or less in relation to their degree of Hellenization. This was clear xenophobia, bred partly by religion -- the nature and history of Judaism -- but partly also by nationalism, the newer reaction to long centuries of foreign rule. The two responses were fused together in the first century with explosive results. Even while some Jews adopted Greek ways, part of the Israelite people moved to be more "zealous" in religious practices. Thus the Jewish nation remained in conflict internally, within itself. The zealous "Hebrews" and the "Hellenists" were not entirely comfortable with one another. In the first century AD that discomfort became more and more acute. Sects were hardening their boundaries, and extremists were gaining ground. Judaism of the first century was by no means a quiet or monolithic faith. In Jesus' time, the people of Palestine were divided into a multitude of sectarian streams of belief and tradition. There were of course the two overarching elements of Jews and non-Jews; that was the greatest divide of all. Jews were people of the covenant made between God and their ancestor Abraham. They were a people apart. In those days an observant Jew could not socialize with gentiles, could not enter a gentile house, could not eat gentile food, and so forth. Yet gentiles comprised about a quarter of Jerusalem's population, and nearly a third of the population of all Judaea. They made up an even higher proportion of the populace in Samaria and in Galilee.

Among the Judaean Jews the most important first-century sects were the Pharisees, Sadducees, Essenes and – after mid-century – the Christians; these predominated amidst a host of minor groups and variant practices. The **Pharisees** in general were strict observers of the Mosaic Law but of liberal mindset; they believed in angels as well as in life after death, and in a Last Judgement, and they were somewhat open to novel ideas. They were not however open to altering the Mosaic Law in any way, even though they might envisage different ways of interpreting facets of that Law. To some extent they sought peaceable accommodation with the "occupying power" – the Romans. They represented an evolving religious faith, and their role in Judaism tended to be as scholars in the Temple and leaders in the local synagogues which existed throughout the empire. They prized learning and were often learned themselves. They strove to be righteous through scrupulous adherence to the Mosaic Law and ritual. Some Pharisees were attracted to Jesus' ideas. Another way of phrasing that would be to say that Jesus' teachings were in part concordant with ideas then circulating among the Pharisees. There was plenty of room for discussion, and there was plenty of discussion. The Pharisees, whether they realized it or not, were the main door to the future of Judaism.

The **Sadducees** were a small and more conservative class of Jews. They believed neither in angels nor in a material resurrection after death but focused on the here and now. They tended to be legalistic and highly ritualistic in religion, zealous for punctilious obedience to the Mosaic Law and especially to its set rites. They were not compromisers; they opposed innovations and assiduously punished breaches of the Law. The Temple High Priests were chosen from a small number of Sadducee families, right up to the mid-first century AD when the whole high-priestly system broke down. As a priestly lot they were ritual-oriented and very Temple-centred. There was little in Jesus' teaching that could appeal to conservative Sadducees, and much that offended their materialism. Nor was Jesus fond of the Sadducees. It is not surprising that they considered Jesus a dangerous revolutionary and finally moved against him.

The **Essenes** were members of a small but fanatically strict and ultra-ascetic sect who had their own monastic community out in the desert at Qumran. Their men also could be found living apart in major towns and cities and were commonly tagged with the keyword "zealous". When Jesus instructed his disciples to locate a place for the Last Supper, their clue was to look for a man carrying a water-jug. Since carrying water was normally women's work, that man would be one of Jerusalem's Essenes who dwelt in the southwestern part of the city. The Essenes were an extremist cult and looked devoutly towards the arrival of a national military saviour, the Messiah. The beliefs of the Essenes seem similar to some beliefs of earliest Christianity, but the tenor of Essene ways was very different. Loving your enemies, for example, was not an Essene habit.

Within each sect of first-century Judaism there was a spectrum of beliefs and filling in the spaces between sects were arrays of apocalyptic, nationalistic and just-plain-cantankerous little groups: among these developed – in the Apostolic period -- the **Zealots** (with a capital Z) and also the **Sicarii** or "daggermen" who were given to violent, murderous means of "defence" of their extreme versions of Judaism. These sectarians were the terrorists of their time. We will hear about their fate in a later chapter.

Most Jews of the early empire, perhaps as many as two-thirds, lived outside Palestine in what was known as the Dispersion or Diaspora. These people were scattered all over the empire, but mostly in its eastern half, especially Egypt. There were also large numbers outside the Roman empire in Parthia, especially in Mesopotamia. Unlike the Jews of Palestine, these did not have the Jerusalem Temple close to hand for regular worship. They had synagogues, places for weekly assembly which existed in every major city and town. The synagogues were true meeting-halls, attended by both Jews of the circumcision and by uncircumcised God-fearers sympathetic to Judaism but not actually Jews. This was a first-century phenomenon. Faraway Jews would journey to Jerusalem for some festivals, and the numbers doing that were not insignificant.

The **God-fearers** were non-Jewish individuals (usually non-practicing pagans) who aligned themselves personally with Judaic religion and moral culture without however actually converting to Judaism. They believed in a sole God, they read the Hebrew Bible in its Greek translation, and they often attended Greek-language synagogue services to hear the reading of the lessons and to participate in prayers. Ethically, the God-fearers aspired to Jewish standards of personal behaviour, because they, like most Jews, believed in a future Judgment Day in which all people of whatever religion would be judged and rewarded or punished according to their ethical behaviour. The Gospels mention several God-fearers by name. However, few if any tried to follow all the stringent details of the Mosaic Law.

Occasionally, a God-fearer would go all the way and convert to Judaism. Conversion was a major life-altering decision. Male converts had of course to undergo circumcision no matter what their age, and all converts were expected to keep the dietary rules and the many other laws enjoined on Jews in the Torah. Yet it was a moot point whether full conversion to Judaism actually made the converts part of the nation of Israel – "Abraham and his seed forever" – that entity with which God had made the Covenant. No matter how that was viewed, however, new converts and anciently established Jewish believers were both held to the same standards of righteousness, and both could look forward – in the Pharisaic version of Judaism, anyway -- to a Last Judgement based on the same criteria of merit. Note that the ideas of evangelism, conversion and a Last Judgment did not originate with Christianity; they were all present in the innovative Judaism of the early first century AD.

Ancient Judaism took its religious life very, very seriously, and nowhere were standards stricter than in Judaea. To some Jews and to a great many pagans living around them, this rigour of the Law and "zeal for the Law" was disturbing. Yet for at least as many others it was attractive and admirable, a clear sign of ordered righteousness in life – and of a powerful and well-demarcated Way.

Under the Roman yoke, and inspired by the Temple's presence in Jerusalem, the Jews of first-century Palestine turned in upon themselves and became increasingly obsessed with compliance with the minutiae of the Law and with ritual purity. Any perceived shortcomings, however small, could be and were used to label individuals as backsliders. In long hindsight it seems clear that Judaism in the hundred years from Herod the Great's accession (39 BC) was polarizing between quite strict religious observance and thoroughly fanatical – even violent – ultra-strict conduct. The more relaxed ground of some Hellenists, and the open ground for change or compromise, which still pertained in most of the Dispersion, were being cut away in Palestine.

In the whole Roman imperial realm, no people felt more dissatisfied than the Jews of Judaea. They had struggled long and hard for political and religious independence and in the end they had been conquered and subjected by pagan Rome. Yet they lived in restless hope – even in expectation – that God would send to them a saviour-ruler, a Messiah from the lineage of King David, who would turn it all around and lead his Chosen People to power and independence. Then the Roman yoke would be thrown off and the Jews would become their own masters once again. Indeed, other nations would pay them homage. This sanguine and thoroughly unrealistic expectation was coming to red-heat in the early first century. But the expectation was not clear as to what exactly would happen when the Messiah appeared. Some Jews expected a purely military Messiah; not a few hoped for an apocalyptic transformation of the whole world at God's Messiah's command. With universal peace firmly established by Augustus, with the Temple at Jerusalem restored to full glory, and with the numbers of Jews in the Empire at an all-time high, it was not unreasonable for Jews of Jesus' day to be particularly expectant that the culmination of history was at hand, and that the long-awaited Messiah of Israel would soon appear. Some even found in the scriptures prophecies pointing to a messianic arrival around 30-33 AD. Great and imminent happenings were widely anticipated, though no one seemed sure how these great happenings would come about or play out. Into this over-expectant society, at just this critical juncture of history, were born two babies. One was named John, the other Jesus.

JOHN THE BAPTIZER AND JESUS OF NAZARETH

It is as certain as anything can be that John and Jesus were historical figures; they did exist. They lived, acted and died, and therefore have valid biographies to relate – if only we knew the facts of those biographies. John (Yohanan) the Baptizer is mentioned in ancient writings outside the scriptures, and so is Jesus. Jewish tradition knows Jesus as Yeshua or Yeshu (=Jesu). It's the same name as the more familiar form "Joshua", and means "Saviour" or "Rescuer" or "Redeemer". It was a very common Jewish name in the first century. The written memoirs which we have from the first century all agree tolerably in describing Jesus' life, his work, his teachings, his death and the names and activities of a number of his colleagues and contemporaries. Admittedly there are discrepancies among stories, but there always are. Ask any crime scene investigator.

John the Baptizer was the only child of a Jewish couple getting on in years. Zechariah was a senior Temple priest; Elizabeth was an aunt of Mary the mother of Jesus. The plot is an old one: the couple had no children and so prayed tirelessly for a child. Zechariah served for a month of every year as a senior Temple priest – a usual arrangement in Judaea then. One day while serving in the Sanctuary, he had a vision announcing that in due course a son John would be born to him. And so it happened.

The boy grew into a hyper-religious young adult who possibly spent time in the Essene community at Qumran near Jerusalem. On passing the age of thirty, in 27 AD John went off on his own into the wilderness along the Jordan River east of Jerusalem, and there began preaching the imminent coming of "the Kingdom of God" and the Judgement, and baptizing people who came to him, confessed their sins, and showed repentance. "Repent, for the Kingdom of God is at hand" was his cry. John was a charismatic and ascetic prophet, wearing only an animal skin and subsisting on locusts, wild honey and wild grains. His baptism in the waters of the Jordan was only given once to each person. John's message was simple: the Kingdom of God is about to arrive and with it God's Judgement upon all people. So, all must repent their sins and prepare themselves by a compassionate, righteous and communal life for this great event and for Judgement Day. Let St. Luke's gospel tell it:

In the fifteenth year of the emperor Tiberius, when Pontius Pilate was governor of Judaea, when Herod [Antipas] was prince of Galilee and his brother Philip prince of Ituraea and Trachonitis, and Lysanias was prince of Abilene, during the high-priesthood of Annas and Caiafas, the word of God came to John the son of Zechariah in the wilderness. And he went all over the Jordan valley proclaiming a baptism in token of repentance for the forgiveness of sins, as it is written in the book of the prophecies of Isaiah: "A voice crying out in the wilderness: Prepare a way for the Lord".

John was not thinking all this up out of thin air. Centuries before, the Old Testament Book of Daniel described the Judgement as coming in 70x7 years, and the scholars of the time had calculated that period as ending in John's own generation, indeed in the precise interval of AD 30-33. We may scoff at this "The-End-Is-Nigh" phenomenon, but in the overcharged religious culture of its time, such a calculation had immense credibility. Before long, John acquired fervent followers, including two pious Galilean fishermen – Simon Bar-John and his brother Andrew – who both later became Jesus' disciples. Simon ended up as the Christian "Prince of Apostles", Saint Peter. Jesus too became a disciple of John and worked with him in the desert.

Crowds regularly came out from Jerusalem and the nearby towns to see John and to hear him calling people to repentance, and many people did repent their sins and undergo baptism in the waters of the Jordan. His baptism in the running waters of the Jordan signified a final cleansing of the body. Everyone was talking about the Baptizer. If John was – as he claimed -- but a "forerunner" prophet of someone else even more remarkable, who and what would come next? The Messiah?

The Temple authorities in Jerusalem sent a delegation out to find out what was going on. Their delegates pointedly asked John who he was – perhaps he was Elijah returned? No, replied John unambiguously, he was not Elijah returned. Well then, perhaps he was the long-awaited Messiah? No, countered John, but he was preparing the way for that greater one who was coming after him. Not really much the wiser, the delegation reported back to the Temple.

One hot day in the summer of 29 AD, the thirty-three year old Jesus came before John with a crowd of others to be baptized. John's baptism was the moment of Jesus' own call to proclaim the arrival of the Kingdom of God. John and Jesus operated together out in the desert, preaching and baptizing. At first Jesus was just another of John's disciples. Soon it became a closer partnership, with John working the northern areas and Jesus the south. Each prophet had a few devoted followers with him. The basic message remained John's: "Repent, for the Kingdom of God is at hand".

Jesus became even more successful than John at preaching to the crowds. But John was the more fiery orator, and eventually got into serious trouble by publicly denouncing the recent marriage of Herod Antipas to his sister-in-law (and niece) Herodias. Israelite law did not forbid such close marriages. However, Antipas' brother the ex-husband of Herodias was still alive; the couple had produced a daughter. That made the marriage an unlawful scandal. The Herodian dynasty's marital arrangements were always messy and in many cases were incestuous under Roman law. John's thunderous disapproval of the marriage soon reached the palace, and Herod Antipas ordered John to be arrested. It should not have come as a surprise. In that place and time, anyone with a large following who was publicly criticizing the ruler was a threat to the ever-fragile peace of the region and likely to be clapped into prison. When John was taken away, Jesus and another disciple named Dositheos vied for leadership of the desert mission. Jesus soon left the Jordan area to other disciples of John and went northwest to take up work in Galilee, his home territory, resolved not to get imprisoned and to complete the work of John by taking the good news of the Kingdom of God to the people.

As we know, John was eventually executed by Herod Antipas. In the first century, being killed did not necessarily signify the end, for it was popularly believed that souls could return as spirits or even as re-embodied flesh. Just as the Temple delegation had suspected John of being a re-embodied Elijah, Antipas by and by came to suspect that Jesus, soon reported as preaching around Galilee, might be John the Baptizer returned from the dead. The ancient world was much more amenable to such ideas than is our modern era. However, the Baptizer was truly dead. John had been unmarried, had left no children and had no more willing successor than Jesus. John was the last of the Old Testament prophets, preaching in the style of Elijah and conscious of some great approaching judgmental act of God. In his own time John was as least as well-known as Jesus. His sect persisted tenuously for many centuries and still exists as the tiny Mandaean cult.

Jesus took up and expanded John's mission, subtly changing its character, altering and developing its message. John had baptized whereas Jesus soon ceased that practice. Thus, even Jesus' own disciples who did baptize – especially those like Peter who had earlier been disciples of John -- may have believed that they were still administering the baptism of John. A generation later when St. Saul was evangelizing in

Asia Minor, he encountered new believers in Jesus who had received only "John's baptism":

> *[Apollos, an Alexandrian Jew at Ephesus] taught accurately the facts about Jesus although he only knew about John's baptism. [Saul] found a number of converts of whom he asked, "Did you receive the Holy Spirit when you became believers?" They replied, "No, we haven't even heard that there is a Holy Spirit." He asked, "What baptism were you given?" They answered, "John's".*

Saul explained the relation of John the Baptizer and Jesus, re-baptized the converts "in the name of Jesus" and laid hands upon them, whereupon they received the gift of the Holy Spirit.

The first-century Romano-Jewish writer Flavius Josephus (whom we will get to know in a later chapter) in the 80s and 90s wrote histories of the Jews. He had this to say about John's baptizing:

> *[John the Baptizer] commanded the Jews to exercise virtue, both by righteousness towards one another, and by piety towards God, and then to come to baptism; so that the washing with water would be acceptable to God… not for the remission of particular sins, but for the purification of the body, assuming that the soul had been thoroughly purified beforehand by righteous behaviour.*

John's main successor was Jesus of Nazareth. There was something irregular about Jesus' birth. He was conceived out of wedlock, but probably he was Joseph's son. Whatever the circumstances, Joseph married a pregnant Mary, accepted the child and brought him up. Joseph and Mary subsequently had eight other children: three girls for whom unlikely legends suggest the names Mary Jr, Ashya and Lydia; and five more boys reliably attested as James (Yakob), Jude Thaddeus, Judas Thomas, Joseph Jr and Simon.

No one knows where Joseph was born, nor his parents' names. Matthew's gospel lists Joseph's father as "Jacob" while Luke's gives an entirely different name "Heli" (Eliezar?). Joseph was certainly of the Jewish faith, for which he must have been zealously observant. His marriage to Mary, his first and only marriage, likely took place when he was in his early thirties and she was a teen-ager of 15 or 16. That suggests that Joseph was born around 35 BC – near the beginning of old Herod's long reign. His most likely birthplace is Nazareth, at the time a tiny Galilean village of about 300 people. However, Mary's forebears came from around Jerusalem: Bethany, Bethlehem, Emmaus or Olivet; only her parents became Galileans.

Joseph worked as a "tekton", as the Greek gospels give it, which can mean a carpenter, but equally a woodworker or artisan or builder or even an architect. On a material level, carpentry and building were portable trades, much in demand at the time. Some early writings call Joseph simply a builder. A successful builder, then as now, could become well-to-do. Jesus' family was not dirt poor as often depicted. His mother Mary was the daughter of well-to-do parents and had received a share of their inheritance, and his father Joseph was a somewhat prosperous professional. The family was "middle-class", had some money, and even owned a tiny farm.

Jesus was Mary and Joseph's first child, and eight others followed. If one supposes a birth every two years beginning with Jesus in 4 BC, and just one infant death, that puts eighteen years between the eldest and the youngest children. The last child would have arrived in 15-17 AD by such a calculation, when Mary would have been about 35. That is not quite the end of child-bearing years, so we can conclude that Joseph died shortly after AD 16 – or that he left the family. Unevidenced tradition asserts 18 as his death date, and that may be close to the truth. Matthew's gospel mentions Joseph as alive and well in 9. After that date it is 29 before we next meet the family in the gospels, without Joseph. Joseph must have passed on at the age of about fifty-three.

Father and son worked together in the rebuilding of the ruined town of Sepphoris, 4 kilometers from Nazareth. Joseph and young Jesus walked to and from Sepphoris each day, talking along the way. A perfect setting for a formative influence from Joseph.

Jesus' mother Mary was of decent family and may have been dedicated to God in the Jerusalem Temple and lived there as a youngster. Upon approaching puberty, she had to leave the Temple and was betrothed to Joseph of Nazareth. Mary became his ward before disaster struck Sepphoris. She was with her parents there when the Roman sack of 4 BC occurred and the sixteen-year-old Mary somehow became pregnant – by Joseph or by the Holy Spirit or by a Roman soldier or... and in due course Jesus was born. In Nazareth, or maybe in Bethlehem, very late in 4 BC.

At first Jesus taught what John the Baptizer had been teaching. Then, going beyond the Baptizer's "imminent" Kingdom of God, he preached that the Kingdom was already starting to appear on earth, and that all who wished to be saved from the judgmental consequences of their sins should repent and actively seek to enter that Kingdom now. He talked much about the Kingdom in parables and stories. The Kingdom itself was understood as spiritual and immaterial, "not of this world", but rather a state of being and a mental outlook which were present and waiting within the mind of every person and in relationships among people. But, everyone must search for the Kingdom and find it within themselves in order to enter it and become fully alive – "saved". Jesus seems to have believed that as more and more people found their internal and enveloping Kingdom and lived according to its precepts, the Kingdom of God would spread throughout the world. Or at least throughout the world of Judaism. He once mused that he was kindling a fire (the inner fire of the Kingdom) and tending it until it blazed up.

Through instruction, parables and stories, and through example, Jesus showed and explained what the Kingdom was like, and how it worked. It was the Kingdom of a kind, loving and infinity generous God, whom Jesus consistently referred to as his Father. To enter it, men and women had also to be kind, loving and generous to one another. No pretending!

The Kingdom was not for those who feigned belief or followed the rules reluctantly, but rather for those who like little children approached it eagerly without reservations or shame or self-consciousness. For the Kingdom was utterly different from the oppressive structures of contemporary Palestine. Entering it first brings astonishment, and then marvel, and finally "repose" – deep inner peace of mind. The journey from the ordinary world into this Kingdom was akin to moving from death to full life; and from darkness into light.

Jesus exhorted his audiences to love God and love their neighbours. Treat others as you would have them treat you. Love them even if they are strangers; even if they are opponents. The parable of the Good Samaritan was about loving those whom you weren't supposed to love. Love your enemies; pray for those who are cursing and abusing you. Forget about revenge and getting even. Instead, forgive. And relax; don't live your life in uptightness. Discipline your mind but be happy. Enjoy simple meals, be content with simple clothing, and have a drink with your friends now and then. Jesus himself loved parties. In a society honeycombed with "thou-shalt-not" rules and minutely specified obligations, this joyful message was a liberation that not everyone could grasp. It was a message about living a life of instinctual goodness, about being entirely good as the Heavenly Father is entirely good, about returning to the life of Light for which human beings are truly meant.

Scholars have shown time and again that most of what Jesus taught was already there in the Hebrew scriptures. Yet Jesus' teaching brought a revolution. It also brought fierce opposition. Jesus was an observant Jew, up to a point. However, he preached that in the Kingdom the Mosaic Law would be construed differently, and he offered some different interpretations. Even more, in the Kingdom people do not feel God's will as a burden, they fulfill it happily.

The religious Establishment in Judaea accused Jesus of wanting to alter the Law of Moses. He declared that the Sabbath – wound around with innumerable petty restrictions – was made for people, not people for the Sabbath. He taught that divorce – another issue hedged with many man-made regulations -- was never possible in the Kingdom of God. He denied the value of ritual sacrifice of animals – as occurred on a massive scale at the Temple -- and he downplayed the whole notion of ritual purity; what God really wants is simple purity of mind and thought. The Temple authorities soon became well aware of Jesus' antipathy to their expensive rituals and never-ending sacrifices. Jesus minced no words on these subjects.

He was best-known as a prophet, healer and exorcist, healing physical ailments, blindness, paralysis, mental illness and leprosy. He resurrected his presumed-dead friend Lazarus. And he taught the importance of faith. Jesus was always highly critical of ritualism. Fullness of belief was everything, everything. Mark's gospel contains this remarkable passage in which Jesus says:

> If anyone says to this mountain "Be lifted from this place and hurled into the sea" and has no inward doubts but believes that what he says is happening, it will be done for him. I tell you then, whatever you ask for in prayer, believe that you have received it and it will be yours. [Mark 11: 22-24]

Such belief is a tall order. Not surprisingly, Jesus' movement ran into bitter opposition from the Law-obsessed religious Establishment, from many uncomprehending Pharisees and even more so from the ritual-bound Sadducees. Jesus' teaching also raised the hackles of secular authorities by its talk of a kingdom not ruled by Caesar. Most ordinary folk just didn't get it – didn't comprehend what Jesus was announcing. When he described his teachings as "living waters like a bubbling stream from my mouth" many simple folk didn't understand that he was talking about his message. Only a small minority of the Lord's hearers comprehended and were truly touched by that message. But those few were the beginning of much greater things. They were the new-kindled flame which would soon blaze forth.

Jesus was laid-back and could on occasion tease and make jokes. In the Gospel of Thomas, a collection of Jesus' reputed sayings which many experts consider authentic, the Prophet advises those who want to find the Kingdom of God. He has just urged his hearers to seek the Kingdom, and someone in the audience has piped up, "But where shall we look for it?" Jesus' reply:

If your leaders tell you to look for the Kingdom up in the sky, then the birds of the air are going to get there before you do. And if they tell you to look for the Kingdom far away over the waters, then the fish of the sea are going to get there before you do. I'm telling you: the Kingdom of God is within you, and right around you. [Gospel of Thomas, logion 3]

This same exchange appears, much truncated, in Matthew's gospel as simply "the Kingdom of God is within you".

Jesus' feelings about his own family were initially not very positive, to say the least. Jesus was caustic about family life in general, curt with his mother, and unsympathetic to family ties. He wouldn't even take time while passing by his hometown to see his mother and siblings. And early in his mission the feeling was mutual, Mary calling her son "not quite right in the head". Some testimonial from your mother!

It seems irreverent to compare Jesus' tour through Galilee with a circus coming to town, but parallels do exist. For in those times most people's lives were dull and hard, relieved only by the occasional religious festival or family wedding. As Jesus' group went from village to village preaching the Kingdom of God and healing sick people, excitement soared. It was an Event – a prophet and healer was arriving. Jesus was everywhere surrounded by crowds wanting to hear his teachings about the Kingdom, and desperately hoping to be healed of their illnesses and infirmities. Soon a secondary group of seventy followers had to be created under the direction of Jesus' brother James (Yakob) to cope with the logistics of crowd control and with the arrangements necessary in each little town for the lodging and feeding of sizeable numbers of followers who congregated wherever Jesus went.

There were many healing "miracles". How did Jesus restore sight to the blind, hearing to the deaf, or movement to the lame and paralyzed? Perhaps Jesus employed auto-suggestion and hypnotic techniques with proven power to effect amazing changes in people. He would have taught the techniques to his closest disciples as the "secret of the Kingdom of Heaven", but not to other people. That does not trivialize the healings. People thought them miraculous, and so they must have been. In our own times we are familiar with the phenomenon of faith healing, and with the "placebo effect" in scientific drug tests. Some subjects are given pills containing the test drug, others are given pills which contain no drug. The experimental subjects are not told which pills they have been given. Always, some of those in the no-drug group nevertheless experience real, verifiable relief from their condition.

There were roadside preachings, conversations and debates. Not only throngs of nameless poor showed up but also learned scholars and men high in the social hierarchy came out from the towns to see, hear and test the Prophet: Pharisees, rich men, synagogue officials, military officers. Even gentiles turned out to hear Jesus, this self-proclaimed Son of God, and to witness his entourage. It was spiritually powerful stuff, and many would never forget the day that Jesus of Nazareth visited their town and spoke inspiringly to them from a hill or in a meadow, or from a rowboat to crowds lining the shore. Then he had healed sick people ... On Sabbath days Jesus might read and teach in the local synagogue, and rest. When he needed more respite time he would go to remote places or meditate in a boat moored out in Lake Galilee.

John the Baptizer, languishing in Herod's prison for more than a year, sent some of his people to find out what was happening, and to ask whether Jesus was the Messiah. This was reasonable since John had heard of marvels but did not know that they were being worked by his cousin Jesus. Jesus gave a non-committal response:

"Go and tell John what you have seen and heard: how the blind recover their sight; the lame walk; the lepers are made clean; the deaf hear; the dead are raised and the poor are hearing good news – and happy is the man who does not find me a stumbling block."

Jesus was tireless in announcing the arrival of the Kingdom of God and in telling parables about what that Kingdom was like. It was a world turned upside-down where the poor and the meek would live in security and peace, while the rich and arrogant would be cast down. It was a place where the disconsolate and sad would find comfort, and the downtrodden would find freedom, while the proud and powerful would be humbled. It would be a place of serene righteousness – not puritanical, repressive ritualistic righteousness but righteousness bubbling up from inner joy and love. "God loves you; God is with you; God's kingdom is within you and around you; God forgives your sins; and I am telling you right now that if you repent, your sins are forgiven!"

For two years Jesus worked his way back and forth through the Galilean villages, through Samaria, north into Phoenicia, and south into Samaria and Judaea. And back again. In part he was trying to ensure against arrest by keeping on the move. However, Herod Antipas was not really very interested in arresting Jesus though he certainly did want to meet him. Also, Jesus believed that by preaching all over Palestine he was making the Kingdom of God appear and take hold. The simple folk of the regions began well and then fell away. His hearers didn't seem to appreciate the urgency of repentance and of readiness for that imminent event, the great Day of Judgement expected in AD 30-33; and already it was 32! Jesus soldiered on, then went to ground with his inner circle over the winter of AD 32-33, preparing for what had to be done next. In the spring of 33 Jesus decided to go to Jerusalem at Passover time, to being matters to a head, and to bring in the Kingdom or perish in the attempt. The mission group left its wilderness lair and once again took to the roads of Judaea, now heading south.

Jesus' forgiving of sins – a prerogative which in Judaism was considered uniquely that of God – was by no means the only source of friction between himself and the strict Judaean religious Establishment. From time to time, Jesus deliberately committed acts forbidden under the Mosaic Law. For example, he repeatedly healed ("worked") on the Sabbath; he allowed his hungry disciples to harvest handfuls of field grain on the Sabbath; he pronounced a rule on divorce different from the Mosaic rule; he sometimes declined to wash his hands before eating; he consorted with notorious sinners. He contradicted the dietary laws by declaring that what goes into one's mouth cannot defile. With good reason the priests came to believe that Jesus was teaching blasphemy. Jesus also told parables denigrating the supposed righteousness of the Sadducee priests and some Pharisees. Sometimes he scolded them publicly for their hypocrisy and materialistic but joyless way of life. The Temple came in for particular criticism. At one point, Jesus uttered these enigmatic, fateful words:

Destroy this temple and in three days I will restore it.

Most listeners took it literally and scoffed. Destroy the largest building in the world? And then restore in three days what had taken ten thousand laborers a half-century to build? He's crazy! But Jesus had in mind the temple that was his own body. Some Pharisees understood what the Prophet was driving at, and they tried to help him. Even two members of the Jewish High Council, Nikodemos and Joseph of Arimathea, became secret disciples. Jesus expected that the Temple authorities in Judaea would try to put him out of the way, yet he wanted to spend time at Jerusalem. Was that to help the Kingdom of God? Or did Jesus hanker to follow the Prophets of old to a martyr's death in the Holy City? Or was it

-- as some have suspected -- to provoke an earthly coup-d'etat in Judaea which would make Messiah Jesus himself the King of Israel?

What offended the Jewish Establishment was, first, Jesus' claim to be the Messiah of God. Worse, in that capacity Jesus repeatedly and publicly pronounced repentant people's sins forgiven, usurping the unique prerogative of God alone. The Jewish authorities were afraid of his reputation, afraid of his denunciations, afraid of his razor-sharp intellect and his awesome powers, and afraid that with so many followers he might well lead an insurrection against them. They sought time and again to catch him in the capital crime of open blasphemy. For his part, Jesus was unafraid. At last, in late March 33 after more than two years of itinerant preaching in the regions, Jesus and his followers reached Jerusalem. He was enthusiastically received by the people. The Prophet was warned that he would be arrested. He expected that much and was at first careful to leave the city to spend the nights on the Mount of Olives just east of the walls. Each day after dawn he returned to the Temple's outer precincts and preached there.

He had lots of followers in Jerusalem. They welcomed him as their King. Was there a political insurrection in the making? There had been earlier attempts to acclaim him as King. As he entered the city the week before Passover, the accompanying crowd chanted "Hosanna to the Son of David", openly accepting him as their legitimate ruler. Jesus' rough ousting of commercial dealers from the Temple precincts the very next day signaled to the Temple authorities that things were slipping completely out of hand and that the Prophet was taking up the reins of royal authority. Other provocations were taking place in the city in Jesus' name. The idea that Jesus was the rightful King of Israel was spread about, and that title would soon be blazoned on his cross: "*Jesus of Nazareth, King of the Judaeans*".

The Temple authorities moved to rid themselves of a dangerous presence and to forestall open rebellion. What Jesus did not expect was the fine-tuned planning of his eradication: arrest, charges of blasphemy and sedition; a lightning-fast informal trial before priestly Elders; and the immediate imposition by the Roman Prefect of a death sentence. The Jewish leaders would turn him over to the Roman Prefect to be sentenced for blasphemy (a capital offense under Jewish law) and for sedition (a capital offense under Roman law), to be lawfully condemned to death by crucifixion -- nailed to a cross and left to die. The whole process once set in motion would take less than thirty-six hours.

Joseph Caiafas was by far the most astute and successful High Priest of the first century. Much as Christians may deplore the events, it must be admitted that Caiafas managed the whole Jesus affair to perfection from his viewpoint. He wanted to destroy the emerging movement by selectively removing just one man, its charismatic leader. Caiafas' nephew Ananus {=Annas) was the titular high priest in 33, but Caiafas remained the brains behind the office. He felt sure that with its leader dead the Jesus Movement would also die. That was his only miscalculation, but it proved to be a fundamental one. Caiafas chose his timing so as to avoid priestly embroilment on the days of Passover[2] and to take advantage of Pontius Pilate's brief presence in Jerusalem for that festival (Pilate and troops always came up from headquarters at Caesarea on the coast to ensure order at the great festivals). The arrest was made late Wednesday night, following the Apostles' last supper, with a Jewish trial committee already assembled and waiting at Caiafas' mansion. Judas Iscariot guided the big Temple police squad to Gethsemane Garden east of the city, where he knew Jesus would go to pray and meditate. It was full night when they found him there with his Apostles and other followers. Jesus offered no resistance. He was bound and taken away. His terrified followers, including most of the Apostles, ran off in all directions.

Jesus was marched back into Jerusalem and past the south face of the Temple to the mansion of the High Priest, where a number of Temple officials were assembling. From the first light of pre-dawn, they interrogated Jesus on charges of blasphemy – Jesus' claim that he could or would

---

2 In Jewish and Christian religious timekeeping, a new day begins at sunset. Passover in 33 AD began at sunset on Thursday and the weekly Sabbath Day followed at sunset on Friday.

destroy the Temple, and on his claim to be the Messiah. The unspoken issues were Jesus' forgiving of people's sins, his rejection of Temple sacrifices, and his insurrectionist potential. There was much discussion, but the main charges succeeded to the satisfaction of the meeting. Jesus was deemed to warrant the death penalty. He was immediately sent off to the Roman prefect Pontius Pilate for imposition of the death sentence, something that the Judaeans themselves could not do.

In the late morning of Thursday 2 April 33, Jesus appeared before Pontius Pilate in the courtyard of the governor's residence in the Antonia fortress adjacent to the Temple. There was a good deal of preliminary talking. When Pilate learned that Jesus came from Galilee, he first attempted to foist the judgment upon Herod Antipas, the Romans' client ruler of Galilee, who was also in Jerusalem for the Passover festival. Jesus was marched over to Herod Antipas' residence – the old Citadel palace at the north-west corner of the city wall, well west of the Temple. The tetrarch had long been very curious to see Jesus and held an impromptu outdoors audience in front of the palace, with most of his court in attendance. Antipas tried to initiate a conversation but Jesus would not respond to any of Antipas' questions.

"So you are Jesus the prophet?"

No reply.

"I have wanted for a long time to meet you and talk to you."

No reply.

"Governor Pilate has sent you to me thinking that I may want to pass judgment on you. You are, I understand, a Galilean?"

No reply.

"Some people tell me that you profess to be the rightful king of Judaea. Is this true?"

No reply.

"Although as a Galilean you are my subject, your supposed offence is about Judaea and really does not concern me. I am not sitting in judgement of you, understand. Can we not then converse?"

No reply. There is a long pause.

"Do you not speak Greek? Do you not even speak Aramaic? Or do you simply choose not to speak at all to me?"

No reply.

Stymied by such communication difficulties, Antipas cannily declined to intervene further. Let Pilate handle this hot potato himself. "Send this fellow back to Pilate". So, Jesus and his following crowd of detractors and supporters appeared again before Pilate in the afternoon. Antipas' herald and Pilate's adjutant gave Pilate full reports on what had and had not transpired at Herod's session. In answer to Pilate's direct question, the herald stated that Herod had not proclaimed Jesus guilty of anything and indeed had not pronounced any judgment at all. Pilate, not displeased that Herod had rendered no judgment at all, then proposed to release Jesus, but when some of the assembled Temple Jews began shouting that Jesus had preached sedition – a kingdom other than that of Caesar – Pilate found himself politically cornered and after considerable stalling he agreed to the death sentence on that account. However, Pilate had one more card to play; he offered to release Jesus as a "Passover pardon" gesture. But the mob clamoured instead for the release of another condemned man, also named Jesus: Jesus Bar-Abbas who had been "involved in the insurrection" and had committed murder. The well-rehearsed crowd then called loudly for the crucifixion of Jesus of Nazareth: "Crucify him! Crucify him!" It was late afternoon when the judgment was finally ratified. Jesus Bar-Abbas was produced, his chains were removed, and he was pushed off unceremoniously into the crowd, a free man.

Following usual Roman practice, Pilate next had the condemned Jesus of Nazareth taken to the military headquarters in the Antonia Fortress to be scourged, beaten up and held overnight while the soldiers erected a cross. Early on Friday morning – Passover Day -- Jesus was marched out beyond the city wall and nailed up on that cross at an execution site known as The Place of the Skull, just to the north of the city. The day was hot and by noon Jesus was beginning to die of suffocation on the cross[3]. He remained conscious until the very end of the afternoon, then slumped and abruptly died. The soldiers speared him to make sure, but they did not need to break his legs. Somewhat before sunset Jesus was pronounced dead and taken down, and the grieving – or just curious -- onlookers went their ways. The body had been claimed and was taken by the Pharisee Joseph of Arimathea, that secret follower of Jesus. The corpse was wrapped in simple grave-cloths and laid hurriedly in an unused tomb not far from the execution site. Then the sun set and the Jewish Sabbath began. Nothing more could be done. Night fell.

The next day (Saturday) was Sabbath, but it brought a steady stream of visitors to the tomb. A few were Jewish but most were from among the gentile residents of Jerusalem's population. They chatted with the four militia guardsmen placed near the site by Pilate at Caiafas' request, they gossiped with one another about Jesus and Pilate, and they discussed the events of the previous days as far as they were known. It went on all day. When night again approached, everyone melted away. Four

---

3 Suffocation and shock were the usual causes of death by crucifixion as the victim was unable to breathe freely. If necessary, the execution squad would additionally break leg bones and shove a spear into the torso to hasten or certify death. However, leg-breaking was only used with Jews, who needed ritually to be buried before sunset on the day of death. Non-Jews might take days to die in agony on a cross.

freshly-arrived relief guards – this time Temple guards, since the Sabbath was over – took over from the Roman squad.

During that second night, the Temple guards received unexpected visitors. Two men wearing the white robes of junior Temple priests showed up, talked briefly to the guards, then opened the tomb and entered it. They shortly came out again, carrying a third man on an improvised stretcher as they moved slowly away into the darkness. A couple of hours later, yet another man, similarly robed in priestly white, appeared and instructed the guards to leave, and not to talk about anything they had seen during the night. A generous dole of money was handed to each guard. The guards understood that for some reason their Temple masters had taken away the body of the man whose tomb they had been guarding; it all seemed in order, with proper papers of authorization. Everyone then departed the site, but before long the same white-robed "priest" returned and took up the guards' vacated place beside the tomb. At the first hint of morning light, other people arrived: three middle-aged women. They were obviously surprised to find the tomb open and empty:

"Put the bag of spices down, Mary, and lend me a hand to roll back the sepulchre stone." Mary Magdalene was the youngest and strongest of the three women. The other Mary – Jesus' mother – was fifty years old, and her sister Salome was in her late forties.

"Look, it's already been rolled back. That's strange." They cautiously approached the tomb, looking in obliquely from a distance but unable in the dim light to see any occupant.

At this point the "priest" informed them that Jesus was risen and would be going north to Galilee where his disciples could meet up with him. The women hurried off to share this dis-information. An hour later two men, one in his forties and the other barely beginning a beard, came running up, looked in the vacant tomb, and received a similar message from the "priest". Then they left. Finally, as the sun rose and tourists arrived again in numbers to view the tomb site, the "priest" gathered up the remaining grave-cloths and departed.

Thus, against all expectations, came the Resurrection on "the third day". The Romans, unlike us, counted days inclusively, so that the three days from execution to resurrection comprised Friday, Saturday and Sunday. Even though Jesus expired near sunset on Friday and the tomb was found empty before dawn on Sunday, while it was still quite dark, the ancients counted it as three days. We would reckon it as around 36 hours. No matter: with Good Friday's date pinned down, the rest follows unambiguously. The Resurrection took place on Sunday 5 April in AD 33, in the closing years of the reign of the emperor Tiberius.

After hearing of crowds visiting the site, Joseph of Arimathea had returned with the other secret priestly disciple, Nikodemos, as soon as the Sabbath ended at sundown on Saturday night. These two, like the three women, brought the necessaries to give Jesus' body proper burial rites, and to move it to a permanent resting place. The men knew exactly where they had placed Jesus, and they sent two white-robed junior priests under their authority to remove his body (they themselves did not want to contact the corpse as it would make them ritually impure). As priestly bigwigs they could collect Jesus' body in spite of the Temple guard, and indeed they had written authorization from Pontius Pilate himself for doing that. Expecting a corpse, Joseph of Arimathea soon heard talk from his servants of a living Jesus.

We now come to historically unanswerable questions about Jesus following his Resurrection. The gospel accounts of these post-resurrection "sightings" are so highly discordant with one another that they cannot be brought together as mere history. And at some point, according to orthodox Christian tradition, comes Jesus' ascension up to heaven-in-the-sky, where he lives on eternally. On this the gospel accounts are again discordant, most of them not mentioning an ascension. We can never discover exactly what happened. Mystics of secular disposition have speculated about Jesus' post-resurrection life on earth, and have wondered if he suffered death again somewhere, sometime. Did he really go back to Galilee as St. John's gospel account relates? It's not wrong to ask such questions, but they bring no useful answers. Believers of gnostic inclinations suppose that the Resurrection itself was metaphorical and involved visions – albeit God-sent -- of Jesus-alive. The gospel accounts are however adamant that the risen Jesus was flesh and blood, eating and drinking. St. Saul – the first to write about the Resurrection little more than a decade later -- came to believe that Jesus had not been raised in his own flesh but in a new and incorruptible "spiritual body" -- whatever that meant to Saul. Maybe it doesn't matter, for Jesus' earthly mission had been completed. His followers came to believe fervently that he had been resurrected to eternal life by God, and they took that as proof of the truth of his teachings and of his messianic claims. Jesus' departure was not the end but rather the beginning of his huge impact on the first century. The tiny flame that he had kindled and guarded was about to blaze up.

IV
TO THE ENDS OF THE EARTH

JAMES (Yakob), the brother closest in age to Jesus, was most like him: intelligent, literate, zealous in religion, and an ascetic vegetarian. During Jesus' mission years, James headed a group of seventy followers which acted as the mission's "advertisers" and as its intelligence, administrative and supply arm. James grew into a superb manager and within a decade of Jesus' departure he became the overall chief of the whole world-wide Jesus Movement, almost a kind of pope. James was on the conservative side of Judaism and was certainly "zealous for the Law". He acquired the reputation of a holy man of highly ascetic character – reminiscent of John the Baptizer. "James the Just" and "James the Righteous" were his two sobriquets. He must have been quite striking. "His knees were hardened from long hours at prayer" according to the second-century Jewish-Christian historian Hegesippus. In imitation of the prophets of old, James never shaved or cut his hair with a metal razor, and allegedly he bathed every morning only in cold water. In addition, James like Jesus remained unmarried.

By no means was this James a bumpkin or a martinet. It was thanks to James that the Jesus Movement reached out successfully to include gentiles as well as Jews. James did not like St. Saul's tactics in winning gentiles who remained "non-Jewish", but he had no trouble welcoming ex-pagan converts into the Jesus Movement within Judaism. Yet he worked with, around and even through Saul. He masterminded the Jesus Movement's missions program very effectively for more than twenty years. James was convinced that his elder brother Jesus had indeed been the promised Messiah – the Christ of God. He believed in the gospel of the Kingdom of God. He believed in the Teachings. He believed in the Resurrection. Yet James also remained a strictly observant Jew.

He presided over the Christian movement for almost a quarter-century. James was in his time a better-known figure than Jesus, and he was largely responsible for the incredible success of the Movement in its early years. The Temple authorities' opportunity to eliminate the increasingly powerful James came in AD 62 in the middle of Nero's reign. The Roman procurator for Judaea, Porcius Festus, unexpectedly died in office in AD 62, and the new procurator Clodius Albinus had not yet arrived in Judaea. A temporary power vacuum existed, and into it rushed Ananus II, the brand new High Priest of the day, arresting James, condemning him on a trumped-up charge of subverting the Mosaic Law, and having him stoned to death -- or thrown down from the highest point of the Temple and then beaten to death -- for alleged blasphemies. Several of James' colleagues were also done to death. However, most of the Pharisees in Jerusalem hotly disapproved of these arrests and executions. The executions were highly illegal, having been carried out without the permission of the Romans. Pharisees blew the whistle and the High Priest was swiftly dismissed at the behest of the incoming procurator. But the damage was done. Later tradition claimed that James had been pushed over the pinnacle-wall of the Temple – a drop of some 40 meters -- and then finished off below with a fuller's club. Could be. The incident seems to have been recognized even at the time as blatant judicial murder. James was buried somewhere within sight of the Temple wall.

In 2004 Israeli archeologists unearthed a stone burial box outside Jerusalem near the Temple wall, bearing the Hebrew inscription "James son of Joseph and brother of Jesus". World-wide excitement! It took eight years of scientific testing and rancorous debate to convince some scholars that the ossuary inscription is a twentieth-century forgery. Yet some well-recognized experts still believe in the box's authenticity. The research and the lobbying go on…

—

Another brother of Jesus was prominent among the missionaries: **Judas Thomas** called "Didymus" (= twin, someone's twin, but not Jesus' twin) – who went on missions to Parthia and to India, and was martyred there in 72 AD. He is sometimes confused with Jesus' other brother Jude the Farmer who worked a small parcel of land owned by the family. That Jude may have been the other twin. Unlike Jesus, Thomas and James, Farmer Jude married and produced offspring, all staunch Christians. Jude's Christian grandsons were farming the same family fields in Galilee when the first century ended. They became celebrities on account of their interrogation by emperor Domitian in Rome. We'll meet them later in our story.

The gospel accounts, when not completely silent on the individual Apostles, do not paint any of them in particularly bright colours. Peter appears as a none-too-cerebral, impetuous guy who denies knowing his master when put in a tight spot. John is the disciple whom Jesus most loved (according to John). He was also the youngest Apostle, a teenager. Bartholomew appears as learned in scripture yet a credulous simpleton in practicalities. Thomas is a doubter, slow to believe but then enthusiastic. Andrew is portrayed as a fix-it man; and Judas Iscariot is always painted as a scoundrel, thief and traitor. So they have come down to us in scripture and tradition.

Jesus had thousands of followers in his lifetime, and still more afterwards. There are only a few whose works and lives are both to some extent known. Apart from the Twelve Apostles, these other individuals became important follower figures in the apostolic period.

—

Yosef Bar-Nabas was a Jewish landowner from Cyprus, a substantial donor to the earliest Christians in Jerusalem; he sold an estate and gave the proceeds to the Jesus-community. Barnabas was well acquainted with all the Apostles. That implies a familial relationship with one or more of them. He was a cousin of John Mark the evangelist, according to scripture, and if that same "John Mark" was St Peter's son "Mark", as stated in 1 Peter 5: 16, then Barnabas was Peter's nephew. Barnabas appears in the New Testament as an early colleague of St. Saul. The two worked together in Antioch for some time. Barnabas, the senior man, was Saul's first significant contact in the Christian community, courageously linking up with Saul at a time when other Christians were still terrified of him and dubious about his amazing conversion. Barnabas provided Saul with introductions to the Apostles at Jerusalem and went there with Saul. The two men afterwards made a "certified" missionary journey to Cilicia in southeastern Turkey and to Cyprus -- their respective home areas.

Barnabas was certainly no peasant. Like Saul he had been taught by the sage Gamaliel in Jerusalem, and he possessed Roman citizenship. The two men may have been classmates. We may fairly assume that Barnabas' family like Saul's was well-to-do, since he owned disposable property, had received a first-class education, and held Roman citizenship. Unlike little Saul, Barnabas was a big man, a powerful speaker and preacher. Among his first converts for Jesus was Mary his "kinswoman", probably his aunt who was John Mark's mother and Peter's wife. Of Barnabas' later travels and death, we know little. Some traditions have him dying as presbyter of Milan in Italy. Another tradition asserts that Barnabas went back to home territory on Cyprus.

Luke: the Greek form of his name is Loukas and we have no Aramaic name for him – for he was not Jewish. He came from Antioch, was highly educated in Greek, articulate and notably rational for his time, maybe a physician but most knowledgeable in civil law. Luke was taken on by Saul as a legal expert and general secretary; he may even have been Saul's slave. Highly-educated slaves were common in the first-century empire; they didn't come cheap and they almost always were treated very well indeed by their owners, for whom they performed demanding highly-skilled services. Slave physicians were common among the wealthy.

Luke will forever be known for his twin writings: the <u>Gospel According to Luke</u> and its sequel the <u>Acts of the Apostles</u>. For his Gospel, Luke researched what had already been reported in writing about Jesus' career. He drew on material which had been available also to Matthew and Mark, but in addition he studied other documentation which he assembled and examined critically. The organization of the material and the writing style are impressive and bear the stamp of a well-educated man who has delivered what he promises in his own gospel Introduction:

THE AUTHOR TO THEOPHILUS: Many writers have undertaken to draw up an account of the events that have happened among us, following the traditions handed down to us by the original eyewitnesses and servants of the Gospel. And so I in my turn, Your Excellency, as one who has gone over the whole course of these events in detail, have decided to write a connected narrative for you, so as to give you authentic knowledge about the matters of which you have been informed. [Luke 1: 1]

Your Excellency?? Who was this Theophilus? We don't know; he may well have been Saul, who as a Herodian aristocrat would have merited the "Excellency". He reappears in the opening sentence of Luke's Acts of the Apostles:

In the first part of my work, O Theophilus, I wrote about all that Jesus did and taught from the beginning until the day when, after giving instructions through the Holy Spirit to the apostles whom he had chosen, he was taken up to heaven. [Acts 1: 1]

—

The name of **Mark** has always been connected with the second New Testament gospel account, "Mark's Gospel". The name was a common Greek and Roman one. Our Mark may also have borne the Hebrew name John (Yohanan) – his grandfather's name; that would explain the joint form John Mark which occurs in <u>Acts of the Apostles</u>. According to scripture, Mark was St Peter's son. Many have treated this sonship only as a metaphorical phrase but it was literal, a biological fact. That Peter was married is attested in scripture, where Jesus heals his mother-in-law. Mark or John-Mark, travelling the missionary trail with Saul and Barnabas (his first-cousin) in the mid-40s AD, can have been born no later than 20 AD. Such a date would fit very well indeed with Mark's being the biological son of Peter. We know this Mark's mother's name, for "Mary's house" in Jerusalem was where Peter's son was residing. Peter's wife's name was Mary; Mark was Peter and Mary's son. Luke relates an incident following Peter's jail-break in AD 42:

> [Peter] went to the house of Mary the mother of John-Mark, where a large company was at prayer. He knocked at the outer door and a maid named Rhoda came to answer it. She recognized Peter's voice and was so overjoyed that instead of opening the door she ran back and announced that Peter was standing outside. "You're crazy," they told her, but she insisted that it was true. [Acts 12: 12-15]

The maid knew Peter's voice; he was no stranger to the house. Where better could Peter – just released "miraculously" from prison – go than to his own usual residence in Jerusalem, where his wife and son were living? Peter was a man on the run, staying only long enough to leave a message for the other Apostles and to say goodbye. Then he fled Jerusalem and King Agrippa.

Peter and his wife Mary produced Mark as their only child, and then they separated so that Peter could go with John the Baptizer and Jesus on the quest for salvation. Mary somehow acquired a comfortable house in Jerusalem where she and Mark lived. Peter's in-laws' house in Capernaum then took in Peter's brother Andrew to help care for Peter's mother-in-law there. Later, Jesus' whole family and mission team moved in and used the Capernaum house as their headquarters. Upon reaching the age of 13, young Mark followed along with the Jesus team and was present at Jesus' arrest – as the young man who fled away naked (mentioned only in "Mark's" telling of the gospel story). Mark continued in the Jesus Movement, often as Peter's assistant and secretary, sometimes with Barnabas or Saul. He performed a useful buffer role between Peter and Saul, and ended up as the editor of Peter's notes -- the basics of "Mark's" Gospel. Mark traveled with Barnabas and Saul in the early 40s, then went with Peter in AD 43 to Rome. Peter and Mark went back east again around 47. Soon after emperor Claudius' expulsion order on Jewish Christians in Rome lapsed in 56, Peter and Mark made their circuitous way back west to sort out difficulties in Asia Minor and Greece arising from Saul's preaching of "heretical" doctrines. These traditions find supporting testimony from early writers such as Clement of Alexandria (writing at the end of the second century). Clement had access to early draft versions of "Mark's" Gospel, and said in his <u>Secret Gospel of Mark</u>:

> *During Peter's stay in Rome, Mark wrote an account of the Lord's doings, not however including them all nor yet hinting at the secret ones, but selecting what he thought would be most useful for increasing the faith of those who were being instructed [prior to baptism]. When Peter died a martyr, Mark moved over to Alexandria, bringing both his own notes and those of Peter, from which he transferred to his earlier book some things suitable for progress towards knowledge. Thus he composed a more spiritual Gospel for the use of those who were being perfected.*

Mark never married. His traditional death date is AD 68. He would have been approaching fifty. He was allegedly buried in Alexandria and his supposed tomb there was known throughout antiquity and into the early Middle Ages. There is a bizarre follow-up, however. Moslem Arabs overran Egypt in the mid-600s. Although the population remained overwhelmingly Christian through the next two centuries, Egypt gradually slipped out of the Christian orbit. In the year 828, the Venetians decided to "rescue" the body of St Mark from Moslem Alexandria and transfer it to Christian Venice. The operation was a piratical raid. It was apparently successful, and it has been believed ever since that St Mark's Cathedral in Venice is where the body of Mark the Evangelist now rests. But recently, the British historian William James has produced evidence suggesting that a dreadful mistake was made during that Venetian raid 1200 years ago. The raiders were not historians, nor well-acquainted with the history of Alexandria. Professor James believes that the illustrious body which was removed from its great tomb and taken to Venice was not St Mark's at all, but rather that of Alexander the Great, no less -- the founder of Alexandria -- who was gloriously entombed nearby! Research continues...

MISSIONS EAST AND WEST

After the Crucifixion, Jesus' followers could have settled down to a quiet practice of Jesus' "Way" and might in that fashion have slowly engendered a small new Jewish sect – as almost happened. But they did not settle down. Feeling that they had been commanded by Jesus to carry his teachings into every corner of the world, they pulled themselves together for a mighty evangelical effort. This effort, between the Resurrection in 33 AD and the beginning of the Roman-Jewish War in 66 AD, established Christianity across most of the Roman Empire and in the Parthian Empire. It was a remarkable feat. The Jesus communities established then were in the main small but organized and fervent. There were many, many problems and no little amount of muddle and chaos. But thirty years of determined missioning transformed a backwater Galilean experience into a world-scale if still tenuous religion. Right after the Resurrection, the Apostles under Peter's energetic leadership began missioning in Palestine itself. Jesus had enjoined his followers to "begin at Jerusalem". Peter preached in Jerusalem – indeed right in the Temple. The brothers James and John were associated closely in this. Even at this early stage, the Temple authorities attempted to repress the message of Jesus as Messiah. Peter and John were jailed and all the apostles were strictly enjoined to cease their preaching entirely. They declined to do so, thus ensuring the continuing disapproval of the Establishment of mainstream Judaism.

The deacon Stephen was the earliest martyr, stoned to death for alleged blasphemy around AD 36. James the older brother of John was executed by the sword in AD 42. Both episodes were precipitated by the Temple authorities, but King Agrippa I – a grandson of Herod the Great who was made king of Judaea by emperor Claudius -- sanctioned James' execution. Agrippa (ruled AD 41-44) was a firm friend of the Romans but at the same time he made strong efforts to be the friend and champion of the mainstream Jews of Judaea. He attempted to execute Peter as well, but Peter escaped from prison and fled Palestine. James' younger brother John was sent out of Jerusalem at this time. Remarkably, James the brother of Jesus rode out the storm in Jerusalem, untouchable.

A mission team generally comprised two lead men, thereby mitigating the risks which faced lone missionaries. Each mission team was sent to a specific place or region. It was financed by funds provided by established Christian communities. For example, Antioch was the sponsor for Barnabas' mission with Saul-Paul to Cilicia and Cyprus. This system was clever in that established communities financed the creation of new communities, and then those new plantings provided financing for still further missions. It resembled a kind of pyramid scheme, and it worked well. Given good management and determined, capable people, this system had the potential to reach vast areas in a short period of time. And that is exactly what happened.

At first, Jesus' brother James was in the background, but as leader of the Seventy Disciples with an organization of his own making, he soon became part of the Jesus Movement leadership team. Moreover, as Jesus' closest living male relative, this James possessed a very strong claim to lead the Apostles, who after all were mostly members of Jesus' family. True, some of the Twelve went back to their former jobs and families in Galilee and ended their connection with the Movement at a time when it appeared to have shipwrecked. Only a few of those returned to the fold or undertook mission work for the Movement once it got underway again. Yet the movement did get underway rapidly and with great energy. The Resurrection put new heart into the followers. Jesus had also provided clear instructions: the followers were to preach the news of the Kingdom of God to all nations. They were to begin by preaching to Jews, for (it was thought) the time was urgent. The followers undertook this mission at once. Jerusalem became the Jesus Movement's headquarters, Palestine its first field of action.

Within a decade of the Crucifixion, Jesus' brother James became the leading figure in Christianity. He was remembered under the title "Bishop of Bishops" and was certainly the closest thing to a pope that Christianity possessed during its first century. However, in the first few years after the Crucifixion, Peter acted as leader of the Twelve and took the Movement on a curious course, in some respects retrogressing to the days of John the Baptizer.

Unfortunately, Peter was not a great organizer, nor possessed of an outstanding intellect. A vague group of followers known in Jesus' day as the Five Hundred melted away under Peter's inadequate governance, for as a hands-on do-it-yourselfer he was more interested in preaching to crowds and making converts then and there, rather than in long-term organizational strategy. Peter believed in the imminent arrival of the End Time. The cool strategic genius of the Jesus Movement was Brother James. It seldom takes long for the best organizer to rise to the top; it took James only five years.

Cracks soon developed in the Movement, beyond the inevitable leadership strains. It happens in every movement, and religious movements are notoriously fissiparous. To understand how the Jesus Movement spread during the generation after Jesus, it is essential to appreciate the ideas, tensions and conflicts that existed among "Christians" even at that very early time.

The Movement was initially a tiny Jewish sect, founded in the work of John the Baptizer and shaped and energized by the teachings of Jesus. Those two prophets had called out to all segments of Judaism to repent, for judgment was coming. The first cracks appeared between the stricter ethnic Hebrew Jewish Christians ("the Hebrews") and the Hellenist Jews in the Movement. The latter were Greek-speaking Jews, as often as not originating outside Judaea. They sometimes failed to conform strictly to the whole Jewish Law, especially those who lived outside Palestine. Yet there were Hellenist names among the first followers of Jesus; for example the Pharisee Nikodemos. Even two of the Twelve Apostles had Greek names.

This Hellenist group of Jewish Christians in Jerusalem complained that its poor were getting shorted on food charity from the apostolic funds. One suspects from this that the Hellenists as a group were not always fastidious about eating only kosher foods and that dietary practices were an underlying issue. The solution chosen by the Apostles was to designate seven men, all with Greek names, as deacons ("servers") to attend to food charity for poor Hellenists in the Jesus community. These "servers" soon became responsible for much more than serving meals to Hellenist poor. They took charge of the entire charity program for Hellenist Jews, and then for evangelical work among Hellenists. All this worked well enough in practice, but only papered over this first division within the Jewish Christian community.

Other issues appeared. Sympathetic gentiles who accepted monotheism -- "God-fearers" – often attended Jewish synagogue services to hear the lessons read in Greek. Most God-fearers went some way towards adopting Jewish practices. However they were certainly not recognized as "people of the covenant" in any sense. Nor were they accepted into the Temple. They were ex-pagans in a stalled transition to monotheism and to the Judaic religion. Jesus had not addressed this group openly. The God-fearers constituted a group standing somewhere on the long, ragged spectrum between paganism and Judaism. The most ardent God-fearing men could become full Jews "of the Covenant" by being circumcised and adhering to the dietary and other parts of the Mosaic Law. Few went that far, but many professed monotheism and adopted some attractive features of Jewish practice – for example the ethical teachings and Sabbath Day rest.

The willingness of Peter and Philip to proselytize monotheistic pagans and to accept uncircumcised converts into the Jesus Movement became a highly controversial issue. In the minds of most observant Jews within the Jesus Movement, the ex-pagans who had entered the Movement were still pagans in their uncircumcision and their unorthodox dietary practices. It troubled Peter himself. Peter was pragmatic and willing personally to extend his preaching and baptizing to God-fearers among the gentiles. He was probably something of a Hellenist himself, "living like a gentile" as Saint Saul charged. As long as he remained the apostolic chief, Peter could get away with it. But it was an issue which helped bring Jesus' more conservative-minded brother James reach the top of the leadership group after 38 AD, the very time of Peter's conversion of the Roman centurion. James would have suppressed the God-fearer issues had he not come up against a person of singular intractability – Saul.

History has a habit of not moving along straight lines. James knew that the Hebrew scriptures explicitly called for extending God's worship to the gentiles. Many gentiles wanted to come into the Jesus Movement, and some (especially at Antioch) had already slipped in, with or without circumcision. As time went by, James came to see not only the inevitability of gentile missions but also the benefits of more inclusiveness. James, if by our standards rigid and obsessed with sin, ritual purity and the Law, was also insightful. He proved a great deal more capable as an organizer than Jesus had chosen to be, or than Peter was capable of being. By the time of Saul's first visit to Jerusalem around AD 39, James was already near the top of the leadership ladder there.

James never went on the mission trail himself, but he forcefully managed a comprehensive and effective missions program for the Movement. He lacked the charismatic personality of his brother. James operated the Organization, sitting like a spider in Jerusalem, weaving his mission webs across the Roman and Parthian empires. He insisted on a clear, consistent message in his missions, and so he "certified" the missionaries sent forth. He studied the regular reports to headquarters which he required from all his missionaries. James attended endless meetings of committees and like the capable general of an army he orchestrated operations in ways which proved extremely adroit and successful. He and his staff managed the funds which flowed in abundantly from the faithful. Soon Jerusalem became the model for far-flung apostolic centres which extended into all parts of Judaea, into Samaria and Galilee, Syria, Egypt and beyond in all directions.

—

The Apostles lost no time in activating a mission program directed at Palestine and the eastern centres of the Jewish Dispersion. The very earliest targets in the 30s were near to hand: Judaea itself, Caesarea on the coast, Damascus, Antioch and Edessa in Syria. Nearby Parthia and Alexandria in Egypt were also targeted. All these places had large concentrations of Jews. The Jews of the Dispersion – with the exception of those in Alexandria -- tended on the whole to be less militant about their religion than were the Jews of Palestine. Strict adhesion to the intricacies of the Law seemingly fell off with distance from the Temple. Thus most Jews dwelling far from Palestine lived partly gentile lifestyles, and many did not even attend synagogue regularly; their Judaism was a family practice and a cultural matter. The Jews of Rome fitted that pattern.

Antioch, the number three city of the empire after Rome and Alexandria, lay to the north of Palestine. Like Alexandria, Ptolomeis,

Caesarea and many other Greek-founded cities, it held a mixed population of Jews, Jewish-Christians and pagans. In Antioch the term "Christian" originated in the 30s. Further north, Edessa too had a Christian community very early – possibly even during Jesus' lifetime. Damascus was another ancient centre in the region where Christians show up in the 30s – they were already there to receive St. Saul right after his conversion. Wealthy Antioch became a base for missionary work to the north (Armenia), northwest (Galatia, Pontus & Bithynia), and east (Mesopotamia, Babylon, Edessa and Parthia). St. Saul and his associates were originally based at Antioch; that community funded their early mission trips.

What exactly was the gospel message and how should hearers respond to it? The lack of success of Jesus' own mystical and often difficult style was well appreciated. At this early date there were no New Testament writings; the gospel story was transmitted in an oral tradition. The mission message chosen by the leadership was thus extremely straightforward and hung on three assertions: First, that Jesus was the long-expected Messiah of Israel (the Christ); Second, that he had been resurrected by God from the dead; Third, that his teachings were the God-inspired basis for the salvation of souls in preparation for the Day of Judgment. Those Jews who accepted this message were baptized into the Jesus Movement.

The Apostles who had studied with Jesus himself were presumed to have received correct instruction and to hold a correct understanding of it. But even that was not certain. The presbyter Papias at the very end of the century described the twelve apostles as a bunch of "ruffians of the deepest dye". As soon as Jesus departed the scene, the problem of correct teaching and correct beliefs arose. The Jesus Movement leaders agreed that Simon Peter and young John Bar-Zebediah possessed the best understanding of Jesus and his message. Peter and John were therefore assigned joint mission work in Samaria and Galilee at a very early date. The most important part of this mission was to visit newly-evangelized areas and make sure that the correct gospel message had been planted there. Peter preached mostly to Jews but maintained interest in the idea of

Gentile conversion as part of the apostolic mandate to proclaim the good news to "all nations". He persuaded James the brother of Jesus to allow him a little slack in that direction. Later Peter took up work as presbyter in Rome and in Antioch, which both had a mixed community of Jewish and God-fearer Christians.

The whole East and West beckoned. On maps showing both the Roman and Parthian empires, Jerusalem stands near the middle, close to the boundary. Christian traditions have certain Apostles evangelizing particular countries or regions. In the east, for example, Thaddeus was sent to Edessa in Syria immediately following the Resurrection. Judas-Thomas went off to Parthia and eventually reached India. St. Saul himself traveled to Arabia to negotiate his new missionary role with his mother, but he did not mission there. Bartholomew went to Armenia (which at that time extended down to the borders of Syria). There were almost as many Jews in the Parthian Empire as in the Roman Empire. They were heavily concentrated in Mesopotamia, around Babylon. Those Jews were early mission targets. As years passed, the Jerusalem headquarters organized mission teams for evangelism far and wide, within and beyond the Roman Empire – wherever there were sizeable numbers of Jews to be told of the Prophet Jesus and the Kingdom of God.

The so-called "Stephen persecution" of 36 led to a local dispersion of Hellenist Jewish followers from Jerusalem. Next, the tougher Agrippan persecution six years later sent the Apostles scattering further afield during 42-43. However, King Agrippa I died unexpectedly the very next year and his realm returned to direct Roman rule. The next twenty years were relatively quiet ones during which Christian missions reached far and wide across both the Roman and Parthian empires. That was the second phase of the apostolic effort.

The Jews in Parthia and Mesopotamia (largely modern Iran and Iraq) were a remnant of mass deportations from Israel perpetrated by the Babylonians six hundred years earlier. These were not ragged refugees but well-established and prosperous residents of Parthia, whose religious and intellectual attainments were at least on a par with those of Judaean

Jews. There were Jews too in Armenia. The apostles Bartholomew and Thomas have always been popularly connected with these easterly missions beyond the frontiers of the Roman Empire. Legends plausibly have Bartholomew evangelizing Armenia – sometimes in company with Thaddeus the evangelizer also of Edessa, and then working in adjacent Parthia. The Apostle Thomas was active in Parthia too, being first based in Edessa, then going further east to the Indus Valley, and later still from there to southern India. If, as seems likely, the Jerusalem church followed its customary practice (which was also Jesus' practice), Bartholomew and Thomas would have been sent together as companions to Parthia. Though seemingly very far-away, this was well within the Roman trading area, and was certainly not terra incognita in any sense.

A story which Eusebius the fourth-century historian insisted was true and documented, tells that King Abgar V of Edessa wrote to Jesus, asking him to come and cure some malady from which the King was suffering. Jesus wrote back that he would shortly send a disciple to Abgar. Right after the Resurrection, Thomas sent the disciple Judas Thaddaeus ("Addai", Jude the farmer) to Edessa, who cured and converted Abgar, making Edessa a very early centre of organized Christian activity. This much-derided tale just might be true in its essentials.

Judas Thomas – like his elder brother Jesus a builder by trade – next headed east and worked for a time in the city of Taxila[4] (in present-day Pakistan) as a builder for a local prince named Gundapur. This potentate was long thought to be legendary. In the eighteenth century a series of princes of that name were shown to be real historical figures whose realm lay around Taxila in the first century. In AD 52 Gundapur's little princedom was overrun by invaders from the north. Thomas then joined – again unwillingly, it seems -- a voyage down the west coast of India, sailing to a port named Kalluz in modern Kerala. There, as a peripatetic prophet and teacher, he preached and healed among the local people for 15 years, until he ran into trouble with the rulers of the area. In response,

4 A city reached by Alexander the Great in his 335 BC expedition.

Thomas moved his mission to the eastern part of the tip of the peninsula. There he encountered trouble anew and was martyred. His martyrdom is traditionally dated at AD 72, at which time he would have reached an age of about 65-70 years. His reputed burial place can still be seen. The churches in south India established by Thomas long remained under the supervision of the mother church in Edessa, the arrangement which Thomas himself had initiated.

There are few counter-traditions about Bartholomew and Thomas. The documents which we possess about their supposed missions show a good knowledge of the geography and history of their alleged mission regions. Bartholomew is well-recognized today as the founder of Christianity in Armenia, and a first-century tomb site said to be his still can be seen in the eastern Turkish city of Erzerum.

In some respects Parthia was a more welcoming place for Christianity than was the Roman empire, and the Jesus followers were from the first able to operate and proselytize openly there. The Jesus Movement provided not only the gospel message of faith, it provided important material supports for members of its communities, such as meals for the poor, mutual support and social-services help. That followed Judaic practice. In addition, Christian communities often functioned as self-insurance societies which provided for members in case of catastrophic needs, and as burial societies -- common in the Roman empire – providing the means for a simple but dignified burial.

—

The western portions of the Roman empire were not at first included in Jerusalem's mission assignment list: no Apostle was sent off to Gaul or Germany or Spain or to the western parts of North Africa. At that time in the early 40s Britain was just being brought into the empire. The reason for omitting these regions is evident: there were few Jews in these places.

It is clear from the New Testament that in addition to missionaries "certified" by Jerusalem, a lot of enthusiastic independent preachers and "prophets" were wandering the world proclaiming the Jesus message as they construed it. That was the very reason for Jerusalem's certifications. They moved from village to village, from town to town. Their messages were sometimes bizarre and off-course. Such independents appear in the New Testament. Simon the Magician came from Gitta in Samaria, was a sometime disciple of John the Baptizer, and was proselytized into Christianity by the Apostle Philip in the mid-30s. He performed wonders and marvels in his district but his theology was out-of-bounds: he declared himself to be no less than the Father who had been mentioned so often by Jesus. This Simon was a renegade.

We hear in early Christian writings about the need to test wandering prophets and teachers by their works -- and to encourage them to keep moving on. These wanderers are mostly unknown to us because unlike St. Saul they have left no writings. The overall picture of early Christian missionary activity is murky and very incomplete and will always remain so. Yet in the earliest decades it was wandering teachers who held the highest positions and esteem in the communities they visited. In later generations this influence was gradually transferred to resident community officers – the local presbyters and (if one existed) the local bishop.

All the missions organized from Jerusalem had three objectives. First, the good news of Jesus the Messiah and the Kingdom of God had to be preached, and believers among the Jews of the Dispersion had to be brought into the "Jesus community". Second, non-Jewish believers had to be encouraged to convert to full Judaism of the "Jesus Movement" variety – to be baptised, circumcised, made subject to the Mosaic Law, and incorporated into some local synagogue sympathetic to the "Jesus message". That full-Judaism objective was modified after AD 50. Third, new followers were expected to become active within the Movement, contributing money and effort to the mission program, and providing the customary Jewish offerings for charity. Further money for the Jerusalem Temple was raised separately through a Temple Tax levied on all Jews in the empire and collected by the Roman tax collectors throughout the whole imperial realm.

Missionaries faced daunting problems. One big challenge was getting the gospel message out widely, for there were initially no written gospels – no "New Testament" existed. This was an age without newspapers or media, without mass communications, without printing, and without a widely literate populace. The message of the gospel had to be proclaimed orally and it varied with the preacher and with the circumstances of the hearers. So long as the message was predicated on the imminent Last Judgement, all that mattered was to make oneself ready. As John the Baptizer had proclaimed, "Repent, for the Kingdom of God is at hand." Everything else mattered little. Most preachers of the gospel had heard only parts of it from Jesus' own lips, and thus could pass on only these portions with any accuracy and confidence. But as years went by and Judgement Day was deferred, people wanted to know more about Jesus, his teachings, and about how Christians should live day to day. What exactly should a Christian believe and do in order to practice the "Way of Jesus" and find the salvation of God? The message had to bend to these realities.

One of the greatest challenges for the early missionaries arose with the "God-fearers" which they constantly encountered in their mission journeys. St. Saul and his circle, Barnabas and even Peter empathized with God-fearers. When faced with the circumcising knife and with the strict dietary laws which would bring social estrangement from old friends and even from family members, most God-fearers and Judaizing ex-pagans backed away from becoming full Jews -- of the Jesus variety or any other variety. They simply lived a gospel-inspired life as non-Jews.

The responses of the various Jesus-Movement leaders to these problems differed very markedly. Jesus' brother James initially insisted that converts must become Jews first and from that vantage point follow the Way of Jesus. Salvation was through the Law of Moses; Jesus' teachings had perfected that Law but the Law was still in force and necessary for salvation. James altered his position in 50 AD and approved conversions of non-Jews direct to "Christianity" that did not require circumcision or adherence to all the Jewish dietary laws, only acceptance of a few token restraints quite easy to bear. James could see that his stricter position was neither required by the scriptures nor practically tenable. His Jerusalem colleagues were not all so open-minded.

St. Saul on the other hand was much more flexible on this issue, and much more at ease with Hellenism and the society of cultured paganism – the society in which he had been raised. Perhaps too flexible, Saul tried to be "all things to all people". He could easily conceive of pagans becoming followers of Jesus without taking on the full burdens of Judaism. St. Saul had principles, but they tended to keep evolving, and they became grist for unpleasant rumours about his own Jewish faith that travelled back to Jerusalem. Saul was not popular with the Jerusalem disciples and the feeling was mutual. They knew he was a Herodian, and that in itself prevented a good rapport. Then there were his quirky beliefs. In a very real sense, Saul was the first great Christian heretic. Saul sarcastically called the Jerusalem team "those super-apostles" and "reputed pillars of the church". The feeling was mutual, but they needed each other.

Peter was an honest broker in all this, the man in the middle, and the man who kept the movement moving forward in the early years. Peter favoured missions to the Jews and himself participated mostly in these. But he also was quite willing to convert gentiles, specifically Judaizing ex-pagans. This he did in Rome and elsewhere. He no doubt believed like Brother James that conversion of such pagans to full Judaism was the ideal, but he knew well the reluctance of most pagans to make that conversion. He eventually decided that he could live with God-fearing gentile monotheists who wished to be part of the Jesus Movement, without the dietary laws and circumcision and all the rest of the Jewish regulations. Peter like Saul had seen life in Antioch and the pagan West and appreciated – as James may not have – the often slack observance even of mainstream Jews in places like Greece and Italy. Jesus himself was not entirely clear on the matter, as the gospel records show.

The leaders at this early stage of Christianity had to be concerned at all times with maintaining the unity and concord of the Christian communities, yet in the first generation after Jesus there were no long-established communities for models, no community rules, and few guideposts other than what Jesus was remembered to have taught or what individual apostolic missionaries or prophets taught. The only firm standards and scriptures available were those of Judaism itself. This meant a great deal of fluidity and too many options for the emerging movement.

On a few key points the emerging Christian sect was agreed. Jesus was the Christ – the Greek term for Messiah. Hence he was called from earliest days "Jesus, Christ". It soon became "Jesus Christ" or just "Christ". Another point of unanimity was the resurrection of Jesus. Even if there were wide differences of opinion about exactly what "resurrection" meant and how it had played out after Easter Sunday, Jesus' rising from the dead was undoubted. Jesus was alive. The role of the Mosaic Law in attaining salvation was long an undecided point. The value of dietary laws was a particularly perplexing topic. The requirement (or not) for celibacy among Christians was never settled by Jesus and remains unsettled to this day. Saul fulsomely circulated his own opinions but he prudently prefaced them with the words:

> On the question of celibacy I have received no instructions from the Lord. Yet I offer you my own judgement as one whom God's mercy has rendered fit to be trusted. [1 Corinthians 7: 25]

Thus, at first it was not clear exactly what it meant to be a Christian and to live a "Christian life". Judaic cultural practices long remained the model. All through the first century that model was dominant in both material practices and in Christian thought. Not until the third century did a strong internal Christian culture emerge, and even then – as still today – the ethos of Judaism remained strongly entrenched in the new religion's framework.

Christianity began as one more sect within Judaism, yet there were notable departures from Jewish practice. Christians seldom if ever participated in the Temple sacrifices of animals. Indeed, outside of Judaea they did not sacrifice animals at all. That custom was replaced by the bread and wine which represented the symbolic "body and blood" of Jesus himself as a sacrifice. Even the Passover celebration was gradually overtaken by celebration of the Day of Resurrection – Easter Day. The Jewish Sabbath (Saturday) gave place to the Christian day of Resurrection (Sunday) as the weekly day of communal worship and rest. As the nascent Church slowly became a gentile-controlled organization, especially in the West, the old Passover rites faded out more and more. Last but not least there was (and still is) in Christianity a notable and conscious tendency to level all distinctions. This tendency was not so strong in Judaism or in paganism; it was uniquely Christian and was a powerful tool in evangelism. As Saul put it:

> *In Christ there is neither Jew nor Greek, circumcised nor uncircumcised, fellow-citizen nor foreigner, slave nor free, male nor female. For Christ Jesus is all and is in all. [Colossians 3: 11]*

SAUL

Of the great names from the apostolic age, "Saul" (Paul) stands in the very front rank. Most of what we know about him derives directly from the writings of his colleague Luke, and from Saul's own New Testament letters to young churches -- the earliest-written parts of the New Testament. The ideas which Saul's letters contain have had overwhelming impacts on the course taken by the early Church. They became Holy Scripture, a destiny which Saul himself never foresaw. Saul – along with his companion Luke -- wrote half of the New Testament. His importance requires us to get to know him better.

Who was "Paul", whose original name was Saul? Saul himself claimed to have been born in Tarsus (southeast Turkey) of parents who were both Pharasaic Jews and both Roman citizens. Full Roman citizenship for Jews was a rare phenomenon in those times, but Saul's parents Antipater ben-Costabar and Cypros bat-Herod were most exceptional individuals.

Saul's father Antipater was the son of Herod the Great's sister Salome by her second husband Costabar, an Idumaean prince. Moreover, Saul's mother Cypros was a daughter of Herod the Great himself. She was a "Princess of Judaea". Saul was therefore doubly a Herodian, though in a non-ruling branch of the family. Saul's parents should have been very wealthy by virtue of their ancestry, since Antipater was the son of old Herod's rich sister Salome. But when grandma Salome died in AD 10 she willed most of her vast assets and territories not to her children but to empress Livia, the wife of Caesar Augustus. Some of Salome's estate passed to Antipater – enough to keep him in fine comfort but not enough to propel him into the dangerous power games of the Herodians. Antipater and his wife Cypros II lived first in Jamnia and Ashkelon, then in Tarsus, then again in Jamnia, and finally in Jerusalem. Antipater had also visited Rome several times. Just as their son would be, they were travellers.

Antipater was in the mold of his mother Salome: a schemer and trouble-maker in the family, but able and well-educated. He was ever at odds with his cousins Archelaus, Antipas and Philip, who had all been made rulers after old Herod's death. However, Antipater and Cypros got along well enough and both became rather pious Jews. At Tarsus their eldest son Saul was born in 6 BC, the Saul who became St Paul. Saul's childhood was somewhat disappointing for his family, for he never attained normal stature or the egregious good looks typical of the Herodians, and his legs were misshapen by some illness in his early years so that throughout his life he walked with a noticeable limp. In adulthood, Saul was barely five feet tall; on the mission trail he was disparagingly nicknamed "the three-cubit preacher". By his twenties he sported a small dark beard in the Jewish-Herodian fashion, but already he showed signs of premature baldness. Despite his unprepossessing appearance, there was certainly nothing wrong with Saul's intellect. He was educated at home by a Greek tutor rather than in Rome as was customary for Herodian children of ruling lines, and he proved a good learner. Having a religious bent, he was then sent, at age sixteen, to study in Jerusalem under Gamaliel the famous sage.

Let's call him Saul, or occasionally St. Paul in his Christian contexts. Saul's full birth names were Saul Alexander Thaddeus Herod. Scripture records his name switch to Saul [Acts 13: 9] but offers no explanation for it. Saul was an observant Jew like his parents, and highly educated. He knew his Bible thoroughly, and he could in addition spout Greek poetry. His religious education under Gamaliel would have been expensive and could not have been accessed without good connections. However, Saul's parents, as Herodians related to the kings and ethnarchs of Palestine, had money and enjoyed high social standing. Saul had a brother Costabar II (named after his grandfather) and a sister known as Cypros III. This sister married the Temple Treasurer Alexas Helcias and produced a daughter (Cypros IV) and two sons – Saul's nephews – all living in Jerusalem. Saul's two nephews are both known to history: they were Julius Archelaus ben-Helcias and Antipas ben-Helcias. Whether Saul himself was ever married is an open question. The answer seems to be no. No wife or children are alluded to by either Luke in Acts or by Saul himself in his letters.

Saul's identity as a Herodian aristocrat explains how he got educated by the finest of Pharisaic masters; why he wrote in his letter to the Roman church "Give my regards to my relative Herodion"; and most of all, how as "Paul" he got his incredible contacts and pull in high official circles -- contacts that could only have been obtained by someone of elite social standing. Here are examples of that social power: Following his time with Gamaliel (ca AD 30) Saul landed a highly responsible job as an agent of the Sanhedrin, the Jewish High Council in Jerusalem. Saul chatted with the governor of Cyprus during his mission trip there in the mid-40s. Much later, having been taken into Roman protective custody (AD 58), Saul was sent from Jerusalem to Caesarea with a full troop and cavalry escort – 200 men and seventy horse! – and with a horse supplied for him. That was not how the Romans normally treated their prisoners. He was on friendly terms with the Roman governor of Judaea (Marcus Antonius Felix, who served 52-60), and the reason is clear: Felix' wife Drusilla was also a Herodian, a first cousin of Saul. Saul although a prisoner of the Romans got invited audiences (AD 60) to chat with King Agrippa II and Queen Berenike – both his cousins. Then Saul got VIP treatment on his voyage to Rome (60-61) to have his appeal heard by Nero. Upon his shipwreck in Malta he was entertained by the island's governor. Once in Rome, Saul was kept only under open arrest (AD 61-63) in his own rented apartment pending the trial and was not hindered from going about his work.

Before his conversion to Christ, when Saul was engaged by the Jewish High Council as an anti-Christian police agent, he carried out his assignments with great vigour. Rabidly anti-Christian and energetically active in many persecutions and prosecutions carried out by the Judaean Temple authorities, Saul was present at the stoning of St. Stephen and approved of that act. How did he become a Christian?

In late AD 36, in the final year of emperor Tiberius' reign, Saul was on his way from Jerusalem to Damascus to take a listed group of Jewish-Christians into custody when he experienced his profound, exceedingly dramatic, sudden conversion. Whatever happened, he afterwards immediately became an energetic (not to say obsessed) proponent of and propagandist for Jesus-as-Messiah and for Christianity. Saul's famous conversion experience occurred on the main road just west of Damascus. A plain reading of two relevant scriptural passages strongly suggests that Saul was struck by lightning:

> *Suddenly a light flashed from the sky all around him. He fell to the ground and heard a voice saying, "Saul, Saul, why do you persecute me?"*
>
> *"Tell me, Lord, who you are."*
>
> *The voice answered, "I am Jesus, whom you are persecuting. Get up and go into the city, and you will be told what you must do."* ... *He was blind for three days. [Acts 9: 3-6]*

Typically for a lightning strike, Saul was knocked unconscious, literally blasted off his horse. His travelling companions were also thrown to the ground. The horse was killed outright. We can pass over the scriptural reports of Saul's apparitional conversation with Jesus as interpretative hindsight. Again typically for a lightning strike, Saul was temporarily blinded but gradually recovered sight after several days. Most telling of all, he later asserted that his body was "branded with the marks of Jesus":

In future let no one make trouble for me, for I bear the marks of Jesus branded on my body. [Galatians 6: 17]

This odd statement, at first sight puzzling, probably means that his body was indeed marked permanently with the strange fern-shaped marks – medically known as "Lichtenberg figures" -- which lightning leaves imprinted in and under the skin of many who suffer a direct strike. The marks represent the fern-like pattern of damaged ("fried") nerves and blood vessels. "Branded with the marks of Jesus" is an apt description.

Yet Saul's life was spared. It is no wonder that Saul was suddenly and utterly convinced that God had spoken and struck him down for his anti-Christian role. The conversion seems triply miraculous: first in that the chances of being struck directly by lightning are very small; second in that the chances of surviving such a strike are not good (though not nearly so poor as commonly supposed – nearly half of those struck survive); and third that Saul was able to turn himself completely about-face intellectually as an immediate and lasting result. Thanks to the ubiquitous superstition of his age, Saul drew a fateful new conclusion about Jesus' messiahship and about God's powerfully demonstrated support of Jesus' claim to that messiahship. Saul's horrific conversion was lasting, and it changed the history of the western world.

Saul became a powerful missionary for the Jesus Movement, channeling his formidable knowledge, intellect and incredible energy now in support of Christianity. Only his former classmate Barnabas – already a Christian -- was willing to chance a meeting with him, at which he became convinced of the sincerity of Saul's conversion. From there on, Saul gradually became integrated into the Damascus church community. Only three years after his startling conversion, and with Barnabas' assistance, he dared to visit Jerusalem and meet James the Lord's brother and the Apostle Peter. Then, a few years later, Barnabas in Antioch recruited Saul as an associate for a missionary tour and Saul began his amazing missionary career in the western empire. Saul made five significant missionary journeys. The timeframe was as follows:

- 36-39 AD: Conversion followed by time in Arabia, Damascus, Tarsus and Antioch
- Brief visit to Jerusalem (39 AD) to meet Simon Peter and James the brother of Jesus.
- 40 AD to 44 AD: Saul resides in Antioch, working in the Christian community there.
- 45-46 AD: Years of famine throughout Palestine.
- 46-48 AD: Saul travels with Barnabas and his cousin John Mark on mission to Cyprus and to Galatia in Anatolia. They return to Antioch.
- 49-50 AD: Second visit to Jerusalem where Barnabas introduces Saul to all the apostles there. The "Council of Jerusalem" takes place whereat Saul's strategy to evangelize Gentiles is approved.
- 50-53 AD: This time in company with Silas and Timothy, Saul travels to central and western Turkey, Macedonia, Greece and Syria, ending up again back in Antioch.
- 54 AD to 58 AD: Saul, now in company with Luke and others, makes a long mission circuit through central Turkey, Macedonia, Greece, Ephesus and the Aegean coast regions, finally going back to Judaea by ship, arriving in Jerusalem with crates of money collected for poor relief. In Jerusalem Saul becomes embroiled in strife with mainstream Jews in the Temple, a riot ensues, and Saul is rescued by the Roman garrison.
- 58 - 61 AD: Saul remains in Roman custody for two years through a protracted series of legal hearings about his case. He

appears before the procurator Antonius Felix, Felix' successor Porcius Festus, and King Herod Agrippa II. Exasperated, Saul at last files an appeal to Caesar.

- 63 - 66 AD: Acquitted by Nero, Saul carries out a short journey to Spain, then returns east
- to Greece and Crete. He reaches Jerusalem just before the Roman-Jewish war begins.
- 66 AD: Saul leads a group to Corinth to report to Nero on the imminent war in Judaea.
- 66 - 67 AD: Saul goes on from Corinth to Rome in the wake of the persecution following the Great Fire, where he and Peter are arrested. After his second trial in Rome, Saul is condemned and beheaded (29 June 67 AD). He was about 70 years old – not such a remarkable age amongst the long-lived Herodians.

—

Saul the Christian missionary became more and more involved with non-Jewish converts. Both he and Peter worked diligently on their respective mission trails, and both were successful. However, it is difficult to escape the conclusion that either Peter was shadowing Saul or Saul was avoiding Peter. They went to some of the same places; the churches at Corinth and at Rome claim both Peter and Saul as their co-founders. It sounds nice, but it came about because the two great saints worked separately – and at different times -- in Corinth and Rome for the hearts and minds of the nascent Jesus communities there. The "certain people" that Saul fulminates about in his letters to Corinth on account of their teaching a different gospel line from his were without doubt apostolic missionaries from Jerusalem – possibly including Saint Peter himself.

The same thing happened in Rome: Peter and Saul were not "partners in Christianity" until the very end, in the mid-60s. Peter felt that Saul had become almost an apostate from Judaism. Saul felt that Peter and his circle failed to grasp the cosmic significance of Jesus' appearance on earth. Peter and James considered Jesus to have been a great prophet and teacher, a son of God, and the Messiah of Israel, but for all that just a human being. Jesus was only James' brother, after all. Saul evolved the idea that Jesus was in some degree divine as the Son of God. That Hellenistic idea was taken much further by others in later times. But it was too much for Peter and the apostolic group.

As a man bearing two personalities, Saul was neurotic, and he drove himself very hard. He wrote much, and in his letters to various church groups he laid out his thoughts about what it means to be a Christian. The question had never before been raised outside the context of Judaism, and many of Saul's thoughts have passed the test of time:

> Love is patient, kind and unenvious. Love is never a braggart or a boor, never selfish or hot-tempered. Love keeps no score of wrongs; never takes pleasure in others' mistakes, but rejoices in truth. There is nothing that love cannot face; no limits to its faith, its hopes and its endurance. Therefore, love will never come to an end. [1 Corinthians 13: 4]

> Everything is summed up in one rule: Love your neighbour as yourself. Love cannot mistreat a neighbour; therefore the whole Law is summed up in love. [Romans 13: 9]

However, Saul's thoughts were not always so full of tender love, so that he has also left us a few passages like this:

> You stupid Galatians! You must have been put under some spell, you before whose eyes Jesus Christ was displayed on his cross. Answer this one question: did you receive the Spirit by keeping the Law or by hearing and believing the message of the gospel? How can you all be so stupid?? [Galatians 3: 1]

Saul's missionary travels took him repeatedly to Corinth in Greece, Philippi in Macedonia and Ephesus in Asia Minor. He spent the central 50s there. His fateful trip back from Greece to Jerusalem took place in AD 58. His relaxed views vis-à-vis the Law preceded him, and his Herodian identity was well known in Palestine. James the Righteous dressed him down in no uncertain terms about his religious heresies and insisted that he go straight to the Temple and undertake rites which would demonstrate to all that he was still a faithful, conforming Jew. Saul made no argument and did so. In the Temple he was recognized by a pilgrim Jew from Asia Minor who mistakenly thought that Saul's companion in the Temple was a gentile. A major riot ensued. It is uncharitable to think that the onlooker in the Temple who shouted "Why, there's that $%^&* Saul of Tarsus!!" might have been primed by certain Jerusalem Jewish-Christians.

Saul was rescued from certain death by Roman soldiers and taken to the adjacent Antonia Fortress in custody. A political hot potato, he was then passed from official to official – magistrates, governors and even princes -- for two full years, without being either charged or exonerated, until his patience was exhausted, at which point he exercised his citizen's right and appealed to Caesar's judgment in Rome. To Rome he went in the autumn of 60 AD in an epic sea-voyage, during which they survived storm and shipwreck on Malta, where the passengers had to overwinter. In Rome Saul waited comfortably for a further two years for his hearing, his companion and servant Luke with him. In AD 63 Saul was finally brought to trial before Nero.

—

The Apostolic team in Jerusalem worked under increasingly difficult circumstances. In proportion to its success in growing the Jesus Movement, the traditional Jewish Temple Establishment sought to cut the Movement down to size. The Romans more gradually became set against the Movement. By the end of the century arose Christian reluctance to offer sacrifice to the genius of the emperor, or to respect the state gods and the deified emperors. Christians were widely seen as "outsiders", inimical to Roman society generally and to the traditional protective gods of the pagan empire.

The Jewish Establishment at least understood the theology and practice of the Jesus Movement. It was after all still a variety of Judaism. Also, Christians used the Hebrew Bible as scripture and thus were familiar with, and indeed shared, many Jewish beliefs and practices. First-century Christians liked to see themselves as the "true Israel", a self-identity which strengthened greatly after the Roman-Jewish War of AD 66-71.

While missions prospered east and west, in Judaea tensions continued to rise between Roman occupiers and the nationalistic Jews. Judaea was coming apart. Riots, demonstrations, insurrections, false messiahs, corruption, provocations and plots became everyday occurrences by the end of the 50s. Inter-class gaps turned into open confrontations and the Zealot extremists gained ground steadily. A big part of the problem was economic, with the poor becoming poorer and the rich holding tight to their wealth. The imperial authorities had no solution. Rome kept sending incompetent procurators who used their two-year terms mainly to enrich themselves. We see from hindsight and from the experiences of our own age that there may have been no solutions short of the apocalyptic ones – revolution and retribution -- which actually did come about. Pontius Pilate was recalled to Rome in AD 36 by Tiberius, and sent into forced retirement. After three years of full rule by a quite competent king (Herod Agrippa I, AD 41-44), Cuspius Fadus served as Judaea's procurator during AD 44-46, the opening years of Claudius' reign. Fadus accomplished nothing. Neither did Julius Tiberius Alexander who followed him during AD[5] 46-48. Two-year appointments continued to be the rule, and none of the appointees left a positive mark on Judaea.

---

5 However, this same Alexander later served with real distinction as the Governor of Egypt.

After eight long years (52-60) as procurator of Judaea, Antonius Felix[6] was succeeded by Porcius Festus who appears prominently in the <u>Acts of the Apostles</u>. Festus was the one and only effective procurator the Romans ever sent to Judaea; but he died in office. Next came Clodius Albinus from 62-64, another incompetent, and finally the incredibly stupid and venal Gessius Florus took over. By that time Judaea was entering an irretrievable state of anarchy. Wise heads foresaw the coming explosion.

CHRISTIANITY COMES TO ROME

The message of the Jesus Movement reached Rome at an exceedingly early date, in the reign of the emperor Tiberius, during Jesus' lifetime. Saul refers to a woman called Junia and a man called Andronicus as among the very earliest members of the Movement there. Perhaps they were Jews who had visited Judaea for one of the great festivals and there had heard Jesus teach, or heard his message proclaimed by his followers. The message kept reaching Rome in pulses, from different sources, all through the 30s.

<u>Acts of the Apostles</u> mentions Jewish visitors from Rome and other faraway places listening to apostolic preaching in Jerusalem within a few weeks of the Resurrection and becoming believers. That was AD 33. They took their new belief to Rome, and each year new pilgrims were exposed to apostolic preaching. By the end of Tiberius' reign in AD 37, a tiny but committed group had formed a Jesus-community in Rome. Its members were all Jews. <u>Acts</u> describes a confrontation in Caesarea Maritima between Simon Peter and a Samaritan Christian called Simon Magus ("Simon the Sorcerer"). In AD 35 when Philip was making a mission sweep up the Samaritan coast, he baptized the Sorcerer. Simon came from the town of Gitta in Samaria and had been a follower of John

---

6 Felix was the brother of Pallas, emperor Claudius' powerful and very rich finance minister. Felix was more or less a suave crook. He married into the Herodian family: his wife Drusilla was a sister of King Agrippa II. Saul was a cousin to Drusilla.

the Baptizer. After John the Baptizer's arrest in AD 30, his movement fissured, one branch continuing under Jesus and another under a follower named Dositheos. This Dositheos acquired Simon Magus as a disciple, but Simon subsequently switched camps and allied himself with Jesus' wing of the sect. Having been baptized into the Jesus Movement by the Apostle Philip, he began preaching locally on his own. Simon's teaching was spectacularly unorthodox: he advertised himself as no less than the Father whom Jesus the Son had talked about. Simon received corrective religious instruction from Peter, who was sent out from Jerusalem for that purpose, and then the Magus took up some kind of leadership position in the Samaritan Jesus-movement. That did not work out, for the Magus fell back into sorcery and strange claims of personal divinity. At some point Simon drew in a woman named Helena as an associate in his preaching and miracle-working.

The Magus was frightened by King Agrippa's crackdown on Christian leaders in AD 42. Simon Peter was also on his case. The Magician took ship for Rome that year and began grossly heretical preaching to the Jews there. As a consequence, Peter himself journeyed to Rome in 43 to rein in the Magician and to straighten things out in the capital.

At the end of the fourth century, St. Jerome wrote that St. Peter reached Rome in "the second year of Claudius" – AD 43. That perhaps underlies the Roman Church's claim of having been "established" by Peter. There had been earlier beginnings by others, not to mention Simon the Sorcerer, but it was Peter who actually organized the Roman community and put it on an apostolically orthodox track. Peter stayed until around 46 AD. In Rome, Peter quickly ousted the Sorcerer, first by verbal sparring and then thanks to a near-fatal accident as the Sorcerer tried an elaborate illusionist trick of "flying" in Rome. Simon recovered and (with King Agrippa newly dead) went back to Samaria where yet again he resumed his former religious teaching as "The Father". He found followers, and there were still a few Simonians in Samaria two hundred years later.

Having dealt with the Sorcerer, Peter stayed on with a distinguished gentile Christian family in Rome – the family of the senator Lucius Pudens -- and preached out-of-doors near the Viminal Hill, by the crowded trans-Tiber area of Rome where most of Rome's Jews dwelt. He also taught in friendly local synagogues. There were five synagogues in Rome of which the prestigious Augustan Synagogue and the Synagogue of Freedmen were some distance away. The trans-Tiber area, poor and crowded, was the site of three synagogues. Peter's favorite place for Sabbath worship was the Olive Trees Synagogue near the river. It was Jesus-friendly. Peter performed Christian baptisms at the nearby Spring of the Nymphs, and over the years the Olive Trees Synagogue came to be known as a "Jesus" assembly. The Apostle baptized both Jews and a few God-fearers into Christ, and frequently he – just as Saul would later have to do -- had to deal with demonstrations by irate mainstream Jews who did not acknowledge Jesus as the Messiah and who did not approve of baptizing pagans who had not agreed to become full, circumcised, thoroughly observant Jews. Sometimes the Roman authorities had to disperse noisy crowds to quell their altercations.

At this same time, in the mid-40s, Barnabas, Saul and young Mark were evangelizing on Cyprus. There they met and converted the Roman procurator, a man named Sergius Paullus. That was when Saul started calling himself by the Roman name Paul. According to an inscription in the Vatican Museums, this same Sergius Paullus – still a supporter of the Jesus Movement? -- was back in Rome in 47, appointed to the prestigious municipal water commission. Almost from its beginnings, the Jesus community of Rome included sympathetic upper-class gentiles like Paullus as well as Jews. As we will presently see, these gentiles included some wealthy families and even aristocrats in addition to more ordinary folk.

Through his link with the Pudens family, Peter met other God-fearers of some social standing. Peter's most momentous conversion occurred during his very first year in Rome. Julia Pomponia Graecina was a member of the top level of the Roman aristocracy, and a woman of high character. Her husband was General Aulus Plautius, the conqueror and first governor (AD 43-47) of Britain. He was not a Christian but was a God-fearer, and was deeply in love with his wife. After her cousin the emperor Claudius had unjustly put her aunt Julia to death, Pomponia defied the emperor by going into public mourning in 42 AD. Her mourning was said to have continued all through Claudius' long reign and those of his successors, but at some time around 44 she accepted Christ in consolation and quietly became a Christian. At that time it would have been difficult for the average Roman to distinguish between mourning behaviour and the typically subdued Christian behaviour. She took the baptismal name Lucina.

Many years after Governor Plautius' return to Rome, in the opening years of Nero's reign, a nosy magistrate brought charges against Aulus' wife for alleged "foreign superstition". Nero generously allowed Aulus to hold a "family court"; in 57 it found Pomponia not guilty. Clearly Aulus was complicit in his wife's religious ways because subsequently their two children were baptized, and Christianity spread through their descendants. Even the historian Tacitus noted Pomponia's case:

> A lady of distinction, Pomponia Graecina, wife of Aulus Plautius, was accused of practicing a foreign superstition and left to be judged by her husband Plautius. He followed the ancient procedure of holding a family court, since the matter related to her status and reputation, and he pronounced her innocent. [Tacitus, Annals 13: 32]

Their daughter Petronilla (named after her great-grandfather Petro, not after "Peter") took the new faith, as did a grand-daughter Plautia. Their son-in-law, Petronilla's husband Titus Flavius Sabinus, was, or became, another closet Christian. He served for twelve years (57-69 AD) as the City Prefect ("Lord Mayor") of Rome under the emperors Nero, Otho and Vitellius. People noted how reluctant he was to shed blood or engage in violence – unlike most Prefects. There was also the senatorial

Pudens family, many of whose members took up Christianity. These were some of the fruits of Peter's evangelizing in the 40s.

The widely disliked Christian sect of Judaism slowly became ill-famed in Rome and then illegal, and so moved outside the traditional exemptions accorded to Jews. There was never any actual legislation; the illegality of Christianity simply germinated from public distaste for the new cult. No doubt the Jews asserted that "those people are not real Jews". Christians on the other hand were anxious to retain their special status as Jews. As with Julia Pomponia Graecina, most Christians seemed dour and unsociable. Another reason for public rejection was the mistaken belief that the Christian rite of the Last Supper with its references to the body and blood of Christ involved real flesh and blood –- cannibalism. And if any more negatives were needed, it was well known that the Christians' founder had been a criminal who ended up crucified.

Judaism – secure in its privileges and exemptions -- encouraged the Roman authorities to treat Christianity as outside Judaism and as illegal. The language of Roman charges brought against Christians was always similar: "atheism" (refusal to worship the state gods); "sedition" (preaching a Kingdom not ruled by Caesar); "disrespect for Roman institutions" (refusal to attend state-religion festivals and to venerate deified Emperors); and "disturbing the peace" (public preaching, altercations with mainstream Jews).

After Claudius' expulsion in 49 of all Jewish-Christians from Rome, the Jesus community there came under the control of the gentile Christians who remained. This was the first example of a primarily non-Jewish Christian community. The ex-pagan converts took charge in Rome. Claudius died in 54 and his expulsion order died with him, since Nero declined to renew it. Many of the expelled Jewish-Christians then trickled back home to the capital, only to find that Rome's duly elected gentile church officers were in no hurry to return to the previous state of affairs. About this time the Greek word for "church" (*ekklesia,* basically meaning an assembly) began to replace the term "synagogue" (also a Greek-derived term for assembly) previously used for Christian as well as Jewish meeting places. The Roman church was never again controlled by its Jewish-Christian members, for its subsequent growth derived largely from gentile conversions.

A big problem at this time arose from Saul's teaching of his own novel theological ideas to new Jesus-communities in Greece, Rome and present-day Turkey. In Jewish eyes, Saul was preaching blasphemies about a "divine" Jesus. He was also admitting monotheistic ex-pagans to the Jesus community without requiring them to become jn any sense full Jews, and he was alleged to be discouraging even Jews from adhering to all the Law of Moses. The allegations had some grain of truth and lost nothing in retelling.

Peter, his brother Andrew and Mark were sent forth from Palestine in AD 55 to rectify the situation. They traveled together slowly from Antioch through northern Galatia and Pontus-et-Bithynia, then they parted. Andrew's team crossed the Bosporus and evangelized along the west coast of the Black Sea as far north as Olbia in present-day Ukraine. This was all territory familiar to the Romans and effectively under their control. Peter's group veered south past the important coastal cities of Ephesus and Smyrna, then crossed to Greece, following in Saul's tracks to Corinth, the seat of major internal problems that seemed to be occurring. Saul had by then (spring 58) gone back to Palestine. Peter stayed in Greece for several months, countering certain ideas preached there by Saul, and working hard for the conversion of local Jesus followers to more conservative Jewish-Christian views. It was not easy, for Saul had left a strong and well-organized contingent behind, a cadre which stoutly defended his views. Peter then returned at last – in late 59 – to Antioch. By that date Saul was in Roman custody in Caesarea.

If Peter was keen to correct Saul's teachings, Saul for a long time avoided opportunities to introduce himself into Peter's mission territory. Nero's formal repeal in 56 of Claudius' expulsion order against Rome's Jewish Christians allowed many to return home to Rome. Aquila and Prisca, Saul's close associates in Corinth and Ephesus, were among the returnees. They carried back to the capital the Pauline slant on belief and spread it there. It was well after the returnees' departure from Greece that Saul learned that Peter's people were starting a new mission out of Antioch; it took Saul by surprise.

Saul longed to go to Rome himself. Almost alone among the Herodians, he had not been sent to Rome as a child to be educated there; his father wouldn't hear of it. Saul prepared a magnificent essay-letter for the Roman Christian community and sent it off with a colleague Phoebe, a woman deacon who was making a business trip to Rome. This essay-letter, Saul's <u>Letter to the Romans</u>, is his finest work, designed to elicit an invitation to Rome. Saul displayed in it a good second-hand knowledge of Christian individuals in Rome; and the letter set forth Saul's views ably. Peter eventually read a copy of the letter, and even he was impressed.

Saul got to Rome in 61, but only as a prisoner sent there to be tried before emperor Nero. During two further years under token house arrest in Rome awaiting the trial, Saul was able to inject more of his outlook into the life of the Roman church. Saul was acquitted by Nero (63) and went to Spain briefly before returning to the eastern Mediterranean in the summer of 64.

When Rome burned in mid-64 everything changed for the Christians. The savage punishment of Rome's Christians in the late autumn of 64 and the spring of 65 following the fire eventually brought both Saul and Peter back to the city to comfort the traumatized Christian community and to help get it back on its feet. During that last period together in Rome, Peter and Saul were reconciled, because the situation had changed in several ways. Brother James in Jerusalem had been silenced by murder in 62 and was no longer their leader. Saul's letters had been a step towards reconciliation, for they showed the two great Apostles growing together in their views of the new faith and in their positions on gentiles as converts. Peter acknowledged that Saul had been essentially right in the matter of bringing monotheistic gentiles to Christ – and Saul on his part recognized that an original Apostle like Peter really did have authoritative insight into what Jesus had believed, taught and done.

In Rome Peter lodged once again with a well-to-do convert, Lucius Pudens Jr, the son of the senator whom Peter had converted back in the 40s. Saul, arriving in December 66 from Corinth, once more stayed at the villa of Julia Pomponia Graecina in the suburbs. Pomponia was by then well over fifty years of age and the serene matriarch of Rome's Christian community. The Roman-Jewish War was getting underway. Immediately a Roman dragnet started to round up prominent Christians in Rome. Jewish-Christian leaders were especially wanted. Peter kept out of the walled city at night. Saul, a bigger and more conspicuous fish, was caught at once. Too many people wanted him out of circulation.

Back in the 40s, Peter had welcomed a Roman youth as an eager convert; the man's name was Flavius Clemens. He was a freedman serving as the secretary of Titus Flavius Clemens. In 61 Saul met this secretary, was impressed, and assented willingly to appointing him as an elder in the Roman church community. In AD 66 Peter and Saul made two other joint presbyterial appointments to the community at Rome. The first and older of the new presbyters was named Linus; he was from northern Italy and had been a Christian since the 50s. He was originally a follower of Saul but got on well with Peter. The second presbyter was named Anenkletos (usually he was called Cletus in Rome), a younger freedman from the Greco-Roman community, who had been baptized by Peter. The well-educated Clemens attended to the Roman community's correspondence and liaison with other Christian communities throughout the empire. He had been doing that work since the late 50s. Clemens was making Rome a new liaison hub. By the late 60s the outlines of a real Christian organization were appearing in Rome and elsewhere. Slowly over the next century and a half, these outlines would solidify and become "the Church".

Despite the setbacks of the years 64-66, Christianity in Rome experienced a growth spurt during the Neronian years 55-68, and under that most unlikely emperor. Nero was certainly odd; but before Nero, two equally odd emperors sat in turn on the throne of the Romans. Their names were Gaius Caligula and his uncle Claudius.

VI
MID-CENTURY CALM

THE AGRIPPAS

In the late 30s the long reigns of the two brother "tetrarchs" Herod Antipas and Herod Philip came to their ends. Philip, whose territories were larger but poorer than those of Antipas, died in 34 as he had lived – peacefully and unobtrusively. Apart from maintaining the peace of his kingdom and keeping the favour of the Romans, he left no great accomplishments. But he had been a good ruler, liked by his people and a moderating influence on his more mercurial half-brother Antipas. With that influence removed, Herod Antipas quickly got into difficulties. His troubles had started in AD 29 when he married Herodias the wife of his still-living brother Herod II. Herod II had for a time been the crown prince of the Herodians, the designated successor of old Herod; but like so many of Herod the Great's sons he fell out with his father and was struck from the succession in favour of his half-brother Herod Archelaus. So he went to Rome and lived there as a very wealthy and influential but indolent private citizen. Herod II married within the family in AD 16. His niece-and-wife's name was Herodias, a granddaughter of the great Herod and a sister of the man who would become King Agrippa I. They produced just one child, a daughter Salome born in 18. This child was the infamous "Salome the dancer".

The purloining of Herodias from Herod II by Herod Antipas drew vociferous criticism from John the Baptizer and led to that prophet's death. But there were other consequences too. In order to marry Herodias, Antipas had summarily divorced his existing wife Phasaelis. She was the daughter of Aretas (=Horeth), the King of Arabia, and her father took a dim view of the divorce. First there were diplomatic repercussions. Soon the Arabian King found a pretext for war in a disputed little stretch of border territory between his and Antipas' lands. In early 37 Aretas declared war on Antipas and sent an army into his territory. The Arab king's forces were completely victorious over tetrarch Antipas' army and sent the tetrarch fleeing to Rome for help. The Romans never accepted that their client rulers could wage war on each other, so emperor Tiberius, now at the very end of his reign, angrily ordered his Syrian governor to launch a punitive counter-offensive against Aretas. Before the governor could organize that, old Tiberius died and the authority for war disappeared. The new emperor, Gaius Caligula, simply threatened Aretas, who thereupon withdrew his troops. Yet Antipas was still not in the clear, for Caligula had for unknown reasons taken a dislike to him, but had earlier taken a liking to a younger and more rakish member of the Herodian clan: Antipas' wife's brother Herod Agrippa.

Marcus Julius Herod Agrippa was a reckless young Herodian prince, son of King Herod's son Aristobulus and Berenike the daughter of King Herod's sister Salome. As usual these parents were closely-related Herodians: Berenike was a cousin of Aristobulus. Agrippa was a consummate schemer and also a phenomenally lucky individual. He led a tumultuous life. Educated in Rome with Tiberius' son Drusus, no less, he soon went through his inheritance there and ran up enormous debts. Broke, he settled briefly in Palestine but after raising a big loan in Alexandria he went back to Italy, where to his surprise and indignation prim old Tiberius refused to put him up at court until his tax debts were paid off. He simply took a new loan to pay off the debts, and thus secured a court post as tutor to Tiberius' grandson Gemellus. While at Capri he also made the acquaintance of young Gaius Caligula, Tiberius' presumed heir. In a supposedly private conversation with Caligula, Agrippa was very indiscreet:

"The emperor is looking tired".

"Well, he is nearly eighty and still puts in full days".

"I look forward to the day when you will take over from him. May it be soon!"

Caligula said nothing in reply.

An eavesdropping slave heard the exchange and reported it to Tiberius, who immediately had Agrippa thrown into prison. Yet Caligula remained his friend. Within a few months, Tiberius was dead and Caligula was emperor. The new emperor then rewarded his friend with liberty and a little kingdom – the territory of his late uncle Philip the tetrarch. Herod Antipas was livid, for here was a poor relation, just a kid, becoming a king – something that Antipas himself had dreamt of all his life. At his wife Herodias' urging, Antipas attempted to stop the rise of Agrippa by denouncing him to Caligula, but Antipas didn't appreciate the odd temper of the new emperor. First, Agrippa was given opportunity to lodge counter-allegations, then there was a full confrontation before the emperor himself. It resulted in AD 39 in Antipas' banishment to southern Gaul, and the transfer of all his territories to King Agrippa. Herodias – even though she was the sister of King Agrippa -- chose voluntarily to follow her husband Antipas into exile. He was 60; she was 56.

King Agrippa I remained a confidant and friend to Caligula. Caligula did not have many such friends. When the emperor was assassinated in 41, Agrippa I had the further luck to be visiting Rome and to support the dead emperor's eccentric uncle Claudius for the emperorship. In return, grateful emperor Claudius added Judaea and Samaria to Agrippa's kingdom. Agrippa then had essentially all the territories which Herod the Great had held.

Agrippa the First was not personally pious but for astute political reasons he supported orthodox Jewish views and policies, and energetically combatted the Christian movement, executing or imprisoning Apostles and others. At the same time he very actively cultivated the continued friendship of Rome and Claudius. In Palestine he behaved as a pious Jew, in Rome as a convivial pagan. As host at a spectacular Games held in 44 at Caesarea in Claudius' honour, the king wore a silver-thread toga to deliver a sunrise oration to the pagan crowd. The speech was a hit and the effect of the sun on the silver garment was awe-inspiring. The pagan audience hailed Agrippa as a god come to earth. But during his speech he was seized by sudden pain – a burst duodenum. Five days later he was dead of septicaemia, leaving behind (in Rome) his 17-year-old son, also named Marcus Julius Herod Agrippa. Emperor Claudius deemed the boy too young for kingship, and so Agrippa's kingdom once again reverted to the status of a Roman province under procurators.

Strictly speaking, the 17-year-old son was already Agrippa I's successor "Agrippa II". It was just a matter of time until he came into his kingdom, for the Romans still looked with favour upon the Herodian clan. Claudius kept Agrippa II at Rome and sent out Cuspius Fadus as a procurator to administer Agrippa I's old territories including Judaea. As young Agrippa waited at the court, he was careful to make no trouble. It was soon evident that here was a Herodian prince of some intelligence and refinement, who could manage his own affairs and thus could no doubt manage the affairs of a small kingdom. So, upon the death of King Herod of Chalcis in AD 48, Agrippa II was given his modest dominions -- but still only as a tetrarchy. Things would soon improve, however, and Agrippa II would find himself on a rocketing rise to royal splendour.

CALIGULA

As old emperor Tiberius breathed his last in AD 37, all attention in Rome focussed on young Gaius "Caligula" Germanicus, the youngest and only surviving son of the famous Roman general Germanicus – the man who, had he lived, would have succeeded Tiberius. Next day the whole city broke out in spontaneous celebration – partly celebration of Tiberius' demise and partly of Gaius' accession. For there never was much doubt that Gaius would succeed to the throne. Everyone looked forward to a new golden age under this golden youth. His throne name was Gaius; Caligula was just a nickname (meaning "little boots"), acquired in childhood when he often wore a scaled-down version of his father's military boots (**caligae**). Gaius was moderately tall and well proportioned, spoke articulately, and was thought to have some of the flash and dash of his famous father. Great things were expected from this grandson of both Augustus and Mark Antony. The new emperor resided at Rome; Capri was forgotten. The first year, 37, went by smoothly enough. However, those who worked closely with the emperor Gaius soon found him vain, bad-tempered and given to cruelly sarcastic remarks. But then, Tiberius had been no model of politeness or tact.

Caligula was not muscular, but was well-formed, fairly bright, well-educated and in some ways very able. But there was a downside. He had inherited the mental instability syndrome of the Claudian line. That instability had been noticeable though well-controlled in his famous father general Germanicus. Germanicus had been vain and self-promotional, loved power, and played to the common crowd. Yet the talents of Germanicus were real enough, and his pedigree was impressive by any measure. His paternal grandmother was Livia, Augustus' wife, by her earlier marriage to Tiberius Claudius Nero[7]. Caligula's maternal grandparents were Augustus' sister Octavia and her husband, the celebrated general Mark Antony no less. There is no doubt that Caligula's

7 An ancestor of the later emperor Nero.

father Germanicus would have succeeded Tiberius had that emperor not outlived him. Germanicus left three sons but two of them – along with their mother -- were executed one after the other in the 20s through the dark machinations of Seianus. Was there really a plot, or not? And so Germanicus' youngest and only surviving son Gaius "Caligula" succeeded to the throne in late 37 AD. His only potential rival Gemellus – Tiberius' mentally challenged biological son, who lived in a sort of banishment -- was promptly liquidated.

Gaius showed himself able to attend to the gruelling business of emperorship, but he was an autocrat through and through. He often worked hard and effectively, though unevenly, but he was dangerously hard to please, and possessed an unbounded ego. It is uncertain whether his frequent outbreaks of apparently uncontrolled rage were authentic or whether they were (as with Adolf Hitler) careful play-acting to impose his will upon others. The emperor was also a large-scale spendthrift; that was certainly not play-acting. Tiberius' carefully accumulated financial surplus soon began to shrink, and within three years it was gone, with little to show for it.

Early in the reign there was trouble in Alexandria, where the always-festering relations between the Jews and the pagan Greeks broke out in open fighting. The Jews, who comprised almost a third of the city's population, were agitating for a fuller role in the municipal government. The Greeks, egged on by governor Avidius Flaccus and his cronies, opposed this demand and decided to make their opposition felt via a pogrom. In the summer of 38 Greek mobs assaulted the Jews and forced them out of the Greek wards of the city into the one ward which was reserved for Jews. Naturally the Jews defended their homes and persons. When emperor Gaius heard of pitched battles in Alexandria, he rashly ordered Flaccus to send in the legionaries and subdue the "insurrectionists" – that is, the Jews. Flaccus was more than ready to oblige and the result was thirty thousand dead, almost all of them Jews, and the burning of part of the city.

Both Flaccus and the emperor were horrified by this unintended disaster. Caligula invited the Alexandrians to send a delegation to Rome to discuss the situation. The Greeks, in a triumphal mood, sent pagan extremists to the emperor while the Jews sent a separate all-Jewish delegation headed by their most illustrious philosopher and writer Philo. Neither delegation gave or obtained satisfaction. The emperor, annoyed that two hostile delegations had arrived, was rude to the Greeks, rightly feeling that they had caused the damage; but he was ruder still to the Jews, keeping them cooling their heels for weeks while he was "busy" with other matters. In fact, Caligula had expected the Alexandrians to send only one delegation representing Greeks and Jews alike. Now the emperor was forced into judging between the opponents. He took the only way out, sacking Flaccus and setting everything back to where it had been before the trouble erupted. But his remarks left no doubt about his own private feelings: "Now the Jews had better behave!"

—

No sooner had the Alexandrian matter been put on hold than a crisis erupted in Germany. The governor there was another man with big ego. Lentulus Gaeticulus treated his northern fiefdom almost as a personal possession and didn't like constraints. He had successfully faced down even emperor Tiberius, and Tiberius had left him in place since he was quite competent; but Caligula would brook no off-leash governors. When Gaeticulus and his German legions mutinied in 39, the emperor sped to Germany with astounding speed – arriving there with an army in just three weeks -- and crushed the revolt briskly. Everyone was surprised at this feat by an emperor whom they had supposed to be indecisive and un-military. But more was to follow. Instead of returning to Rome, Caligula took his army west into Gaul and overwintered in Lugdunum (=Lyons). His parents had lived for some time in Lugdunum – his uncle Claudius had been born there – and the place was full of happy memories for Caligula. But the side trip was yet another manifestation of the young emperor's sudden, erratic decision-taking.

By the end of 39 it had become abundantly clear to the Roman Senate and to most other people in Rome that Caligula was not quite right in the head. The emperor had suffered some mysterious illness early in the year which involved a high fever, a period of delirium and a good deal of pain. After his recovery his ideas and actions were decidedly stranger, and his increasingly threatening manner offended and frightened everyone. Basically that attitude was "I'm the boss and I can do anything I want -- to anybody" – his very words. The emperor wanted to develop the monarchy along the lines of earlier Greek monarchies in the East, where the ruler was accorded divine honours as a god and possessed unlimited powers. Caligula especially made it very clear that he wanted to be worshipped as a living god. He had several senators executed for no very strong resistance, and he was soon publicly proclaiming himself a living god in the style of the old oriental despots. In Syria where the idea had some historical currency he built two small temples to himself and got himself worshipped after a fashion. But his grip on reality was slipping. According to himself, he had had sex with all of his sisters (and many others). Indeed he had seduced one of his sisters, Drusilla, with whom he was infatuated. Was he lying about the rest? He said he intended to make his horse a Consul, but that also was idle sarcasm. He routinely threatened his associates and his few friends with death, and he occasionally made good on that threat, as in the case of his nasty chief minister Macro. Caligula made increasingly lunatic decisions and spent money wantonly. Was the emperor really insane? Most ancient writers thought so. Yet he retained evidence of occasional competence. We moderns might diagnose unmanaged anger, or a bipolar mind, or schizophrenia. He reveled in power, thought himself above the law – indeed thought himself divine and above all humanity -- and he would experience fits of insensate rage over rather trivial matters.

In AD 40 Caligula decided to conquer Britain. We don't know why. His immediate reason may have been to put a stop to the Britons' annoying interference with affairs on the Gallic side of the Channel. Vanity may also have played a large part. Julius Caesar had invaded southern England back in 54 BC, but no lasting Roman occupation had resulted. Now the emperor's intelligence people were saying that conquest would be easy. Caligula gathered forces and made elaborate preparations for a combined army-navy assault on the south coast, in present-day Kent and Sussex. The army assembled en route from Germany and Gaul, and after delays it arrived at the Channel coast near Calais. The fleet presently joined the legions there. There was much murmuring in the ranks. They were going into Ocean and overseas, with all the real and imagined terrors of the unknown. Superstition made the real dangers much worse. The autumn winds were contrary and the narrow sea was storm-tossed for weeks on end. Rain fell almost every day. The augurs who consulted the will of the gods obtained a steady string of negative results; the gods were against an invasion. The emperor eventually caved in, for he shared in full the superstitious nature of his comrades. Convinced by the foul weather that the gods were not cooperating, and faced by inauspicious auguries by the priests, he decided to abort the expedition and try again next year. Most telling of all, in spite of Caligula's strong exhortations, the troops themselves remained cowed by the prospect of crossing Ocean to some wild land beyond. After a long stand-by, the emperor ordered the legions to strike camp and head back to Germany. Typically, Caligula turned it into a cynical, witty pun. Ordering his soldiers to gather up their equipment (**musculi**) could also mean in Latin to gather up seashells (**musculi**) on the beach. Some hearers took it one way, some the other and began collecting shells. The emperor promised that they would resume the invasion the next spring when conditions would be better. In fact his failure threw him completely out of sorts; the trip back to Rome was sombre. He never did invade Britain.

The remainder of the brief reign of Gaius Caligula was marked by many impetuous, even crazy, decisions, by an extraordinarily scandalous personal life even by the abysmal standards of the time, and by a streak of viciousness and cruelty never before seen in an emperor. Besides all that, he had no morals. After two short marriages and at least one incestuous relationship he married an aristocratic woman named Milonia

Caesonia in AD 39 and produced a daughter Caesonia by her. Some of the time during 40, Caligula continued to function administratively at a quite reasonable level; at other times he was decidedly off the track. Caligula was above all else unpredictable, so that everyone who had to deal with him did so in constant fear and trembling. Long having talked about it, he now built more temples to himself in the eastern parts of the empire, where his person could be worshipped. In the West he ran into a senatorial wall of opposition, but the Senate was terrified of him, with good reason. He didn't hesitate to have people executed on whims. He had become power-mad.

The case of his statues, his last mania, is illustrative. It was normal practice for emperors to have effigies of themselves set up in towns and cities in places where oaths to the emperor or the State would be administered by local officials. These statues were in places such as public markets where people offered a pinch of incense as a token of their loyalty to the empire and the emperor. Often the effigies were perfunctory affairs, a plain slab of stone showing only the imperial face; but sometimes they were fully-finished statues. For no discernable reason, Caligula decided in AD 40 that full-featured oversized statues of himself should be very prominently displayed in every major city. In Rome itself such a statue was installed in the Temple of Jupiter Capitolinus, the most ancient and prestigious shrine, right alongside Jupiter, Juno and Minerva. He preferred his statues to be set in majestic existing temples and explicitly ordered that in Jerusalem, his statue should be placed in the Jewish Temple. This decision was retaliation for a Judaean destruction of his town statue in a rural part of Judaea. His officials were aghast, knowing that putting the imperial image into the Temple would be seen as blasphemy of the highest order, and would lead to immediate mass revolt. The Jews confirmed in no uncertain terms that they would die *en masse* rather than acquiesce. A couple of courageous delegations pleaded with Gaius for reason, but to no avail.

Petronius Turpilianus, the new governor of Syria where the Jerusalem statue was to be manufactured, realized the folly of the project and decided to "go slow" and hope for second thoughts. At first Caligula would brook no such resistance, and in a rage threatened Petronius with death. Then the unpredictable emperor did have second thoughts, prompted by his confidant the Jewish King Herod Agrippa I, and he agreed not to erect the Jerusalem Temple statue after all. Unfortunately, in the meantime governor Petronius had talked to a huge delegation of Judaeans, concluded that the statue project was unfeasible and counter to the interests of the empire, and he wrote that much plainly to the emperor. Caligula, on receipt of the letter, fell into another rage and changed his mind again – he would after all have his statue in the Temple no matter what. He sent out a warrant for the governor's execution on the grounds of disloyalty. By sheer chance Caligula – just 29 years old -- was assassinated a few days later, and a further letter, countermanding the death warrant, was at once rushed off to the harried governor in Syria. Governor Petronius, who must have dreaded the arrival of mail from Rome, received that latest missive just days before the execution warrant, and so he kept his head[8].

Next year never arrived for the emperor. At the very beginning of AD 41 Gaius Caligula was assassinated by an elderly officer of the Guard who had a personal grievance with the Princeps. The emperor had viciously and repeatedly insulted the officer. The assassin was immediately struck down, but he had support from many senators and guardsmen. More brutally, the Praetorians hunted down Caligula's wife and infant daughter and murdered them in cold blood. Gaius, being in his twenties, had given little serious thought to his successor and – most unrealistically – had designated his lover-sister Drusilla as his heir. But at the end of 40 AD she died unexpectedly and the presumptive heir was then construed by some to be her husband Lucius Aemilianus Vicinianus. Aemilianus certainly didn't want the throne, and neither the Praetorians nor the

---

8 Given the circumstances, Petronius was an outstandingly brave and honourable official. He continued in high office in Claudius' reign.

Senate wanted Aemilianus (who was soon murdered, just to make sure). Who then would be the next emperor?

The Senate dithered, wanting to end emperorship altogether and to restore the old Republic, but it was unable to agree on anything specific. In typical fashion, after two full days of discussion the senators could not even decide who the two new Consuls of their restored Republic would be. Meanwhile, the soldiers acted.

UNCLE CLAUDIUS

Tiberius Drusus Claudius was the elder brother of the famous Germanicus, and therefore the uncle of emperor Gaius Caligula, as well as the nephew of emperor Tiberius. So great had the attrition been in the murderous Julio-Claudian "August Family" that this Claudius was the last male left in the direct line. But there were decided problems with Claudius as a potential emperor. He was strange. Rumour had it that he was an idiot, and an eccentric idiot at that.

Rather unexpectedly, Gaius was followed on the throne by this eccentric uncle (reigned 41-54), who came to the emperorship most reluctantly, and apparently by a chance of fortune, pressured into it by the Praetorian Guards. Or so the story has come down to us. The Guards wanted to continue the monarchy – their employer – even though the Roman Senate, disgusted by Caligula's dreadful performance, had decided to do away with the imperial office altogether. The Guards acted first by acclaiming Claudius as emperor. The fifty-two-year-old was the only member of the ruling Julio-Claudian family that the soldiers could locate on the spur of the moment. They found him hiding behind the curtains in the palace. They whisked him away to the Praetorian camp to be acclaimed, if he were willing. Claudius being the brother of the famous General Germanicus carried the day for him. A visitor at the palace, the earlier-mentioned King-to-be Herod Agrippa I from Palestine, urged Claudius to take up the offer of the throne. He did. Essentially, then, Claudius got the throne by accident. Herod Agrippa got a better throne too: a grateful Claudius gave that grandson of Herod the Great the reconstituted kingdom of his grandfather. But this succession tale sounds fishy; it's just too neat. More likely the "by chance" accession of Claudius was a well-planned takeover. King Agrippa was on the scene to butter his own bread.

It's hard to know what to make of Claudius. His contemporaries – those in Rome who knew him, saw him up close and worked with him -- thought him a stammering, drooling idiot, and he did have a speech impediment. He walked with a limp caused by some childhood disease, perhaps cerebral palsy or polio. His own mother Antonia had called him "a work which nature had begun but never finished". Before his elevation to the throne, Claudius had never been given any responsible civil or military posts, except that Caligula had whimsically made him a Consul for a year. He was a voracious eater, though he never grew fat. He was spastic and at times trembled inexplicably. Either Claudius had some biochemically-based medical condition, or (a recent idea) he suffered from lingering effects of juvenile cerebral palsy. None of this recommended him to his own family or to the Roman public. For the Romans, any infirmity rendered a person inferior. Claudius' multiple health problems precluded him from taking any public role, according to the considered opinions of both Augustus and Tiberius. Caligula considered Uncle Claudius a harmless old fool. But if not a genius, Claudius was certainly no idiot. He was just different. For years he feigned stupidity in order to escape the notice of his bloodthirsty relatives, especially his ever-suspicious nephew; and that probably saved his life. On becoming emperor, his "stupidity" vanished -- though not his eccentricity.

The Senate was non-plussed by the military acclamation of Claudius, having intended to end the monarchy after Caligula's assassination and to name new Republican Consuls from among its own ranks. Nonetheless, faced with Claudius' fait accompli, the senators sourly voted him the full powers that were by now expected by each new emperor. But they grumbled.

Claudius was 51 years of age on his accession. The son of Drusus the Elder and Antonia the daughter of general Mark Antony and Caesar Augustus' sister Octavia, he was born in Lugdunum (=Lyons) in Gaul while his father had been posted there. He was medium-tall with rather thin legs. Although his body was not prepossessing, his brain was quite a good one. He had arcane scholarly interests and considered himself a historian. Indeed, he had authored several scholarly works of history (which have not survived, alas). Especially, he was author of a history of the Carthaginians and a history of the Etruscans, and in addition he had a working knowledge of the old Etruscan language which today can no longer be understood. Claudius was well read, perfectly bilingual in Latin and Greek, and had a head full of interesting trivia. He tried to govern much as Augustus had done – but he had no proper training or prior experience and anyway he lacked the innate flair and the Augustan "presence". His efforts at imperial dignity did not come off well, for Claudius had in some measure the body of a clown and the soul of an academic. Neither quality evoked praise or respect in the Roman political world.

In his fifties, Claudius was another old man at the helm. His concerns as emperor tended to be for plain-Jane "practical" projects. But in certain key ways uncle Claudius was a great improvement on his two predecessors: he was affable in public, was extremely hard-working, paid due attention to the administration of justice, and possessed a great fund of knowledge about the empire. The Romans snickered at him, but people in faraway parts of the empire came to like his mild, beneficent style of rule. He respected all the peoples of the great empire and sincerely tried to give them good government. In considerable measure he succeeded. His reign was well-remembered as a time of prosperity and contentment.

The Romans denigrated his shaky body, his stammering speech and also his "odd" sexual habits. For he only slept with women, something the Romans found quite strange. In addition, though he was in his fifties, he kept up a vigorous sex life. He was four times married, and of course his sex life was not entirely confined to his wives. By his second wife

Julia Urgulanilla he had sired a daughter Antonia, by his third (Valeria Messalina) a daughter Octavia and a son Britannicus.

Eccentric he was, however. Claudius had esoteric interests, such as anthropology, geography, history and linguistics. He devised three new letters for the Roman alphabet to express sounds not adequately covered by the 22 existing letters[9]. His speeches, such as have survived, have a distinct quality of long-winded lectures rather than of the rhetorical speeches usual at the time. Claudius tended to be long-winded both in speaking and in writing.

Claudius did work extremely hard as emperor, and with considerable result. He took a keen personal interest in judicial cases but for other duties he often relied on his equestrian and Greek freedman "ministers". At least he chose competent ones, and he knew the art of light-handed supervision. Pallas and Epaphroditus served for finance, and Narcissus was his secretary. There were several lesser officials too. Claudius improved the imperial administration in various ways, especially in the provinces, where his interest was backed by his good knowledge of their various histories and cultures. However, Claudius had intermittent memory problems which grew worse over the thirteen years of his reign. Many decisions were seemingly made in a fog. Fortunately for the emperor, the imperial economy remained strong at this time, and political and financial stability were well-maintained all through his reign. He himself was parsimonious with funds, and overly fearful of everything that might possibly go wrong in projects. Claudius was a worrier: where others saw the road, he saw the rocks on it. Claudius was knowledgeable about, and interested in, the whole empire – not just Italy -- and he was the first emperor since Augustus to travel extensively and see parts of his realm first-hand. As a consequence, Claudius was able to ameliorate some of the most resented features of Roman rule and was able to nudge along the long process of making a cohesive state out of the many cultures and

9 One new letter differentiated between the sounds "U" and "W" which in standard Latin were both rendered by "V"; the second new letter rendered a guttural sound; and the third provided the Greek "PS" sound.

regions which made up the Roman realm. Claudius was far more popular outside Italy than within it.

The empire mostly thrived under Claudius. Pallas and Epaphroditus the finance ministers kept the money flowing in (to both the state's coffers and their own pockets), while Narcissus the chief secretary kept Claudius' heavy paper traffic moving. Of course, all the ministers became wealthy from sharp practices, but the emperor didn't seem to care about that.

Claudius had not held any military commands before his accession; he had been left to his antiquarian interests instead. Even the usually perceptive Augustus had written him off. As emperor he became determined to demonstrate his martial qualities and took the field in Britain personally – very briefly -- to participate in the conquest of the island (43-47). He rightly felt that military experience would be a political asset. Emperor Caligula had already carried out the planning and a trial run in 40, so the project got moving fast. In high spirits the emperor journeyed northwest to Lugdunum and from there continued north to the Channel coast, where a Roman naval squadron was waiting to ferry him across Ocean to Britannia.

Preparations for that invasion were well advanced by the summer of 41, but it was not until 43 that the new emperor set it all in motion. Claudius found a very able leading general – Aulus Plautius – for the endeavour, and assigned him no fewer than three legions, roughly following the plan that Caligula had envisaged. This time there was no dithering at the seaside and no forbidding winds or waves. The auguries were good. The troops crossed safely and advanced easily because the Romans had many willing allies among the disunited tribes. These allies saw the Romans as the enemies of their own enemies, and hence their friends. The war was not particularly bloody, and within two months the south of Britain had been overrun and put under effective Roman control. General Plautius was soon approaching the town of Camulodunum (=Colchester) which served as the capital of the main hostile tribe, the Iceni. The emperor was contacted and invited to come command the legions during the taking of Camulodunum. Claudius wanted to do that and indeed was already waiting anxiously at Calais when the message came. He crossed and spent sixteen glorious days as active Commander-in-Chief of his forces. Camulodunum was such a walk-over that everyone suspected – correctly – that a deal had been done between the Iceni and Plautius. In any event, Claudius was inordinately pleased with himself in his role as conqueror, and with General Plautius. The General was made the first governor of Roman Britannia and promised an Ovation on his return to Rome. Claudius was as good as his word. Plautius got his Ovation in 47 – the highest military honour possible since by then Triumphs were reserved for emperors only. The emperor even limped along part of the way beside Plautius' chariot. The Roman crowds loved it; it had been many, many years since they had experienced the old thrill of conquest.

General Plautius' wife was a strikingly beautiful woman of ancient lineage: Julia Pomponia Graecina. When Plautius left Rome for Britannia in 43 she was already in deep depression over the distressing and unjust execution of her aunt Julia. As has already been told, she found religious consolation through a charismatic Jewish preacher named Simon Peter, newly arrived in Rome. By the end of the year she had been baptized into Christ. She remained very quiet and pensive, but her depression lifted. In 47 she confided to her newly-returned husband what had happened, and out of love for her he accepted her secret Christianity. In those very earliest years of the faith, there were no dogmas or doctrines or set rites, one simply committed to the kind of life advocated by Jesus – a quiet, withdrawing, peaceful life. Many friends thought that Pomponia was prolonging her mourning for Julia; but such subdued behaviour was typical of the primitive Christians. In time she became a friend of St. Saul.

If Claudius was well-intentioned and generally hard-working, he could also be sedentary and indolent at times. He often seemed not to give a damn about the world around him, or about the business of running the realm. Peace, quiet, his books, regular work, punctual meals and frequent sex were what he really wanted. In that he was scarcely unusual. He was certainly not an evil man, but he could be careless and quite callous and bloodthirsty. He enjoyed an afternoon at the amphitheatre watching gladiators butcher each other. Claudius was often poorly briefed on what was taking place right around him. He notoriously had difficulties in making decisions, and even greater difficulties in making right decisions. He was overly susceptible to ministerial "advice" and especially to his wives' advice. Signing state papers without bothering to read them was one of the emperor's most damaging habits, one which sent many people to their deaths. One critic remarked sarcastically that Claudius was careless with other people's blood. He was never a very popular figure in any quarter of Italy. The Senate acquiesced in his rule without enthusiasm and mostly without any great show of cooperation.

Yet his reign was not troubled by any major reverses apart from a few military mutinies and two famines in the East in the mid-40s. Militarily, Claudius' forces obtained signal victories in Britain and on the German border. The economy experienced an upswing as his reign progressed. Claudius re-built some of Rome's aqueducts and gave Ostia at last a proper port facility for receiving vital Egyptian and African grain destined for the capital. These were important non-triumphalist projects. It's good that the situation of the realm remained calm, for Claudius had few plans or ambitions, beyond Britain, to extend or even defend the empire's borders. During the closing years of his reign the Parthians began (yet again) to give trouble in the east, but even there nothing serious befell the emperor.

Claudius was keenly aware that, apart from his young son Britannicus, he himself was the very last male in the Julio-Claudian imperial line. This caused him to become obsessed with security. Guards accompanied him everywhere, even into the Senate house, and before every audience in the palace all visitors were thoroughly searched for hidden weapons. The emperor maintained that it worked because no assassination attempts occurred. In fact he was fortunate in not being widely hated as Tiberius and Caligula had been.

The emperor Claudius had trouble with the vigorous dissension among the Jews of Rome, right from the beginning of his reign in AD

41. Some of this unrest was residual from the unhappy preceding reign of Gaius Caligula, but most was connected with the Jewish-Christian sectarian disputes mentioned above. In the 40s AD "Christianity" was still a Jewish sect and it was only possible to distinguish Christians from other Jews by their belief in Jesus' Messiahship and Resurrection. Claudius expelled a small number of targeted troublemakers in 41 and briefly closed down some of the city's synagogues. But the ruction continued. The historian Tacitus records agitation by followers of "Chrestus"; read "Christus". It was the familiar pattern of noisy dust-ups between mainstream Jews and Jewish-Christian members of the Jesus Movement who accepted Jesus as Lord and Messiah. The Jewish-Christians were supported by numerous ex-pagan God-fearers who had become members of the Jesus Movement. They possibly encouraged not-very-observant Jews also to think about that same possibility. In any event it was yet another source of friction. The Jewish followers of the new Way were ardent in their belief in Jesus as Messiah and the result was a deep fracture in Rome's Jewish community.

—

Worst of all Claudius' personal faults, he tended to follow the advice of his string of unworthy wives, especially his third wife Messalina. Claudius had four wives, two of whom he divorced. Valeria Messalina, number three, was aristocratic, beautiful and ambitious but no genius, being most famous for her reputation as a nymphomaniac, which was widely known (and widely enjoyed) in Rome. Her interests were not political, rather the personal acquisition of whatever she fancied at the moment, but she was quite prepared to shed blood to get her way. She framed the admittedly unpleasant senator Valerius Asiaticus in order to confiscate his gorgeous gardens in the northern part of Rome. Finally she entered into a clandestine marriage ceremony with a senatorial lover Lucius Silius (who was a Consul) as part of a planned coup d'etat to replace Claudius as emperor while he was out of town in Ostia. Claudius in

Ostia got word, at last took notice and told his minister Narcissus to lower the boom. He did; the two malefactors and several accomplices were executed without trials.

Claudius vowed never to marry again. But soon the emperor did re-marry, this last time incestuously to his niece Agrippina "the Younger" who was a grand-daughter of Augustus, and one of the ill-famed sisters of Caligula. His minister Narcissus advised against the match and was dismissed for his trouble. If the Herodians could marry each other, so could the imperial family. Other courtiers and the Senate obsequiously expedited this crassly incestuous marriage. That scheming, power-mad and overbearing last wife already had a son by an earlier marriage. The son's name was Nero. Whereas Messalina had people liquidated in order to acquire the material goods she craved, Agrippina had people liquidated to open her way to more and more power in the state. By the last years of Claudius, Agrippina was effectively his co-ruler; even her image began appearing on the coinage. Yet she was an effective co-ruler.

Claudius may or may not have met his end by poison in 54. Romans were always keen on conspiracy theories and it was popularly believed that Agrippina had poisoned Claudius. She was undoubtedly capable of it. Modern opinion favours a natural death, but who knows? The emperor was in his mid-sixties when he died, and he had been experiencing worsening health problems. Significantly, under his wife's wheedling pressure he had agreed to be succeeded not by his own son Britannicus but by Agrippina's handsome, clever son Nero – who in AD 54 became at age 17 Rome's first teen-aged emperor. This time there was no senatorial talk of doing away with the monarchy. Agrippina kept Claudius' death secret for a day, during which Nero, with a troop of well-rehearsed, well-bribed Praetorian Guards, was presented to the people with great fanfare and ceremony as their new emperor. If some folks in the crowd wondered "Where's Britannicus?" they had sense enough not to voice that question aloud.

—

This closeness of the imperial family is quite striking. Some of the marital in-breeding would raise eyebrows in our times, and some of it did for the Romans. The son of the deceased general and heir to the throne Germanicus was Gaius "Caligula" (emperor 37-41), and Germanicus' elder brother was Claudius who subsequently occupied the throne (reigned 41-54). Caligula's sister Agrippina the Younger bore a son (Nero, reigned 54-68) to her second husband Lucius Domitius Ahenobarbus, then she married her uncle Claudius while he was emperor. Nero's best army general was brother-in-law Domitius Corbulo, married to Nero's relative Cassia Longina. In AD 70, Corbulo's daughter Domitia married the emperor-to-be Domitian. Nero's second wife was Poppaea Sabina, a thrice-married prefect's daughter who had divorced her second husband Marcus Otho (who later reigned briefly as emperor in 69). That same Otho's sister-in-law Coccaeia was later the wife of the emperor Nerva (96-98). A sister-in-law of the emperor Titus (79-81) became the mother of the emperor Trajan (reigned 96-117). And so forth, one big interbred ruling "family" of dizzying complexity. [See the family charts in the Notes.]

Yet for all the family ties, precautions, plots and plans, the path to the throne could be utterly haphazard, for there was no fixed rule for succession. One of the most remarkable things about the Roman empire from its foundation in 27 BC right up to its final demise in AD 1453 is that it never had a succession rule. As has been told, when Tiberius' successor Gaius Caligula was assassinated in 41, uncle Claudius was literally forced by soldiers to take the imperial helm. And when he died, his adopted son Nero took the throne, just what Nero's mother Agrippina had been working to achieve by fair means and foul.

The quantity of bloodshed and cruelty involved in eliminating real or imagined rivals was large and, because the people eliminated were usually conspicuous in Roman society, it was all highly visible in the capital. Needless to add that young Britannicus, Claudius' biological son, came to an early end under his step-brother Nero. Relatives and friends of the great learned to keep their heads down and their profiles very low. However, this intrigue and violence at the top scarcely impacted at all on the people of the empire. It only played out in Rome. Emperors came and went, but so long as one's own town or city was not the site of a revolt or military action it didn't much matter who occupied the throne. The administration ground on. As a Chinese maxim puts it, "The Empire is vast and the Emperor is far away"; just so too for the Roman empire.

Surprisingly, the situation for many inhabitants of the Roman empire got better rather than worse over the course of the first century, and things improved still further during the second century. The very worst period of bloody rule was the Julio-Claudian half-century from 20 to 70 – by chance the formative period of the Jesus Movement. But through those years, most of the empire as a whole prospered. It was a mid-century calm.

VII
NERO THE GREAT

"THE BEST GOVERNMENT THE EMPIRE EVER HAD"

Nero (reigned AD 54-68) was Rome's first teen-aged emperor. Nero's biological connections might give us pause, for his mother Agrippina was the sister of Gaius Caligula, and his deceased natural father had been a rich but nasty scoundrel named Domitius Ahenobarbus. On the other hand, Nero was a great-great-grandson of Augustus, and that mattered a great deal in Rome. He was reasonably good-looking, with golden hair, sky-blue eyes, a powerful build and a light but blotchy complexion. The precocious young Nero had charm and undoubted talents.

Nero succeeded Claudius without any problem. He was simply presented to the crowds and soldiers as their new emperor -- a fait accompli masterfully engineered by his mother. But after a very promising start, Nero grew into a playboy on a colossal scale, not aspiring to be a great public official but rather the greatest "rock-star" singer, poet, tragic actor and chariot-racer of his time. And he spent money without restraint. Finally, his life went completely off the rails as he became cruel and a drug addict. It ended in suicide – at just thirty-one.

Nero has had a bad press, and he deserves much of it. He was the spoiled child of two nasty parents and grew up into a monumentally spoiled adult. Yet Nero was certainly not as vicious or crazy as Gaius

Caligula had been, nor – until his very last years -- was he egregiously cruel by the standards of his time. In fact his bonhomie was notable – until he felt himself personally threatened. Then he would lash out. For Nero, being too keenly aware that he was the last of the Julio-Claudians, was a great coward about his own safety. Needless to add that the courtiers and schemers around him made full use of that characteristic to settle their own scores; Nero was led to believe in many "threats" that were imaginary. Over time, his safety obsession turned from being defensive to being offensive; anyone critical of Nero's rule became an enemy to be sequestered, banished or liquidated. Anyone thought to be positioned too near the throne could become such an enemy. In the end, even outstanding public popularity would be enough to draw down Nero's lethal wrath on someone. From first to last Nero was a bully, and it got worse over the years.

It is difficult to resist the thought that there was something genetically wrong with the whole ruling Julio-Claudian family, for the same qualities of eccentricity, power-mania, cruelty, obsession with dominating, and extraordinary sexual urges show up time after time. They were palpable in Nero's maternal grandfather Drusus Germanicus, as we have seen. Germanicus' offspring – the emperor Gaius Caligula and his sisters (including Nero's mother Agrippina) -- manifested the qualities very strongly. Nero's late father Domitius Ahenobarbus, by all reports a boor, contributed little positive counterweight. In Nero himself the full picture of abnormal and troubled genius was on display.

Yet genius there was. Unlike his stolid predecessor Claudius, Nero was easily able to cope with all the business of his job, for he possessed youth, intelligence and energy. He was well educated and read well and widely in both Latin and Greek. He wrote and spoke both tongues perfectly; indeed he wrote poetry in both languages which later critics accepted as "not bad at all". Bits of it have survived. Nero had a retentive memory, he possessed a good grasp of Roman law; and he had a knack for select-ing capable officials upon whom he could delegate important work. In his first six years as emperor he was a conscientious and capable Chief

Magistrate – though at first just a teenager -- and important people sought to have their cases brought before him because of his reputation for fair and sensible judgements. His close advisers provided good advice and in addition they carried much of the administrative workload. Initially these advisers were his mother Agrippina, his tutor Seneca, and his Praetorian Prefect Burrus. However, they were all gone within eight years.

The grind of bureaucracy and administration was not for Nero. He was by temperament an artist, a writer and would-be singer and would-be actor, a youth who liked fast chariots and fast, none-too-refined company. He was "creative" -- a dreamer of vast projects[10]. The customary military and administrative enthusiasms expected of Roman emperors were absent in Nero, to the disgust of his principal Roman subjects. In stark contrast to most Romans, Nero was not a militarist at all; if anything he tended to be a pacifist. He thought that as Roman emperor he should be the embodiment of the state, but that the Senate and other regular governmental machinery should see to the empire's day-to-day running. He wanted to reign but not to rule. Or so he sometimes said. Augustus had tended in vaguely similar directions with his distinction between the state's revenues (the **aerarium**) and his private revenues (the **fiscus**), and Tiberius too had experimented with state-court separation. But it just wouldn't work because the emperor held powers and prestige that the state needed to use, and also because the Senate was widely discredited as a management institution by its frequently demonstrated indecision, sycophancy, incompetence and venality. Time after time the senators themselves declined to exercise their responsibilities of rulership. Instead, the sycophantic senators habitually referred all manner of business to the Imperial court, thereby evading decision-taking on its own part. At the same time, of course, senators grumbled about their loss of power and status. Nero's eccentricities, his wilfulness and growing paranoia,

10 Nero's character and career are in many ways reminiscent of Hitler's: the would-be artist vigorously exercising the most absolute power, with visions of grandeur, but with worsening rule over time, and a constant need for mass adulation. Both men came to similar ends.

waywardness and megalomania emerged with the years, intensifying after AD 65 as the emperor became a drug addict. Though intelligent, Nero was in a perpetual state of neurotic anxiety over his personal safety and his personal artistic development. In the end, his mistaken self-focus was his undoing.

Nero's first six years (54-59) were by far his best period. Thanks to his step-father Claudius, the administration of the empire was on a rational footing. Things ran quite smoothly, in large part because Nero was the beneficiary of Claudius' administrative reforms. By 54 the empire had a bureaucracy adequate for its minimal needs. In 59 Nero – then aged twenty-two -- began to change, and not for the better. He hankered to be free of his advisers and to fly on his own wings. And he did. Even as late as 64 he was rational, energetic and "on the job". However, the final four years 65-68 were a sorry time of reverses, decline, self-indulgence and despair amid fast-growing troubles. A generation after Nero, the emperor Trajan praised his early rule highly:

> *The first six years of Nero's reign saw the best government the empire has ever had.*

Most later historians also praised the emperor's early rule but ended up very critical of his later years. However, that was the story of most emperors' records – they started well and deteriorated over the years. Only Augustus and Vespasian seem to have avoided that course. Christians, as we will see, had (and still have) a particular axe to grind with Nero. With long hindsight, we can recognize him as essentially amoral but seldom actively evil, one of those pleasure-loving tyrants who go their hedonistic way without the guidance or constraint of gods or men. Nero scoffed at all religion.

Representing a new generation which had never known the terrible last phase of the old Republic or the struggling reigns of Augustus and Tiberius, Nero began his rule graciously by according the Senate more autonomy. In his first year, he even forbade others to appeal to him with regard to the Senate's enactments. But in the very next year, of necessity, Nero began taking on a more active role as the director of his administration. He had found, just like all his predecessors, that he Senate simply wouldn't take things in hand.

During his first half-dozen years of rule, Nero was under the tutelage his sole Praetorian Prefect Lucius Burrus; his tutor the philosopher-writer (and Praetor) Annaeus Seneca; and his tough-as-nails mother Agrippina. All three were intelligent and competent people. Seneca in particular was outstanding as imperial counsellor and tutor. He carried much of the load of government for Nero during the first six years of the reign. Seneca was something of an outsider. He came from Corduba (=Cordova) in Spain and had laid down a mixed record in the imperial service of Claudius and his last wife Agrippina. Seneca was a notable poet, playwright and philosopher, many of whose works have come down to us. He held some fine opinions about gentleness and kindness, strikingly like those of Jesus of Nazareth, which made the men of the Middle Ages suspect him of being a closet Christian. It's not impossible. His colleague Burrus was also an intelligent and upright man, one of the few Praetorian Prefects never assailed by a lust for more and more power. Burrus, Seneca and Nero cooperated to a remarkable degree, and together they managed to restrain Agrippina's incessant drive for power. That cooperation was doubly amazing because both courtiers were to some extent her appointees (in Claudius' reign) and under her power, but both were principled enough to resist her pressure and clear-sighted enough to recognize the winning side. Agrippina, having co-ruled with Claudius, made no bones about wanting imperial power for herself as well as Nero. As soon as Nero ascended the throne, she insisted on having her portrait on the coinage along with his, and when that succeeded she tried unsuccessfully to participate in Senate sessions and to sign state documents. Burrus, Seneca and young Nero all resisted those moves, but mom would not back off. She had attained virtually equal power with old Claudius and she wanted at least that much from Nero. There was an unsettling incident in AD 55 when Agrippina made an unsuccessful bid to replace her son on the throne with a more pliable man. That incident was swept under the carpet, but Nero did not forget it. Agrippina was sent to live near Neapolis (=Naples), well away from Rome.

Nero generally followed the advice especially of the enigmatic but wise Seneca. Seneca inculcated in Nero the value of gentleness in a ruler, and for a while that bore fruit. It was a golden time of prosperity and peace presided over by a golden youth. But for all that, Nero lacked inner confidence and conscience and had to be fed a steady diet of flattery and adulation. However, that was the standard diet of emperors. The Roman masses in particular loved Nero. But why?

Our popular image of Nero as a blood-crazed madman derives mostly from just two episodes: his murder of his mother in 59, and his appalling punishment of Christians after the Great Fire of Rome in 64 – which we will hear about later. In most respects Nero was decidedly mild. While he sometimes resisted the selfish demands of his rich, higher-class subjects, on some issues in the interests of clemency he opposed the frequent lower-class tendency to sheer bloodiness. For example, the Roman public was thoroughly addicted to gruesome spectacles in the amphitheatre which involved to-the-death gladiatorial matches, the public murder of condemned prisoners, or the cruel slaughter of terrified wild animals. These were supposed to be "entertainment" for the crowd. Where Claudius had enjoyed these bloody spectacles, Nero was revolted and refused to attend. Instead, the emperor liked to spend an afternoon now and then at the chariot races at the Circus Maximus racetrack. Early in his reign he limited the numbers of bloody amphitheatre "performances" to a very few per year, and later in his reign he established alternative shows – the Neronian Games -- in which nobody got killed. This is a side of Nero which tends to be forgotten today.

Though Nero at first took the counsel of others, it didn't last long. For in the background still panting to be in the foreground was Nero's mother Agrippina, actively scheming to rule the empire through her son. She had forced a compliant child-wife (Claudius' 10-year-old daughter Octavia, the child of Messalina) on her 14-year-old son and she routinely bribed and threatened leading men of the empire. Agrippina was much feared, and even Seneca and Burrus fell into her sinister power for a time. She did not hesitate to have opponents ruined, murdered, judicially framed or banished. As Nero grew older, his resentment of his domineering mother and the boring child wife she had foisted on him grew into fear as he came to realize that he was in danger of becoming nothing but his mother's pawn. Or one of her victims.

Relations between the two worsened until, in response to a probably true rumour that Agrippina was again intending to supplant Nero entirely with a new stooge-emperor of her own making, in 59 the threatened Nero finally decided to eliminate his mother permanently. And he did, although with some difficulty. As always with Nero, it was turned into a creative theatre event. An elegantly contrived murder plan used a purpose-built collapsible ship while Agrippina was vacationing in Baiae near Naples. But the collapsible ship plan was a fiasco, for doughty mom managed to swim to shore. There, she was coldly murdered by a death squad sent out the next day by Nero himself for the purpose. The rumours that immediately swept the empire were true, and the scandal of matricide stuck for good. Six years later, when Nero's much-loved second wife Poppaea died, more rumours were put about that Nero in a rage had kicked her to death. Untrue. In Rome, rumours were always being heard. The first century had no newspapers, no "media", just street-corner rumours that gained in the telling. Given her own record of murders, it is difficult to feel great sympathy for Agrippina, but the crime of matricide elicited profound shock throughout the whole empire. It was the first turn downward in Nero's reign.

By 61 the emperor was in his mid-twenties. He was by then impatient of all advisers. In succession, Nero's relations cooled with Seneca and Burrus (who fell ill and retired the next year, just in time to die a natural death). Nero split Burrus' job of commanding the two Praetorian Guard regiments in Rome, appointing the forgettable Faenius Rufus to one of the regiments and an odious but fairly competent horse-trainer pal Ofonius Tigellinus to command the other. These two appointments effectively broke Seneca's power over Nero and set the emperor on a new and questionable course. Seneca sensed trouble and tried to resign, but Nero would not allow it until the following year.

Nero's troubles began in the early 60s, but the period 61-64 AD also saw several imaginative projects bloom. Nero had no military interests but he was interested in exploration. Early in his reign he dispatched explorers north to pinpoint the amber sources on the Baltic Sea. They succeeded, and that success spurred him on. He sent ships to the south-east tip of Arabia and from there on to India, and in the early 60s he also sponsored an upriver expedition to discover the sources of the Nile. It failed only because tropical water weeds far, far upstream clogged the river. For the same reason, no other Europeans got closer to the sources of the Nile until the mid-19th century. Several small land expeditions were sent south from present-day Algeria across the Sahara Desert. Most disappeared, however a few got across and back, reporting on the land and peoples of West Africa. At the same time, the emperor sent ships beyond Gibraltar to explore the African coast and to search for new lands in the Atlantic Ocean. Nothing much came of that. Explorations were also planned in the north of recently-conquered Britain, and into the Caucasus mountains. However, the British revolt of 60-61 prevented the Scottish expedition from launching until much later in the 60s. The Caucasus project never materialized because Armenia, the starting-out point, remained in serious turmoil. Apart from the amber trade and the fast-growing India trade, nothing much of lasting value – apart from information -- came from any these expeditions. Closer to home, Nero took an increasing interest in architecture and in building; those at least were acceptable topics for emperors. He embellished gardens he had acquired on the Vatican Hill and was keen to have trees planted in central Rome.

On great occasions when he was showing himself to the people, Nero would wear egregiously flashy attire which often bordered on theatrical costume. Yet Nero set an extremely casual style within his court. He would attend official meetings in his gorgeous muslin nightgown (studded with sewn-on gold stars) and he would sometimes rush around the city with friends without much thought of his attire or even of taking along guards. Some city perambulations with his cronies occurred at night and involved drinking, loud singing, vandalism and fights. His companions were effectively his bodyguards but it didn't always work. On at least one occasion he was beaten up by an insulted citizen who never suspected that he was punching out the emperor. Nero talked a lot, loudly, and was given to joking and chatting amiably in what were generally thought of as solemn situations, such as religious processions.

In mid-60 Nero's tribulations began. Claudius' conquest of southern Britain in 43-47 had been followed by much Roman maladministration of the new province. The empire was too anxious to extract money from the British, too prone to insulting the tribes and their rulers, and was insensitive to the British tribal way of life. Moreover the Romans persisted in extending their conquest over the island so that one tribe after another was vanquished. Who would be next? Some tribal chiefs threw their lot in with the mighty conquerors, while others resisted and resented the rule of Rome. During the brief rule of General Aulus Plautius, order and some consideration reigned, but both friends and foes among British chieftains tended nonetheless to get mishandled. The 50s were an anarchic time of push-and-shove, when the tribes learned to dislike the pushy, greedy Romans and the Romans learned to dislike the "barbaric" tribesmen. In 60, it blew up. A new military governor, Paullinus Suetonius, proved a most aggressive man. While he was fighting his way through northern Wales, he received news of revolt. As so often, a single outrage had finally triggered rebellion. The wealthy chieftain of the dominant Iceni tribe had died, leaving half his fortune to the emperor and half to his wife and daughters. But his modest palace was pillaged by Roman soldiers and his family and servants were all carried off as slaves. For resisting them, a clutch of Roman centurions had his wife flogged, and they raped his two daughters. Queen Boudicca, the mother, vowed revenge and led the rebellion. Suddenly all the outraged British tribes rose and massacred tens of thousands of resident Romans. The main cities went up in smoke and for a time the Romans seemed to have been defeated. Camulodunum, the largest and most Roman town in Britain, was obliterated, and the atrocities visited on resident Romans were gruesome in the extreme. Other British victories followed. The Romans (including their armed forces) fled with intent to escape the island entirely. The procurator and his staff crossed over to Gaul. The empire fixed its hopes on General Suetonius and sent reinforcements from Germany. The native British forces, hastily raised by the rebels and lacking military discipline and good tactics, were no match militarily for Rome in the long run. General Suetonius moved ten thousand legionaries from Wales to the British midlands and there fought a major battle on the road to London, routing a vast but ragged British host. That was the turning point in the rebellion. The Romans scored a dramatic victory and the Britons suffered a lethal defeat. By late 61 the rebellion had been put down forcefully.

Nero found Suetonius hard to control and inclined to measures of harsh retribution. Moreover, the general was continually feuding with the new civil governor Julius Classicianus (himself a difficult man although half-Briton). Exasperated, the emperor sent a trusted freedman court official named Polyclitus as his legate to Britain to assess the situation. Somehow, Polyclitus struck fear into the legions and their commander and tactfully recommended replacement of both Suetonius and Classicianus. Accordingly, a pliable ex-consul named Petronius Turpilianus became the new commander. For a while Polyclitus continued as the effective governor. He and Turpilianus re-established some kind of peace throughout the island and restrained both the administration and the army.

Nero's devotion to the gods was neither conspicuous nor deep. Nero was amoral as well as immoral, a thoroughly spoiled brat, and a bully who enjoyed pushing himself and others beyond the limits of propriety to explore the new worlds that he felt existed beyond. With his mother out of the way, he divorced and banished Octavia. Later she intrigued against her ex and came to a suspicious death. Then in AD 62 Nero found the great love of his life in Poppaea Sabina. She was married to Salvius Otho, a friend of Nero's who obligingly divorced his wife in order that the emperor could have her. Poppaea, beautiful, bright and tough-minded, wouldn't accept the status of an imperial mistress and held out successfully for marriage and the title of empress (**Augusta**). She was a ruthless but intelligent woman and a serious admirer of the Judaic religion. Born in Pompeii in 30, she had first been married at age 14 to Rufrius Crispus to whom she bore a son[11], then she got divorced and married Salvius Otho. Then they divorced so that she could marry Nero in 62. Nero "thanked" Otho by sending him as Governor to faraway, boring Portugal. But Otho would be back !

By and by a daughter Claudia Octavia was born to Nero and Poppaea, to great celebration. However, the child died in infancy, to the immense grief of both parents. Poppaea herself died (65) during her next pregnancy. "Rumour" said that Nero had kicked her to death, but that was not Nero's style. She may have miscarried, something which often proved fatal in the first century. Nero was overcome with grief and went into a deep and prolonged depression. Very likely his drug habit began at this time, in 65.

But after Poppaea there was a third wife. There had to be, for Nero at 28 was desperate to sire a son as his heir and dynastic successor. He once again opted for beauty with brains. The intellectual noblewoman Statilia Messalina (no relation to Claudius' wife Messalina) moved in late in 65. However, no children appeared. The Roman emperors never lacked for wives or lovers, Nero least of all. Where old Claudius had been laughed at for being a complete heterosexual, Nero was more than just bisexual. He acquired a second "wife" in 67 in the person of a slave boy Sporus, whom Nero ordered castrated to prevent from him from entering puberty. Eerily, Sporus resembled the dead Poppaea and Nero sometimes even called him Poppaea. And as a further part of his utterly bizarre sex life, the emperor in late 65 had publicly and formally married a man named Pythagoras whom he described as his "husband". In addition to these formal bed partners, he kept up other brief liaisons and a tenuous relationship with his long-time lover, the freedwoman Claudia Acte. Those two must have

11 The boy was later murdered on Nero's orders

been true friends, for it was Acte who loyally saw to Nero's burial in AD 68 after he was disgraced and committed suicide, and she who set up a fine memorial to him after his death. He must have treated her well enough. Sporus also proved remarkably loyal to the emperor's memory but came to an unhappy end by suicide in the reign of Vespasian.

The Herodians had a uniformly good relationship with Nero, and he with them. Agrippa II's well-governed realm was modestly expanded. Agrippa II continued on his throne all through Nero's reign – and indeed through the reigns of the next seven emperors too! In 57 Nero created a tiny kingdom for his good friend Herod Aristobulus who had been a long-time fixture at his court. Aristobulus took over Chalcis in northern Palestine and delivered good government in the little enclave.

From 63 onwards, Nero's spending got progressively out of control. He was generous to a fault, and he had a lot to be generous with, always giving large sums of money to someone – friends, friends of friends, hard-luck cases, artists, entertainers and more. Nero never showed any financial restraint and he never did anything by "economy class". When his exasperated Treasurer one day heaped up a million sesterces to show the emperor what a very large amount that was, Nero simply remarked "I hadn't realized it made such a small pile".

MURDER, FIERY TRIALS AND PLOTS

Nero's penchant for theatre and showmanship was always present. The empire itself was his favorite theatre, the common people his favorite audience. The party went on and on. The applause could never stop, and indeed it never did. The emperor needed action and adulation to a pathological degree. Nero gave the fickle low-class Romans the greatest show on earth: his own antics. Until taxes began to increase to pay for those antics, they adored him.

In AD 62, just before Nero's marriage to Poppaea, a big earthquake in southern Italy damaged cities there around Naples. Nero immediately made a trip to the area to announce material help for the cities and to show the imperial concern. He stopped briefly at the port town of Puteoli on his return and enjoyed a memorably warm reception there. Puteoli and Antium (modern Anzio) were full of ethnic Greeks and manifested a decidedly relaxed Hellenic culture of which the emperor was very fond. Indeed, his birth had taken place in Antium. As a result, he began to make frequent trips down the coast to these centres. On his returns to Rome, he always found catch-up work waiting for him, but he somehow managed to deal with a wide variety of business. Nero was not lazy and not yet befuddled by drugs and depression.

The year 62 saw Nero's first public singing and acting performances. He had been taking singing and acting lessons for years, but only with the departure of his adviser Burrus did to venture to take the public stage. That was thought to be scandalous, but Nero didn't care. He first performed in Naples and was enthusiastically applauded by his audience. Before the end of the year he was preparing further performances, and in addition he had taken up chariot racing under the tutelage of his ominous new Praetorian Prefect Tigellinus whose former trade had been in horse-racing. The time spent on public business soon plummeted, but the emperor didn't seem to care.

On his desk among many scrolls in early 63 was a docket for the upcoming trial of a Roman citizen he had heard about from Seneca but had never met, an elderly Jewish man named Saul. Saul, it seemed, was a member of the Herodian clan, and he used the Latin name Paul. The new City Prefect Titus Flavius Sabinus – who claimed an interest in the case -- had already recommended acquittal and suggested that this Saul would be worth a personal hearing by Nero. Nero was on good terms with the Herodians – especially Agrippa II the current King of Judaea -- and was hosting several of the family's youngsters at his court where they were being educated. Since Saul's legal case turned on arcane Jewish complaints, Nero asked his wife Poppaea for her opinion. She was a knowledgeable Judeophile and had just been dealing – on a different matter – with a delegation of ten important Judaean visitors to Rome, including no less than the outgoing High Priest Ishmael and the Jerusalem Temple Treasurer Alexas Helcias. She in turn asked their opinion and elicited from Helcias a strong recommendation to quash the case entirely. Poppaea did not know that Helcias was Saul's brother-in-law. The priest Ishmael did know that, and he knew also of Saul's highly controversial standing in Judaism, but he said nothing. Why get involved? Besides, the Sanhedrin in Jerusalem had failed to press the charges or even to send a prosecutor. Through such back-room manoeuvres the case was easily quashed and Saul was released after a brief but cordial meeting with the emperor.

In the preceding decades the distant Crimean peninsula at the north end of the Black Sea had been occupied by the Romans without fighting, non-militarily. Rome was slowly advancing like an amoeba around the Black Sea coasts. The south, west and northern shores were effectively in Roman hands already. In the mid-60s fresh legions began to be raised for a major expedition – which never happened -- to conquer the whole Caucasus region at the east end of the Black Sea, from the Crimea to Armenia. This was another brainchild of Nero. It would have linked the north-eastern end of the empire with the Crimea and turned the Black Sea into another Roman lake, just like the Mediterranean. And it would have positioned Armenia to be engulfed by the Romans. But it was not to be. The preparations for this vast undertaking yielded an unintended benefit for Rome, for when the Jewish-Roman war broke out in the autumn of AD 66 a host of windfall troops, battle-ready, was available to Nero in Syria. The legions intended for the Caucasus went instead to Judaea; the new word in the Caucasus was Peace.

The Parthian and Roman empires did not get on well and by AD 60 were set to fight again over control of Armenia. A half-century before, Augustus had signed a treaty with the Parthians stipulating that Rome had the right to name the kings for Armenia and to act as their overlord. The Parthians now renounced that treaty and were trying forcibly to take back Armenia. In 52 the long-reigning Parthian "King-of-Kings" Vologases had invaded Armenia for that purpose, but the invasion failed.

The Armenian kingdom, sitting squarely across the route to the Caucasus and to far-off China from which silk came, remained a point of contention for both empires. Under Claudius there had been continuous trouble. In 58 young Nero sent General Corbulo in with a big army. He was Rome's top general. After sharp conflict, Corbulo burned the Armenian capital Artaxata, overwhelmed the Parthian forces, occupied the country and facilitated the takeover of a non-Parthian prince favoured by Rome – Tigranes, yet another member of the Herodian clan. The Parthian King-of-Kings was outraged and stubborn and decided to make a fresh effort to put his own brother Tiridates back on the throne of Armenia. In 61-63 the two empires had another round of war in which the Romans again showed well. The Roman generals again smelled the scent of big victory around the corner, but the King-of-Kings was obstinate. Corbulo next began to put Armenia under effective Roman administration. Then Nero proposed a peaceful solution: the Parthian King-of-Kings would name the ruler for Armenia, but that new king would receive his crown in Rome from the hands of Nero, and peace would be maintained. The generals on both sides thought this idea absurd, but in fact it worked very well. In 63, Tiridates surrendered his crown to the emperor via Corbulo, to be received back in three years' time. Amazingly, peace was then maintained between the two pugnacious empires for more than half a century.

The coronation project got into gear slowly. Three years later it came to climactic fruition. In the summer of 66 Nero feted in Rome the nominated King Tiridates of Armenia and his enormous retinue. The emperor met the bill for the king's travel to Rome and back – with his many followers. The cost was nearly 300,000,000 sesterces plus a gift of 100,000,000 sesterces to Tiridates himself – one of the largest single expenditures made by the empire during the first century. Tiridates' trip to Rome was a logistical nightmare. First, the king-to-be brought a retinue of three thousand Parthian officers. Second, their Zoroastrian religion forbade them to cross salt water. Third, they had elaborate dietary protocols. In the end Tiridates agreed to cross the Hellespont (the Dardanelles) via a bridge of boats, with due propitiations of the gods on both shores. The precedent for this compromise was King-of-Kings Xerxes' crossing five hundred years before. From there they should have followed the land route along the Adriatic Sea and into north Italy. At the last moment there was pressure for haste and the Parthians decided to cross salt water after all to reach Brundisium in southern Italy, which they could see from the Balkan side. Nero and his retinue met Tiridates near Naples and escorted him to the capital. The coronation itself was held in Rome in June 66 and was a huge gaudy oriental-style festival the like of which the capital had never seen and would never see again. It went on for two weeks, climaxed by the three Coronation Days.

On Day 1 the vast open-air theatre was filled with worthy Roman citizens in their best togas; that audience had been carefully selected. This was the day of the crowning; the golden crown was lowered on to Tiridates' head by the emperor himself. Fulsome speeches followed. The audience on Day 2 comprised mostly citizens from Africa, the East and elsewhere, in fine light togas or more colourful ethnic apparel. There were games and music. On Day 3 it was the turn of northerners and western-ers in white tunics, and on that "acclamation day" the core message became clear: the Roman emperor ruled over all races and lands. At all the events there were dancers, musicians, lavish entertainment, food and drink, and a display of thousands of uniformed Praetorians, state officials and court grandees. Swarms of servants attended to every wish of the Parthian visitors. As intended, the Parthians were completely overawed, with the exception of King Tiridates himself, who considered the whole show a colossal waste of time and money. However, it was Nero the Great's ultimate "performance" and may rank as the greatest show of the ancient world.

If 63 was a fortunate year for Nero, the following years were not. In 64 Rome suffered a disastrous conflagration which began in an olive oil warehouse near the Circus Maximus on 18 July and burned out of control for more than a week. The fire swept slowly over most of the vast urban area, climbing hills and snaking its way along low-lying areas. Half of the city of a million people was turned into ashes and ruins. Hovels burned, and so did palaces (including Nero's main palace), but the greatest damage was done in the congested poorer areas which were packed full of multi-story apartment buildings. Some of these stood six stories tall and most were shoddily built by landlords eager to maximize their rental profits. They combusted readily. Thousands of people were burned to death and hundreds of thousands took flight from the city. Some never returned, and the population of the capital never again reached the level of a million which it had before the fire. Nero at once opened his palaces, gardens and administrative buildings to the refugees, and then organized a major relief effort, funding much of the reconstruction from his own very deep pockets. Unwisely, as part of that reconstruction, he began to build the vast **Domus Aurea** (Golden House) which he planned would become his new imperial residence[12]. That project was not popular with any section of the burned-out public. "Rumour" said that the emperor had fired the city to clear space for his new palace.

The Great Fire of Rome marked the second downturn in Nero's reign. Was it accident or arson? The later historians Suetonius and Cassius Dio thought it was arson, and that Nero himself was the arsonist, clearing land so that he could build his new palace complex. That view doesn't fit the known facts, which show an accidental conflagration in a warehousing area where lots of flammable materials were stored. The emperor was away in Antium at the time of the outbreak. Besides, Nero was arguably the biggest loser of all from fire damage, which destroyed his main palace and several adjoining imperial administrative buildings. The historian Tacitus also claimed that it was arson, but he accepted that Christians had committed the crime. According to Tacitus, Nero was the "good guy" who oversaw a big relief effort financed from his own funds, personally took part in the rescue of victims of the blaze, and opened his properties and gardens to provide shelter and food for the homeless. Also chalked up

---

12 Ruins of it still exist. The idea and design of this surreally modern structure still fascinate.

to Nero's credit(!) by the Roman historians was his prompt and condign punishment of the Christians of Rome, who were strongly disliked at the time for their secretive anti-social behaviour and for their supposed cannibalistic ritual practices. All three historians were writing long after Nero's day; none was an eye-witness to the Fire. Yet they all concurred that Nero had acted well in the crisis.

Nero proved no "good guy" to the Christians. To quell the persistent rumours that he had instigated the fire, the emperor fastened the blame on the hated sect and revenged himself in grisly fashion. Under torture, a few hapless women "confessed" and implicated others, and those when put to torture named more names – a familiar story. In the end several hundred Christians were rounded up. There do not seem to have been any proper trials. We may presume that Nero himself truly believed that Christians had set the fire. In Nero's own gardens on the Vatican Hill the supposed malefactors were burned alive. That was the normal Roman penalty for arson, not something special thought up by the emperor. But in addition, some were crucified; some were torn apart by savage dogs. Those were Nero's own touches. He attended in the full regalia of a chariot driver. It was another Neronian "performance", but it actually excited the pity of onlookers, many of whom anyway doubted the guilt of the Christians. The historian Tacitus wrote bitterly:

> To stop the gossip [that he had torched Rome] Nero found scapegoats on whom he inflicted terrible punishments: the Christians, hated for their shameful rites. The man from whom they took their name, Christus, had been executed under Tiberius by the Judaean procurator Pontius Pilate. Their hateful superstition, checked for awhile, was breaking out again in Judaea and in Rome, where everything shameful in all the world comes together and achieves popularity. [Annals XV: 44]

Although the consensus of history has been "accidental fire" there is no compelling reason why the fire could not have been set – even by Christians. At that date the line between Judaism and Christianity was just being drawn. Jews and Jewish Christians had twice been summarily expelled from Rome by the previous emperor, Claudius, but many had either failed to leave or had afterwards returned. By 64 the Christian community in Rome was growing rapidly, and the feeling of an imminent Judgement Day was waxing very strong. With so much conflict and anti-Roman unrest in co-religionist Palestine, might some hot-head have plotted apocalypse on the Romans by torching their capital city? It's unlikely but not outright impossible that something of the kind happened. Or, the Christians may have abetted an accidentally-started fire. There were rumours of people – Christians? -- actively impeding the firefighters. Rumours again. Some Romans certainly thought it possible, even probable. Innocent or guilty, a significant fraction of the city's Christians suffered and died horribly in Nero's wrath. Many others fled the burned city. It took years before the repair of the city was far enough advanced to suggest normalcy; the rest of the year 64 was chaotic indeed, and the retribution continued far into the next year.

In 65 Nero's tribulations accelerated with the attempted coup d'etat of Gaius Piso – which was easily quashed. This was a real enough conspiracy, not imagined or trumped-up, but it was an amateur-night effort. A large group of disaffected senators was behind the plot, and as always the senators could never manage anything properly. Too many people were privy to the plot, and the attempt moved ahead far too slowly. In fact, it is amazing that it gestated as long as it did without becoming common knowledge. The conspirators changed their plans several times, then couldn't agree upon when or where their assassination of Nero would occur. The deed was postponed again and again. Too much talk, and far too many discussions. Eventually it leaked out, and investigations began. In those times, "investigation" always meant questioning non-citizens under torture. Commonly the household slaves of suspect citizens were put to rack and fire. Of course people confessed – sooner or later they would have confessed to anything. The surprise of the investigation was the high social status of the alleged conspirators. They were almost all citizens, equestrians and senators (who could not be put to torture). The apparent leaders of the conspiracy – who included even Nero's old retired tutor Seneca – were executed or commanded to commit suicide. Rumour had it that Seneca, and not the mediocre ringleader Gaius Piso, had been fingered by the plotters to be the next emperor. Rumours again… Seneca cut his veins and bled himself to death.

By AD 65 the situation in Britannia had become normal again, but trouble was brewing in other parts of the empire. Gaul and Germania in the north were becoming restive, and the discontent there involved not only the common people – increased taxation was becoming a burning issue everywhere -- but also the Roman legions stationed in those provinces. For the region was traditionally a trouble zone and had been assigned one-third of all the legionary forces of the empire. In the mid-60s the loyalty, obedience and competence of the legions was still assumed, whether it was true or not. Some thought it was not. A still more worrying trouble spot was little Judaea at the eastern end of the Mediterranean. There were no legions in Judaea, just auxiliary troops of the Procurator and of the regional Herodian King Agrippa II. Tension there had been rising for decades and was soon to boil over. In all the provinces there was concern about the imperial leadership after the Fire of Rome, about the attempted coups, and about Nero's strange personal behaviour, but it was mostly rumour so far. The centre held; the main issues were internal to Palestine and hinged on the troubled relation-ship between pagan Greek-speakers and the Jews. The new governor of Judaea, Gessius Florus (he was the empress Poppaea's choice in 64) would shortly undo Judaea.

In AD 65 empress Poppaea died, and her unborn child perished with her. Nero was shocked and immediately had a nervous breakdown. He coped by giving Poppaea a most extravagant funeral and the post-humous title of Augusta; and he coped also by starting to take drugs – opium and cannabis – which were the age's mainstays for relief of pain and depression.

The following year 66 was an unprecedentedly busy and trying one for Nero. First, another clumsy attempt at a coup-d'etat was suppressed with ease. Then in June came the coronation of Tiridates, the new King of Armenia, described above. The state's business was in a mess and very serious financial problems were appearing. Taxes had been raised and would be raised again this year to meet pressing expenses brought on by Nero. The emperor began maliciously seizing large estates, sometimes ensuring by foul means that the owners died in timely fashion. The emperor – by now deeply dependent on daily drugs – nonetheless felt himself coming apart under the relentless blows of fate. He needed a vacation. Perhaps with the example of Tiberius in mind, he opted for complete escape – not just to southern Italy but to Greece.

A HOLIDAY IN GREECE

In the late summer of 66, with Tiridates' coronation behind him, Poppaea gone, and the recent conspiracies crushed, the emperor took himself and a mass of his officials off for a long tour of Greece, where Nero passed the time in singing competitions, in stage productions, in chariot racing, in tourism, and in enjoying himself immensely. He needed a holiday but he worked himself nonetheless. The great tourist practiced assiduously for his public performances and entered every competition available. Not surprisingly he was accorded "first place" in almost all of them. The games and competitions had of course been re-scheduled so that they would all occur while the emperor was in Greece. Even a chariot race mishap in which Nero's chariot overturned throwing him to the ground earned him a First Prize – no doubt for pluck and luck. He came within an ace of being run over by other chariots and of being trampled to death by the teams of four horses which pulled each vehicle. He was lucky to come away without any broken bones, only badly bruised and bloody. Parts of his charioteer's leather and metal gear were torn away by the force of the hard landing, and he was bleeding significantly. But he took it all in stride and waved to the crowd as they cheered him on. Without any intervening medical attention, Nero re-mounted his chariot and the race was re-started to the applause of spectators. First prize!

Nero felt refreshed by Greece. He liked Greek culture, and the Greeks sincerely liked him. It would have been easy for him just to drift through the motions of competing, but he took his efforts very seriously, rising early each morning to gargle and practice his singing or to rehearse his lines in upcoming plays and declamations. He worked hard at it and was often in a state of high anxiety about the quality of his singing and acting and performing, and about the state of his precious voice. His retinue rolled their eyes and sighed. They longed for Rome.

The emperor had not been long in Greece – he made Corinth his headquarters -- when, in autumn 66 the Roman-Jewish war began in slow-motion, a fateful conflict which over seven years would consume colossal sums of money and a million lives. At first the conflict remained small-scale, stuttering and confused. The emperor assumed that his Syrian generals would put the Jewish rebellion down without undue effort. Too bad for Nero that he had executed his best general, Domitius Corbulo, just months before. He was soon disillusioned about easy victory by several minor reverses and then by a major one (November AD 66) which led to the spread of the revolt to Jews in Syria and Egypt. The governor of Syria had proved militarily incompetent. The Herodian King of Judaea, the durable Agrippa II, with Queen Berenike at his side, made an impassioned speech in Jerusalem urging peace and conciliation. The gist of his speech was:

> Be reasonable, my people. We live in the empire and we must
> expect that from time to time we will receive a procurator not
> as good as we would like. Just bear up, and soon we will get
> a procurator even better than we normally expect. If it is not
> specific complaints about a procurator that you have, then it
> may be the general complaint against being ruled at all by the
> Romans. If that's it, then you must admit that we are ruled by the

strongest power on earth, as are all other countries in the empire.
Rome is invincible, and all talk of defeating the Romans by
rebellion is crazy. Remember the mighty Carthaginians, and the
Macedonians who conquered the east; those great empires were
both in turn conquered by Rome. Some of you may say "But God
will help us". Did not God ordain that the Romans would rule?
There is no justification for rebellion now. And remember also that
if you make war on the Romans and you lose – as you will – the
consequences for Judaea will be utterly catastrophic.

Agrippa spoke in this vein for a half hour. Most of his audience heard
him out and probably, most agreed with him. Certainly the chief priests
did, for they added their agreement with it and tore their garments to
show their opposition to a revolutionary war. But the numerous activist
Judaeans were not listening. They then raised the crowd, chased the King
and Queen out of the city and burned their Jerusalem palace.

Next, an alarmed team of Herodian aristocrats – including St. Saul
– was sent by Agrippa to Corinth in December 66 to plead for decisive
imperial action to avert a full-scale war. But it was too late; war had begun
irretrievably. Nero recalled Cestius Gallus, his ineffectual governor of
Syria, and shortly sent out a new Governor-and-General named Titus
Flavius Vespasian. General Vespasian could not be described as outstandingly well known, but he had a solid background of military command
in the Britannia rebellion and in the Balkans, he had capably filled a civil
post in Africa, and he was the younger brother of Nero's City Prefect
for Rome. Vespasian took up his post in Palestine at the beginning of
67 and proved much more competent and ambitious than anyone had
bargained for.

By 67 Nero was spending money at a terrifying rate. Throughout the
whole year, Nero continued touring Greece in high style, with his followers in tow. That cost bundles. He light-heartedly ordered the construction
of a ship canal through the Isthmus of Corinth. That colossal project was
begun but never finished; it died with the emperor the following year.

By 67 Nero had become thoroughly addicted to cannabis and opium. Now he had to have ever-larger daily doses. The effect may have been euphoria of the mind but at the same time lethargy of the intellect and lassitude of the body. Yet he continued to sing, act and chariot-race his way through Greece for another year, spending less and less time on matters of government. His drugs kept him in good humour even as they robbed him of his vigour, mental clarity and determination. When Nero next decided, on a whim, to exempt all of Greece from taxation, his officials were aghast. Meanwhile, big post-Fire re-building costs were mounting up at Rome, and huge bills were pouring in from the Roman-Jewish War and from King Tiridates' coronation. Such wild overspending brought on an empire-wide fiscal crisis, and in response Nero increased taxes (again) in the taxable provinces. Then he taxed Italy -- up to then a tax haven -- and confiscated every estate and every accumulation of money that he could lay his hands on. Finally he devalued the imperial currency -- the first devaluation in the empire's history. The Roman empire had no financial institutions of the modern kind which would have allowed deficit financing; everything was run by cash and short-term loans. Nero literally ran out of gold and silver reserves and so he resorted to putting less gold or silver into each coin.

Nero was absent from Italy from the autumn of 66 until February 68. In the Greek Games, he "won" 1808 first prizes, which on his return were proudly displayed at the palace in Rome for all to see. That represents more than two first prizes per day. Did he really compete at that killing rate? He would have stayed in Greece even longer had his lengthy absence from Rome not brought the direst of consequences: military revolts and impending state bankruptcy. Nero had left in charge at Rome a devious Praetorian Prefect named Nymphidius Sabinus and a tough "Prefect of Italy" named Helius. Though not geniuses, both were competent enough and kept things in fair order within their limited powers. But there was nothing they could do about the emperor's compulsive spending, or about growing military indiscipline in the provinces.

Nero's style as emperor – which we find merely eccentric and foolish – broke all the basic rules of Roman tradition and manners, and outraged the upper classes who mattered most in the State. Even today, what would citizens think of a head of state who was always on the concert circuit, or racing as a jockey? Many today might blush at a head of state who brought homosexual partners to public banquets, or conducted cabinet meetings in a nightshirt, but those were not the sorts of things that bothered the pagan Romans too much. They bothered Nero not at all. Emperors could and did bed whomever they wanted, and anyway paganism had few qualms about sex, even Nero's pornographic varieties. However, the Roman emperor above all other men was expected to maintain the sacred dignity, gravity and authority (**dignitas, gravitas et auctoritas**) of the Roman state; to ensure the friendship and support of the state gods; to be militarily-inclined and victorious on the battlefields; and to stay in or near Rome for the religious festivals and for ready performance of his many judicial, diplomatic and administrative functions. Nero fitted none of that. The influential classes of Rome – senators, knights, the military, magistrates, professionals, and everyone else pretending to "culture" -- could not bear to see their imperial ruler behaving as the scum of society (as actors, singers and chariot racers were considered). They came to loathe the emperor and to wish he was gone. But Nero was still young and promised to be on the throne for a long time to come.

Nero paid no attention to the feelings of his elites, right to the end. He saw himself as an extraordinary artist, above criticism and above the law. He also came at last to want untrammeled power, much as his nephew Caligula had done. He gradually became cruel, vindictive and paranoid. Cultured rich Romans – the entire senatorial and equestrian classes -- saw only the distressing scandal of their crazy emperor debasing himself time after time on the stage or racing chariots for prizes. And abandoning Eternal Rome for sleazy Greece. By late 67 Nero had no support apart from the military, and parts of it were abandoning him too.

Nero's closest friends and advisers "suggested" ever more urgently that he come back to the capital, where he arrived in March 68. He staged a triumphal entry into Rome, a "triumph of arts, not arms" he called it. But showtime was over. He found everything in much worse shape than he had been told. The confidence of the Senate and other institutions of state in his rule had vanished. Taxes were resented and the people were restive. The economy was plunging. One day, news arrived of an army mutiny in Gaul, led by an odd character named Julius Vindex – an ethnic Gaul. Soon afterwards other mutinies were rumoured. This time it was more than idle rumour. Germany seemed to be loyal, but soon Spain was in revolt. The reality was too much for Nero. Within three months he committed suicide. He was 31.

Yet for reasons hard to fathom, despite all his excesses and failures, Nero remained popular in the memory of the lower-class populace – the vast majority of Rome's million residents. Greece too loved him; so did the East (except Judaea). They identified with his youth, his famous golden-blond hair, his bonhomie, his generosity and kindness to them as a class, his avoidance of wars, and – yes – with his eccentricities and erotic flamboyance. The news of his suicide gave rise to legends that he was not really dead but fled to his friends the Parthians. Nero would someday return from the East and resume his rule. Sure enough, over the next two decades, three pretenders appeared, claiming to be the returned Nero. His popularity, needless to say, did not extend to Christians, but they were then only an insignificant part of the population. They thought him a fiend, an unspeakable sinner, the Anti-Christ. One way or another, Nero gave rise to legends and fantasies which are still with us.

Nero precipitated events which after his death convulsed the empire for three years. The war in Judaea was only the beginning of the disintegration.

VIII
APOCALYPSE

THE CATACLYSMIC END OF ANCIENT JUDAISM

In the 60s the imperial dynasty of the Julio-Claudians which had begun so auspiciously with Augustus a hundred years earlier was winding down in the inanities and excesses of Nero. Under the brilliant Augustus and the dour Tiberius peace had been kept reasonably well throughout the empire, even in volatile Palestine. The brief but tumultuous reign of emperor Caligula (37-41) saw a sudden short downturn, then Claudius' reign (41-54) was marked by lowered tensions, fresh Roman conquests and by useful reforms in the imperial system -- but also by regional famines, a few uprisings, and Roman regional administrators of uneven calibre. By the time of Nero's accession in 54 the empire was at peace but the management of several provinces remained deeply flawed and tensions in the East were moving toward the flashpoint. Judaea was beset with unprecedented sectarian unrest and spiralling violence, and the mis-governed new territory of Britannia was gearing up for revolt. Armenia too was a recurring point of hot contention between the Roman and Parthian empires, contention which flared up sporadically into military actions. There was turmoil in the province of Mauritania (modern Morocco and Algeria), and the usual simmering unrest in Germany. A few Roman landlords were ruthlessly acquiring the majority of the farmland of the African provinces – areas more fertile and productive in ancient times than they are today. Yet the outlook for the empire as a whole remained generally bright up to 60. Until then the system held together. Six years later that outlook had changed, and signs of deep instability and unrest were clearly visible everywhere. The economy of the empire, strong in the 50s, began to deteriorate in the face of Nero's astronomical expenditures.

In Palestine the poor were being triply taxed: once by the Romans and again by Rome's regional puppets -- Herod Antipas until 39, Agrippa I until 44, and Agrippa II right into the great breakdown in the 60s and far beyond. The Jews also paid a small annual Temple Tax, collected by the Romans. As Judaea's economic health went into decline, these exactions became unbearable, and could not be met during the famine years of the mid-40s. By 60, major rural brigandage began along with popular outcries by the poor against the exactions of the state and the rich, and organized resistance began. Banditry and lawlessness intensified throughout Palestine but especially in Judaea. The Zealot party of the pious poor became a force to be reckoned with in Palestine.

In the Christian communities times were changing fast in the 60s. Many first-generation personalities had departed: long-gone were John the Baptizer (in 32) and Jesus himself (in 33). James the son of Zebedee had been executed in 42; the apostle Thaddeus may have been executed around the same time. Jesus' mother Mary died around 54. After a pause in mortalities through the later 50s, the sixties took a big toll: James the Lord's brother, the leader of all Christendom, was judicially murdered in Jerusalem in 62. Around this time too, John Bar-Zebediah disappeared from Jerusalem; he supposedly fled to Ephesus. The "Prince of the Apostles", Simon Peter, was crucified in Rome in 67. St Saul was imprisoned there in the winter of 66-67, tried, condemned and beheaded the following summer. The evangelist John Mark died in 68. Luke too may have died in the late 60s even though his traditional death date is 74. In faraway India Jesus' brother Judas Thomas was martyred in 72. The Apostle Andrew was martyred at Patras, Greece in the same year. Time was felling them one by one. With their passing the threads of direct contact with Jesus and his teachings were cut. People who had seen and heard the True Prophet and who could remember exactly what he preached and taught were becoming fewer with each passing year. Amid these falling trees stood one enduring oak: the Apostle John in Ephesus, where he would live on for a full generation more.

New leaders and the Christian communities left to them were put to severe tests, for the next-generation men and women lacked any direct connection to Jesus. They had never seen him or heard him teach, had received decidedly different messages from various apostles, prophets and teachers, and some of them harboured strange ideas. The writings which we call the New Testament were just coming into being in the 60s but were not yet seen as definitive holy scriptures. The communities tried hard to find their way but the outcomes were not always good. What would happen to nascent Christianity? An impartial wise man in AD 65, surveying what had happened in the Judeo-Christian community since Christ's departure, could have identified three likely scenarios:

FIRST, that the Jerusalem church's apostolic line and zealously Jewish-rooted organization would prevail over the more "lax" mixed Jewish-Gentile communities of Saul, Barnabas and Peter, thanks to greater cohesion and deeper cultural roots. The Law-observant part of the Jesus Movement had the support of most if not all of Jesus' remaining Apostles and of many thousands of Jewish Christians all over the empire. Their Jewish heritage and the synagogue network provided apparently rock-solid religious bases for their Christian interpretations of Judaism, and they believed that their Christian faith and practices conformed closely with what the Messiah Jesus himself had taught – a perfected Judaism. Acceptance of Jesus as the Messiah was still the hallmark of Christians, just as circumcision was the mark of Jewishness. But a man could identify both ways. The Jerusalem church acknowledged Jesus as the Messiah (the Christ); it asserted that he was the Son of God, whatever that meant. It held fast to the view that Jesus was a mighty prophet – like Moses – though not a divine being. And now, for this Jewish-Christian camp, in 67 Saul "the heretic" was gone. We could call this the Jewish-Christian scenario: Christianity would remain a Jewish sect.

SECOND, our prophesier might have predicted that the western communities based largely on Gentile converts to Christ would prevail in the long run because of their potential future numbers. This must have seemed a good deal less likely as an outcome in 65 given those communities' glaring problems -- disunity, poor cohesion, theological problems and scant experience in living the emerging new religion. Even Saul had been driven to despair by the waywardness and fractiousness of his flocks. By 65 AD the gentile Christians did not outnumber Jewish Christians anywhere in the Empire – except at Rome -- but the pagan reservoir for conversions was huge and most of Saul's small groups had more evangelical elan for that direction of expansion than did the Jerusalem-based Jewish-focused groups. Even Peter's communities tended to include numerous Gentiles. This could be called the Gentile-Christian scenario: Christianity was destined to develop into a separate religion.

THIRD, our hypothetical wise man might have concluded that the whole sect of Christians would fade and vanish now that the lead personalities were passing and considering that the enterprise was by no means on a solid organizational or theological footing. The Second Coming so fervently awaited had not happened. Moreover, the Roman state had set its face against Christianity. This fading-away scenario was one that High Priest Caiafas and Gamaliel the sage had both envisaged a full generation earlier. A failure scenario: Christianity would fade and disappear.

These three scenarios are all rational. In 65, any of them would have been a good bet. But events played out in unexpected ways. Judaea was the centre of a coming super-storm. To the Jews it appeared that each Roman procurator was worse than his predecessor and that the Romans were deliberately aiming at demeaning if not destroying Judaism. To the Romans it seemed that the Judaeans were determined to be unruly, intractable, unreasonable, unmanageable, seditious fanatics. Within Judaism the friction among sects and more so between economic classes had triggered near-open warfare by 65. Sectarian militias were being raised, less to fight the Romans than to oppose rival sects and the growing bandit gangs which were supportive of, and popular with, the poor peasants of the countryside.

Gessius Florus was the all-time worst governor Rome ever sent out to Judaea. Recommended for the posting by Nero's wife Poppaea, Florus was vain, pompous and corrupt. In his two-year term as Procurator (64-66) he antagonized everyone, was manifestly stupid and massively venal, and he seems to have actively goaded the Jews into revolt. And revolt they finally did in 66. The issues were what they had been for sixty years: heavy and ruthless Roman taxation; oppression of the common people by the rich and elite Jewish classes; and the seething resentment of all Jews at their subjection to a heathen foreign power. Moreover, the Jews had always intensely disliked their pagan Greek neighbours and the Greeks intensely disliked the Jews. These combustible relationships were laced with red-hot religious zeal, superstition and an end-of-the-world kind of madness on the part of the Judaeans. Florus simply lighted the match. In 66 the crisis broke like a storm, with riots, anti-taxation protests and sporadic attacks upon Roman citizens. As the populace rapidly got out of hand in the summer of 66, the Romans responded by plundering the Jewish Temple treasury to collect taxes allegedly owed to the emperor, and by executing dissident Jews in Jerusalem. In the countryside the Zealot faction – the voice of the poor -- included several well-organized insurgent organizations. The Zealots quickly became a cohesive political force, actively arming and organizing military units. Most common people supported the Zealots; indeed, many desperate peasants had joined the "bandit" military units in the late 50s and early 60s. By 66 AD the Zealots more or less controlled all the rural areas of Judaea, and the Sadducee-dominated Temple establishment was left only with Jerusalem. The Judaean establishment – basically the Temple Sadducees and their friends -- then began creating its own military forces, more for security against the insurgents than for use against the Romans. The military leaders chosen tended to be priests, guiltless of any military experience.

Added to religious zeal, ethnic nationalism and a burning sense of rich-versus-poor within Palestinian society, the feeling of final end-of-the-world culmination now steeled the nerve of the Jews of Palestine, Egypt and Syria. "God is with us, who can oppose us?" The key signal for full rebellion was an unexpected decision by the Temple authorities to discontinue the daily sacrifices made in the name of the Emperor. The decision was announced by the Temple Captain Eleazar, firebrand son of the new High Priest Matthias. That action was tantamount to breaking off diplomatic relations. But by that time fighting had already begun in parts of Galilee and Samaria, led by Zealot bands whose hatred of Rome and of the rich knew no bounds. The Judaean rulers put their improvised militias on active standing. The Temple authorities appointed regional militia commanders, prominent among whom was a 28-year-old priestly scholar Yosef Ben-Mattityahu – better known to history by his later Roman name Flavius Josephus. All that set the stage for a full-scale uprising which commenced in September of AD 66.

Dishonorable deeds immediately set the tenor of the whole war. Roman troops in Jerusalem carried out a pre-emptive search for rebels and they crucified many Jews, including several who embarrassingly turned out to be Roman citizens – even knights. The Jerusalemites labeled it a "massacre". The city Jews then bottled up the soldiers of the Roman garrison in the Antonia Fortress adjacent to the Temple, promising them free passage if they surrendered. But then, after their surrender, they were all slaughtered. This war was going to be vicious.

Naturally the Romans, full of confidence, had expected no major difficulties. Their allies on the spot were much less confident. The pro-Roman Herodian King Agrippa II and local Roman officials first tried mightily to dissuade the Judaeans from going to war; Agrippa came to Jerusalem in person and gave an impassioned speech for peace. It was not well-received. Then the Herodians fled Jerusalem for Syria and the safety of their capital Caesarea-Philippi. From there King Agrippa sent a delegation to Greece where emperor Nero was on tour, to warn him of the seriousness of the situation. That Herodian delegation was led by Saul and included his brother Costabar and his nephew Antipas Ben-Helcias.

Despite the dictates of common sense, Rome's forces in Judaea had always remained small, just a local militia of soldiery and one cohort of cavalry, all stationed at Caesarea Maritima on the coast. Another cavalry regiment was now sent to Jerusalem by King Agrippa to protect the High Priest Matthias in the Upper City against assaults by the dissident leaders Ananus II and his extremist son Eleazar. But then another rebel leader named Menahem[13] appeared in Jerusalem, fresh from his force's capture by treachery of a cache of arms stored at the fortress of Masada in the south. There, events had repeated: the Roman garrison had been promised safe passage out, but when disarmed it was massacred to a man. Menahem and his now-well-armed forces speedily took the Upper City area of Jerusalem, murdering Ananus II, but Menahem was in turn slain by Ananus' son Eleazar. Already this suggested a Jewish civil war as much as a war with the Romans, and so it continued throughout the whole period of the so-called Roman-Jewish War (66-71). In addition to a struggle against the Romans, the war became a civil war among the Jewish classes. That was Judaea's undoing.

The spectacle of initial Roman defeats at the hands of the Jews caused Cestius Gallus, the elderly governor of Syria, to lead Rome's Syrian legions south to restore order and quell the revolt. These were seasoned professional troops and there were lots of them – the equivalent of two full legions. Yet, the leadership proved wanting so that despite initial easy advances, the Syrian armies did not storm Jerusalem. They advanced right up to the walls, made a couple of desultory thrusts against the defences, actually occupied sections of the city, then stopped. Inexplicably, in November Gallus ordered them to retreat to winter quarters on the coast. The Roman withdrawal was seen by the Judaean rebels as a signal victory, and the Judaeans pursued in high spirits. En route northwest,

13 This Menahem was a son or grandson of the famous Galilean bandit Judas who had led a major revolt in 4 BC just after the death of Herod the Great.

the Roman forces were ambushed and defeated by a coalition of Jewish rebels at the pass of Beth-Horon, with several thousand Roman troops killed and their legion's eagle standard captured. That result really shocked the Roman leadership -- right up to Nero. As news of this new Jewish victory spread through Judaea, communal atrocities broke out in many mixed-population centres, exuberant Jews first slaughtering pagan Greek neighbours, and the Greeks then massacring Jews in enthusiastic revenge.

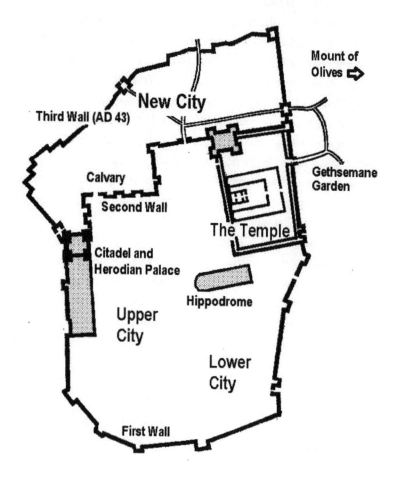

City plan of Jerusalem in the mid-first century

Early battle successes of the Judaean rebel forces encouraged Jews in adjacent Syria and Egypt to join the revolt, and they did. Conflict immediately erupted in Alexandria, Egypt between the Greek and Jewish sections of the vast city. Again, as in AD 38, long-standing antagonisms burst into full flame of armed combat between the two opposed parties. At first the Jews of Alexandria, who comprised one-third of the city's population of a half-million, had the upper hand. However, the governor of Egypt, Tiberius Julius Alexander (himself an apostate Jew), called in legionaries and instructed them to suppress the conflict and, if necessary, to massacre any recalcitrants. The legionaries decided that all the Jews of the city were recalcitrants, and they massacred 40,000 people. No one was spared in the indiscriminate slaughter: men, women, children were all put to the sword. The mass butchery in Alexandria shocked the whole East, especially Palestine, temporarily cowing the spirit of revolt. In Syria to the north of Palestine, several uncoordinated risings were similarly put down by Roman legionary troops, allegedly with a loss of nearly 20,000 lives.

All of Palestine had risen. Judaea remained the heart of the rebellion, but the rebels were neither well-trained nor militarily well-coordinated, nor of compatible religious or political minds. There was no common plan. How could there be when the "bandits" were fighting against the oppression of the Sadducees and the rich as well as against the Romans? Yet it was the Sadducee class which was supposedly directing the Judaean military operations. Jewish sectarianism and class divisions did much of the Romans' work for them. The war was largely provoked and fueled by the Zealot sect, whose strength lay in the countryside and whose program was virulently anti-Roman. The Zealots fought for an independent state of Israel like that which had existed two or three centuries earlier. The Zealots representing the poorest classes, their program had strong egalitarian and communistic tones, wedded to violent religious fanaticism.

In Jerusalem itself, an attempt by the terrorist Sicarii sect[14] -- a homicidal offshoot of the Zealots -- to take control of the city failed. With great difficulty the Sicarii were identified and ejected from the city (they went off to Masada with Menahem and sat out the rest of the war there) and for good measure a radical Zealot peasant leader Simon Bar-Giora was also expelled along with his followers. The High Priest Ananus II who succeeded the murdered Matthias was the same man who had occupied the post briefly in 62-63 AD and had contrived the murder of Jesus' brother James at that time. Ananus realized that the Romans would soon take revenge with irresistible force, and he took the lead in reinforcing the city for that expected Roman assault. The elite classes in fact hoped for a negotiated settlement before Roman retaliation could begin. But most of the population was spoiling for a fight which the people seriously thought would lead – through God's help -- to the defeat of the Romans and an independent Israel. The "bandit" Menahem was sent south to Masada Fortress to capture the cache of royal weaponry stored there. That too succeeded, so that the rebels became well-armed – and still more optimistic.

Certainly, Jerusalem was formidably walled and fortified, and most Judaeans thought it would prove impregnable. Many wealthy people had even brought their movable wealth to Jerusalem for safe deposit in the Temple vaults. Formal Judaean army commands were set up throughout Palestine by the Sadducee rulers. The Pharisee Yosef Ben-Mattityahu was appointed as the commander of the northern Galilee army units; Eleazar Ben-Ananus, the murderer of the brigand and would-be messiah Menahem, became the commander in Edom (=Idumea) in the south – Herodian home-country. Both these appointments turned out badly, but that could not be foreseen at the time.

Early in 67 Nero assigned to the experienced but not very well known Roman general Titus Flavius Vespasian the task of crushing the rebellion

---

14 The Sicarii were ultra-strict extremist Jews who carried concealed daggers (**sicae**) and in crowds quietly murdered opponents, often without being detected.

in Judaea. Moreover, against all precedent, Vespasian's own son Titus was appointed as second-in-command. Vespasian also became the new governor of Palestine, and the governorship of Syria shortly afterwards devolved upon one Lucius Mucianus. Given the new legions which had been intended for the conquest of the Caucasus region and moved to Syria, and assisted by regular Syrian legionary forces, Vespasian invaded Galilee from the north in spring 67. He had something liked 60,000 troops at his disposal. Avoiding the strongly-reinforced city of Jerusalem, the Romans launched a bloody campaign of terror to eradicate secondary rebel strongholds throughout Galilee and Samaria, and to punish the Jewish populations there indiscriminately.

The Romans now brought crushing force to bear. Within a few months Vespasian and Titus took over Galilee, overrunning the key town of Jodapata after a two-month siege. When the Romans took a hostile town, they usually killed the old and the ill – those being of no material use to the Romans – and enslaved the young and able-bodied. No mercy was shown to families, and certainly not to anyone thought to be fighting in the Jewish ranks. Some towns surrendered and received lenient treatment, and some even presented their rebels to Vespasian in return for him sparing the town as a whole. In most districts there was strong resistance, ending in general massacres by the Romans. Flight was the best chance for survival. Driven southward out of Galilee, tens of thousands of peasants, merchants, rebels, brigands and refugees (by no means all Jewish) arrived in Judaea, and headed straight for Jerusalem, creating fresh political chaos there. Sadducee-led Jerusalemites were soon battling ferociously in the city streets with armed Zealot forces arriving from Galilee under the ruthless but able command of John of Gischala. Edomites from the south under the command of Simon Bar-Giora actively aided these Zealots. Whether the Zealot factions included many Jewish-Christians is a question without a clear answer.

The newly-restored High Priest Ananus II was killed in a skirmish inside the city and his faction was militarily routed by the Zealots and Edomites. The main other regional rebel leader, Simon Bar-Giora, commanding 15,000 troops, was then invited back into Jerusalem by the remaining Sadducee leaders to fight against the Galilean Zealots. The Sadducees were desperate, for Bar-Giora had been ejected from Jerusalem only a few months previously. His faction was strictly egalitarian, indeed quasi-communistic, and he himself was an able commander. Simon's forces quickly gained control of most of the city, but John of Gischala's forces held the inner parts of the Temple, and the Sadducees clung to the outer parts. Bitter infighting continued among the factions of Bar-Giora, John of Gischala and Eleazar Ben-Ananus, all through the year 68. They all made their strongpoints the Temple, each faction occupying a different part of the vast structure. It was a year of merciless and bloody sectarian strife in the city, Jew against Jew. Acting together, the Zealots and the Edomites, who occupied the lowest part of the Temple and thus had access to the rest of the city, systematically killed off the entire upper classes of Jerusalem that year and burned all the records of taxation and indebtedness. They made a clean sweep: the Sadducees fell to a man and thus disappeared from history. Saul's nephew Antipas was killed at this time, being a member of the "aristos".

Beyond the city walls, the Romans watched but did nothing. They did not lay siege to the city at this time. For, while bloody strife was going on within the city walls, there was a long lull in Roman military operations in 68, owing to Nero's unexpected demise and the ensuing political turmoil in Rome. Initially, General Vespasian had his troops swear the oath of loyalty to the new emperor Servius Galba and then he awaited orders from Galba. As the year wore on and no orders came, it became apparent that the situation in Rome was disintegrating, not improving, and that the empire was up for grabs. Galba was the first claimant to be acclaimed emperor, in his residence of Spain. The very first rebel Roman general, Governor Julius Vindex in Gaul, had believed that as an ethnic Gaul he himself stood no chance of becoming emperor. So he wrote to a number of governors and generals at first urging them to rebel, and then in particular urging them to support General Galba in Spain as a new emperor to replace Nero. Galba unwisely accepted the offer. At first

Galba was strongly supported by Nero's one-time friend Otho – the first husband of the late empress Poppaea and now the Governor of Lusitania, but once on the throne Galba meanly and foolishly alienated Otho. In revenge Otho had Galba murdered and himself acclaimed emperor in Rome. Galba reigned for just six months, dying in January 69.

Otho's strategy was the very opposite of Galba's. Instead of meanness, discipline and old-fashioned rigour, Otho offered the Romans a return to the "good old days" of Nero. It might have worked but for the prompt emergence of other claimants to the throne. General Aulus Vitellius (ironically an appointee of Nero) was acclaimed as emperor by his troops in Germany on 1 January 69 AD and he promptly sent two armies south into Italy to challenge Galba. However, Galba's murder took place just two weeks later, so that Vitellius' armies ended up contending with the forces of the new emperor Otho.

Thus three men – Nero, Galba and Vitellius -- occupied the imperial throne within the space of nine months. Vitellius proved no more satisfactory than Galba and Otho. General Vespasian in Judaea first conceived the idea of making a pitch for the imperial throne in early 69, right after emperor Galba's murder. The suicide of emperor Otho just twelve weeks later confirmed in his mind the desirability of making his own bid for power. He moved cautiously, building support throughout the East. Then on 1 July 69, he was ready: General Titus Flavius Vespasian was acclaimed as Roman emperor by his armies in Judaea, supported by the Egyptian governor and legions, and by the Legate of Syria, Lucius Mucianus, and his legionary troops. Vespasian had the backing of at least nine legions. He had done his political homework well and had gathered massive support before making his move. He also obtained the support of the Herodian ruler Agrippa II, and indeed the King's sister Berenike helped finance Vespasian's bid for power. Vespasian sent some troops west, and thoughtfully ordered a much closer sympathetic army in the Balkans to march on ahead to Italy, quickly. With his father's departure for Alexandria in the autumn of 69, son Titus took over all the military operations in Judaea. His task was to lay siege to Jerusalem and bring the protracted Jewish-Roman war to an end.

The Judaean war now became a pit of horrors for the Jews as internecine strife within the city of Jerusalem reached fantastic proportions. There, food stocks were burnt – either accidently or deliberately – and famine set in. Those with weapons preyed upon the rest of the population even as it starved, and the Romans treated mercilessly anyone who tried to escape the city. Thousands of poor wretches were crucified just outside the city walls, in conspicuous view of those within the city.

During the first three years of the war, the gates of Jerusalem had remained open each day, giving many inhabitants the impression that the Romans were afraid to attack. In early 70 General Titus moved to besiege Jerusalem closely. His father, though by then solidly acclaimed in Rome, was still lurking in Alexandria controlling the grain supply to Rome. Just before Titus' siege ring closed around Jerusalem, John of Gischala's forces managed by a supreme effort to expel their opponent Eleazar and his Zealot supporters from the city. That still left Simon Bar-Giora's bands as armed opposition within the city. The gates were shut tightly and the siege began.

Those who had not fled Jerusalem were now trapped within it – almost 200,000 people. The city fortifications proved strong indeed, so that despite famine and violence within the walls, the siege dragged on for nearly seven months. When the outermost (newest) wall of the city was breached by Titus, a fanatically stubborn rebel defence prevented the Roman troops from breaking through the two older and still stronger walls which enclosed the residential quarters, the Temple and the adjoining Antonia Fortress. Titus set his legionaries to dismantling the Antonia from the side facing beyond the walls. They used the masonry to build a counter-wall and bases and ramps for siege towers. The outermost wall was similarly recycled to further the siege. The Judaeans fought back ingeniously, mining under the siege platforms and firing the siege towers with burning pitch as they were brought near the walls.

During the appallingly brutal seven-month siege, extremist factional infighting in the city intensified. It was marked by mass starvation, atrocities and even instances of cannibalism amongst the besieged. Terms were repeatedly offered by Titus, yet that elicited no signs of Jewish surrender. Finally, in the early summer of the year 70 AD, Titus' troops succeeded in dismantling the remaining masonry of the Antonia for use in building stoneworks against the second city wall. Soon the Romans breached that second city wall of the weakened Jewish forces – only to discover that behind it the Judaean forces had constructed yet another wall, using their "share" of the Antonia Fortress masonry. That new wall was stealthily surmounted in the middle of the night, and Roman legionaries entered the Temple platform itself. More close-quarters fighting ensued and some of the city was fired. But the Romans having access to the Temple platform allowed them to push back the Judaean forces below. Roman troops began occupying the whole northeast of the city – where the Temple was located. Even then the Roman advance involved hard street fighting and culminated in the storming, looting and burning of both the inner city and the Temple precincts.

For a time the Inner Temple was not attacked, but as the insurgents chose to make its roof a site for their "artillery" fire and rejected all calls to evacuate it, it became a military target. At some point its periphery was set on fire. Then after still further attempts by Titus at an armistice the Inner Temple was set ablaze. It was later put about by the Romans that the Temple burning was accidental but that seems unlikely. The porticos had been burned earlier by the Jews themselves as a defence tactic, and now the Sanctuary was set alight by Roman soldiers. The Temple vaults were immediately looted along with several mansions in Jerusalem, but the palace of Rome's Herodian ally King Agrippa was spared by the Romans (having already been looted and torched earlier in the war by the Judaeans). The few remaining Temple priests themselves handed over the golden ritual equipment to Titus so that it would not be destroyed or looted by soldiers. With much of the city in flaming ruin, resistance finally ceased. Smoke from the burning city could be seen for many days all over Judaea.

The Romans immediately slaughtered 10,000 elderly and infirm captives, who had no economic value. Some 50,000 young and able were sold into slavery or assigned to the provinces as "booty" to be ceremonially executed in the cities' amphitheatres or there sold into slavery. Numerous slave dealers had flocked to Jerusalem in anticipation of its fall, and those now set up slave markets amid the ruins. Ten thousand famished prisoners died of hunger while waiting to be sold. A further thirty thousand were sold at low prices, mostly for re-sale by other dealers. Both John of Gischala and Simon Bar-Giora were captured alive. John and a few comrades had taken refuge in the underground tunnels which honeycombed the earth beneath the Temple, but after not many days they were starving and decided to re-surface. Simon, gorgeously appareled, leapt out from a rubble pile to the astonishment of the Roman soldiers. John was not killed but ended his days in a grim Roman prison. Simon Bar-Giora – whom some Jews thought had claimed royal and messianic status – was captured and taken to Rome, marched in chains in the Flavians' Triumph (AD 71), and ritually beheaded in front of the Temple of Jupiter Capitolinus. By that time General Vespasian was in Rome as emperor and General Titus was there as commander of the Praetorian Guard. It was their double Triumph.

Some time after the apocalyptic fall of Jerusalem, Titus left for Rome, followed by tons of treasure, leaving just one legion behind to reduce the remaining Jewish strongholds at Masada and Herodium. That "mop-up" operation took a further two years, ending only with the fall of Masada Fortress in 73 and the mass suicide of its thousand defenders. Then the war was over.

The more perspicacious inhabitants of Jerusalem – including most Pharisee Temple scholars and the leadership of the Christian movement – had fled the city for the hinterlands before the siege got underway, sensing that disaster was imminent. Neither the Christians nor the Pharisees had backed the rebellion or approved of it. A very few stay-behinds managed to escape through ingenious ruses and incredible luck. The eminent teacher Yohanan Ben-Zakkai was smuggled out of besieged Jerusalem and through the Roman lines in a coffin. A Roman soldier wanted to thrust his sword into the coffin "to make sure" but was dissuaded by the pallbearers on the basis that such an act would desecrate the corpse and look bad. Most Temple scholars who left Jerusalem or escaped the siege re-assembled at Jamnia on the coast where they were protected by Vespasian's orders and by the local ruler. Jamnia was part of the territory which Salome the sister of Herod the Great had acquired and then willed to Augustus' wife. The Christian leadership with many followers went northeast out of Judaea to Pella across the Jordan, on similar terms of local protection. The two religions were parting company both theologically and physically, but in 70 AD both could still see themselves as essentially Jewish.

The Sadducees were completely wiped out in the war and disappeared along with their Temple. The Zealots and Sicarii too were almost all slaughtered in the fighting. The Romans systematically and very deliberately massacred the Essenes in their various settlements, notably at Qumran. At the end, the only Jewish sects to survive the war as viable entities were the Pharisees and the Christians – both representing the liberal wing of ancient Judaism.

The historian Flavius Josephus fought in the war first on the Jewish side, and later on the Roman side. He was a turncoat. In his tendentious history The Jewish War he estimated that the War took three million Jewish lives. Allowing for the gross exaggerations of most ancient authors, this is probably not so very wildly off. Many hundreds of thousands of Jews were certainly killed outright by the Romans, hundreds of thousands more died of starvation or privation, and at least 100,000 were taken captive and sold as slaves or killed in the empire's amphitheatres. Losses in Syria and Egypt, other theatres of the rebellion, were also big. It seems probable that the war was directly responsible for a million deaths. Abruptly, the Jewish Temple-state of Judaea collapsed, and festivals, sacrifices and worship at the Temple site ceased forever. Sacrifices and rituals had continued right up to the final days, even as the Romans were hacking their way into the Temple precincts.

The precious Temple gold treasures, some dating back to King Solomon, were all carried off to Rome. Some remained on display there for four centuries. In AD 459 when Rome fell to the Vandals, those invaders carted the treasures away to Carthage, their capital city in Africa, from where the Eastern Romans (Byzantines) recovered them in 533 and returned them to Jerusalem. They were allegedly hidden near Bethlehem in 613 to keep them from invading Persians – but somewhere along the line they "disappeared". They may still be there.

Most Jewish survivors of the War fled the devastated city for the hinterlands, where food might be found. The population of Jerusalem fell from more than 300,000 in AD 66 to around 30,000 five years later. Ninety percent of the population was either dead or fled. The devastation of war had not extended much into the northern territories of King Agrippa II, so that region became a refuge for many Judaeans and Galileans. The dispirited remnant of the Pharisee priesthood which reached Jamnia on the coast realized that there was no use trying to restore the Temple-worship system or the High Priesthood. Too much had been destroyed. From then onward all Jewish worship took place in synagogues – as it had long been doing in most towns and cities of the Empire. Animal sacrifice too ceased forever; it had been being discredited by Pharisees and Christians for decades but had continued on a massive scale at the Sadducee-run Temple. AD 70 defines the end of Jewish Temple-worship and of multi-faceted ancient Judaism, and marks the beginning of the synagogue-centred Rabbinical Judaism which has endured right up to the present time. The Pharisee teachers became known as rabbis. Many Jewish-Christians vanished too – though their losses were not remembered as high – and the scholarly Pharisees were left to dominate and guide Judaism.

The outcome of the War caused much soul-searching among the Jews, including the Jewish-Christians. What about God's promises of freedom and redemption from the Roman yoke? What about God's failure to protect his own Temple? "My God, my God, why have you forsaken me?" There were no easy answers. Jewish-Christians at this time faced similar questions, and in addition they must have wondered why Christ had not returned in glory or intervened in what seemed to be the promised Apocalypse. The War had certainly fulfilled scriptural passages about "the Last Days" yet Christ had not come back, and on the Jews' side no rescuing Messiah had appeared.

Just as it marked a challenging new path for Jewish life, the War also marked the end of a Jerusalem-based organizational headquarters for the Jesus communities of the empire. Many Jewish-Christians including the leadership group settled away from ruined Jerusalem for some years -- or for good. They survived the war as one remnant group but over time began to fragment into a number of sub-communities with subtly differing beliefs and practices. The scourge of sectarianism wounded Jewish-Christians and mainstream Jews alike. What had been "the Jerusalem Church" under the tight control of James the brother of Jesus soon became an array of congregations of Ebionites (the main and longest-lasting group), of Elchesites, of Nazareans and of other splinter sects. Their main points of agreement were that Jesus had indeed been the Messiah and that he had been resurrected to eternal life by God. They accepted his teachings as those were handed down in the Gospel of Matthew. On certain other points of belief they began to diverge. Some of these Jewish-Christian sects held that Jesus was a quasi-divine Messiah and in some way the literal "Son of God". Others saw Jesus as a fully human Messiah. The Nazareans seem to have treated Jesus as an Israelite prophet, terming him "the True Prophet". In the view of some Palestinian Jesus communities, Jesus had become Messiah upon his baptism by John the Baptizer; for others Jesus had become the Christ only upon his resurrection. No one then believed Jesus to be co-existent with God, nor born of a virgin. Nor that there was a "Holy Trinity". Incarnation theology was still in the future. All the sects practiced baptism, and all had some form of Last Supper rite. Other subtleties developed too. Yet all these small sects remained basically similar to one another and recognizably

"Jewish-Christian", and all maintained an orientation to Jesus' teachings as those were construed in the Jewish context. The western, partly-gentile churches considered the Palestinian Jewish-Christian churches fully orthodox and fully acceptable parts of the faith.

Jewish-Christians remained in full communion and open communication with Christian communities in other regions of the Roman and Parthian empires. The rest of the Church found the Judaean Christians for the most part orthodox and brotherly. Few of these Judaean sects involved gentiles in any significant way, but neither were the sects opposed to the mixed and increasingly gentile communities such as existed in Antioch, Rome and Caesarea. Gentile believers were welcome.

Some prominent Christians fled Palestine altogether. The Apostle John Bar-Zebediah narrowly escaped execution in AD 62 when James the brother of Jesus was judicially murdered. John lived for a short while in Caesarea on the coast. When the war broke out he moved again – along with the Apostle Philip and his family – to Anatolia (Turkey). John, then aged 47, went to Ephesus and Philip to Hierapolis, and they stayed there for the remainder of their lives.

The post of Presbyter of Jerusalem – curiously vacant since the death of James the brother of Jesus in 62 – was formally filled again after the War by election of Simeon the son of Jesus' uncle Clopas. The post may first have reverted, in theory at least, to Simon Peter upon Brother James' death in 62. But by 67 Peter too was dead. Brand new leadership was needed in Jerusalem. Simeon was nearly sixty at the time of his election and allegedly survived for another thirty-some years. In any case, Judaean Christianity remained a "family enterprise" in Jesus' dominant House-of-David family, all through the first century.

Given the scale and ferocity of the Jewish insurrections in Syria, Palestine and Egypt, it seems surprising that in the rest of the empire there was no stir of revolt. Especially in Rome and further west, not a ripple of unrest was noted. The Jews of Rome were, as we have already seen, not Zionist in their outlook, and many were not even particularly strict in their religious and social practices. Despite that inactivity, the

Roman authorities were vigilant all through the War, fearing that the Jews of the Dispersion might well become partisans on behalf of their Palestinian co-religionists, as Jews in Syria and Egypt had done. So there were bureaucratic roundups of prominent Jews and Jewish-Christians in Rome after late 66 when the War broke out. Particular interest centred on members of the "House of David" who were tagged as messianic candidates around whom Jewish independence movements tended to gather. In addition, the Roman authorities, mindful of the Great Fire of only two years before, were still looking for prominent Christian leaders. Nor were the Jews of Rome slow to denounce Christians, frequently easing the Romans' tasks of finding "people of interest".

—

At the beginning of 67 there was a final roundup in Rome. This netted, among many others, St. Peter and St. Saul. Both were arrested and imprisoned. It was easily confirmed that they were leaders of the hated Christian sect and important agents of the sect's headquarters in Jerusalem. At their trials, both men received death sentences (the precise charges are unknown). Peter, as a non-citizen, was crucified after some delay, on the Janiculum Hill or possibly on Vatican Hill just outside the city walls, in spring 67. As a Roman citizen Saul was imprisoned for months until he could have a proper death warrant drawn up and signed. That was a sensitive matter because Saul was a Herodian aristocrat, but his Christian status overrode even that standing. Possibly his warrant was finally issued by the notoriously tough interim Prefect of Italy, Helius, or by the Praetorian Prefect Nymphidius Sabinus -- or even by Nero himself in Greece. Saul had visited Nero in Corinth in December 66 as part of the delegation of Herodians from Syria-Palestine sent to brief the emperor on the impending Roman-Jewish conflict. He knew Nero but Nero knew him only as "Saul". Perhaps Nero signed a death warrant for "Paul" and didn't equate it with the "Saul" he knew. While in Corinth Saul also contacted his old colleagues in the Christian community. His fatal mistake was to proceed on to Rome, where he was arrested and imprisoned. This time it was no matter of a luxury apartment; he went to the grim Tullianum prison. His last letters to Timothy, his deputy in Ephesus, describe his mood in the final days:

> *Already my life is being poured out on the altar, and the hour for my departure is near. I have run the big race, I have completed the whole course. I have kept faith, and now the prize will come, the wreath of righteousness which the all-just Judge will give me on the Great Day... [2 Timothy 4: 6-8]*

Little Saul was beheaded near the Praetorian camp outside the south-west wall of the city, on the road to Ostia, on 29 June 67. He was about 73 years of age. Small groups of Christians from aristocratic circles of the city claimed Peter's and Saul's bodies and buried them together in a simple temporary sarcophagus. A few years later, in calmer post-Nero times, the remains of the two saints were separately re-buried in modest graves near the sites of their executions. Peter's remains were buried on the Vatican Hill, Saul's near the Ostia Gate. Very simple shrines were subsequently built over each sarcophagus. Saul's grew finally into a church called – both then and now – St. Paul's Outside the Walls. Peter's memorial church became today's St. Peter's Basilica on Vatican Hill, where Peter's bones still rest deep beneath the main altar.

BREAKDOWN AND WAR AT THE HEART OF THE EMPIRE

In February 68 Nero finally returned to Rome. By then Nero's decadent lifestyle had made him obese, an addled drug addict, and a man wholly divorced from the real world around him. He landed at Antium in Italy in high spirits and proceeded to a triumphal entry into Rome where his top priority turned out to be displaying the 1808 first prizes which he had won in Greece. He had them exhibited outside his garden-palace on Vatican Hill, the place where Christians had been slaughtered three years earlier. Nero had somehow acquired a pipe organ[15] and while the empire threatened to collapse around him he proudly announced that he would be giving a concert soon. It never happened. Rebellion was spreading in the empire. The first to openly declare his revolt was Julius Vindex, the Prefect of Gaul.

Vindex was nothing if not bold. He wrote openly to fellow-prefects and to governors around the empire asking them to revolt and to support a little-known candidate named Servius Sulpicius Galba as a new emperor. And to Nero Vindex wrote a stream of letters of criticism and rebuke. Nero responded in kind. A bizarre letter-writing war ensued. Both Vindex and Nero next began to issue coins inscribed with provocative messages. Soon everybody knew of Vindex' plan. Servius Galba, then serving as the governor of Nearer Spain, unexpectedly accepted the offer of the throne. It was unexpected because Galba was an old man of none-too-glorious background, and a notably mean-tempered character. Besides, he possessed only the one second-string legion assigned to Spain. In the northern provinces of Gaul and the two Germanies, military rebels were soon squaring off against loyalists, of whom there were still many. Pitched battles were fought between Vindex's Gallic legionaries and the larger Nero-supporting armies of the Rhine region, and in one of those battles Vindex was killed. That should have extinguished the comic-opera rebellion, but it did not. Events began to take on a grimmer motion of their own.

Soon those events were moving very fast. Galba set out from Spain for Rome, detouring via Gaul, preceded by a mountain of promises of bribes for officials and soldiers in the capital. The Praetorian Prefect at Rome, Nymphidius Sabinus, decided too late to take Galba's side. Nero, in an addict's stupor and unable to make decisions, panicked and started talking about abdicating. That sent his courtiers and staff flying for safety,

15 These instruments were known in ancient times, and one was located in Rome's amphitheatre. Another had been situated in the Jerusalem Temple.

and Nero awoke one morning abandoned and almost alone in his palace. A lone official, a Greek named Phaon, remained and persuaded Nero to leave Rome for the supposed safety of Phaon's own country house. They took along Nero's treasurer Epaphroditus and – of course – his "wife" Sporus. After a midnight gallop on horseback through Rome, they reached the suburban villa only to find it deserted too.

The Roman Senate met the following morning and on the advice of Nymphidius Sabinus declared Nero deposed and a "public enemy". However, the Senate did not do anything else for Nymphidius (to his chagrin) who continued in his delicate position. The Praetorian Guards, having been promised large bribes by the Prefect and by Galba's other agents, and had accepted those offers, set off to capture the emperor who had been their commander and employer only that morning. Seeing them approaching his hideout, Nero made his way into a subterranean room and there committed suicide with a dagger. Epaphroditus had to show him exactly where to strike the knife in. Nero died as the soldiers broke in, lamenting "What will the arts do without me?" Somehow, his long-time mistress Claudia Acte retrieved Nero's corpse, arranged for him a full state funeral and official burial, and later erected a personal funerary monument to him. He did have friends. The Senate damned his memory. The armies were divided on his merits. Most common folk cherished his reign.

At this point, the Prefect Nymphidius decided to make his own inept bid for the throne and declared himself the new emperor on the strength of the blatant lie that he was an illegitimate son of Caligula – hardly a great recommendation. One of his first acts as claimant to the throne was to marry Nero's lover Sporus. There must have been something about Sporus… but this was all too much for the Praetorians, who upon Galba's arrival summarily murdered Nymphidius.

Galba's tardy arrival in Rome in the summer was not at all what people had expected. The man was older and even meaner than advertised, and soon revealed himself as a cheat and a martinet for obedience. After Nero's bonhomie, the abrupt return to old-fashioned republican formality and coldness was a rude awakening. Fatally, Galba failed to pay to the Praetorians the bribes he had so fulsomely promised. Galba lasted just six months before being assassinated. His murderer and replacement Marcus Salvius Otho was an old pal of Nero's – and the ex-husband of Nero's second wife Poppaea. Otho had been sent off by Nero to govern remote Lusitania (Portugal) – no doubt to get him well away from Rome and Poppaea. To everyone's surprise, Otho had proved a successful and well-liked governor. At first he assisted Galba in his bid for the throne, assuming that old Galba would be grateful and name Otho as his successor. But Galba never showed gratitude for anything, and on 10 January AD 69 he named an obscure young man – the son of an old crony -- as his successor. Outraged, Otho immediately decided to make a much more forceful bid for the throne. Five days later, Galba was attacked in his carriage by suborned Praetorians, stabbed to death, and decapitated. His recently-named successor, Calpurnius Piso Lucinianus, who should then have become the next emperor, was also murdered by Otho's agents. Galba's head was paraded around the city to show that he was indeed dead. The man behind these murders was acclaimed emperor in mid-January 69. Otho took the throne name of "Otho Nero" to signal that the good Neronian times were coming back after Galba's demise. However, the supposed good times could not be brought back so easily. Others were already claiming the throne, specifically General Aulus Vitellius in Germany.

Unknown to all but the people on the spot, on New Year's Day (1 January AD 69) some of the legions in Germany had refused to swear their annual oath of allegiance to Galba. Instead, they put forward their own General Verginius Rufus for the emperorship. Rufus flatly refused[16]. The German legions then acclaimed a different and more senior general – Aulus Vitellius the governor – as their new emperor. He did not refuse.

16 Rufus was incredibly lucky to live for another twenty years. Once a man had been publicly acclaimed as emperor, even if he refused, he would normally be marked as a political threat and be liquidated by the successful claimant. Yet Rufus lived on, thrived under the emperor Vespasian, and even became a Consul under the emperor Domitian.

Nine days later, Galba in Rome named his own successor, and just five days after that came the murder of Galba and that successor, and the accession of Otho.

Vitellius had been very recently confirmed in the German command by none other than emperor Galba. Though a general, Vitellius was another rather unpromising candidate who possessed the ancestral fame on which Romans put so much store, but nothing else. His father Lucius had at one time served as governor of Syria and was thought to have been fully adequate but somewhat showy in that post. Lucius afterwards had been something of a fixture at the court of Claudius. His tenure there ended under a cloud. His son Aulus Vitellius, in most respects unprepossessing, yet had a streak of kindness and common sense. What he conspicuously lacked was the ability to command the obedience of others – a vital quality in a general and an emperor. When he heard of Galba's death and Otho's accession, Vitellius revolted only at the insistence of his legionaries, no doubt fearing the taint of having been acclaimed. In a somewhat confused series of actions Vitellius set about the business of making good his claim to the throne. Still unaware of Galba's murder, he figured that he would have to defeat the old general in the field. For inexplicable reasons he divided his forces and ordered two none-too-reliable armies to march south from Germany under separate commanders, one along following the Rhone River to near the Mediterranean and then heading east into northern Italy, the other proceeding by a more easterly route through present-day Austria. The two commanders were thus placed in the position of potential competitors with each other. One army under the energetic but hot-headed and self-seeking general Caecina Aliens, marched through Austria, over the Alpine passes near the Trento, and into northeastern Italy, arriving first. The forces of the stolid but more reliable Fabius Valens took the westerly route through present-day France to enter northwest Italy. By March, both armies had reached Italy and had joined up. But their command remained divided. Valens' opinion of Caecina: "He's an ass." Caecina's opinion of Valens: "He's a moron."

Emperor Otho found himself without adequate forces to deal with Vitellius' invasion of Italy. It was necessary to patch together what military units could be found around Rome, and to add such supplementary forces as could be found in the gladiatorial ranks and among veterans. This Otho did to the best of his ability, but it was not a promising solution, nor did time allow any better strategy. The motley forces were sent north to the Po Valley.

The Vitellian armies fought Otho's patched-together forces near the little city of Bedriacum. The battle was bloody but decisive: Vitellius' forces won hands–down, with Caecina taking the lion's share of the glory. To celebrate, the unruly soldiery of Vitellius then spontaneously rampaged through Bedriacum. The date was 15 April 69 AD. Defeated, Otho committed suicide the next day, sincerely not wanting to be the cause of a full-scale civil war of Roman against Roman. He had lasted exactly three months as emperor. He nobly intended that his own end should clear the way for Vitellius and spare Italy further conflict. But peace was not yet to be had. Already in the far east of the empire, yet another general had made up his mind to seize the throne, and other senior generals too were contemplating their chances. Nine weeks later, on 1 July 69, General Titus Flavius Vespasianus in Judaea was acclaimed emperor by his legions and by those of both Egypt and Syria.

The claim of Vespasian to the Roman throne became known to Aulus Vitellius by mid-July. At first Vitellius took little note of such a faraway threat. However, Vespasian had a vice-regent already designated for Rome, Lucius Mucianus the serving governor of Syria, with Vespasian's own seventeen-year-old son Domitian as an associate. These two won the admiration even of some of Vitellius' troops and through astute diplomacy paved the way for the General. Domitian was already ensconced in Rome itself. Vespasian also ordered friendly troops sent to Italy quickly from the Balkans, under a stalwart but over-eager commander named Antonius Priscus. Priscus was on his way west even before Vespasian's formal command arrived. It is remarkable that Vespasian's older brother Titus Flavius Sabinus remained in office as City Prefect of Rome, an office he had filled very satisfactorily under Nero and again since his re-appointment by Galba the previous year. Sabinus readily swore allegiance to Vitellius as the legal emperor and the two men seemed to reach an accommodation. However, that was a sign of these two men's agreeable temperaments, not of the general situation. Despite Otho's parting wish to avoid more bloodshed and strife, the situation now became outright civil war between the Vitellians and the Flavians. It was not a healthy situation for City Prefect Sabinus, nor for Mucianus and Domitian; nor for Vitellius either.

With Otho dead, Vitellius at last made his leisurely way south from his German headquarters to Italy. He relied on the Praetorians to clear his path in Rome. Even when the new emperor joined his troops in Italy, the problem of which of his two commanders should be made the senior leader continued to fester. It was clear that the two distrusted one another and that the two legions looked first and foremost to their respective commanders, and not to Vitellius himself. The evils of the old Republic were re-asserting themselves and Aulus Vitellius was not a strong enough personality to maintain his imperial prerogatives to obedience.

Vitellius made a big mistake at this point. He disbanded the old Praetorian Guard of some 9,000 men and attempted to create a new Guard of 16,000 men. Confusion followed. First of all, the disbanded soldiers bitterly resented their fate, even though some ended up in the new Guard. Second, mixing Vitellians with Guards of unknown political sympathies was a poor idea. There were not barracks or other facilities in Rome sufficient for the new out-sized Guard. Last but not least, Vitellians from Germany were over-eager to become pampered Praetorians even though their loyalty and performance as ordinary legionaries had been sadly wanting. All this worked against Vitellius.

The troops which Vespasian sent ahead from the Balkans under Antonius Priscus proved unexpectedly effective. This was mainly because Antonius was a charismatic and super-charged leader much given to bold action and speed. The troops themselves were as keen for booty as for patriotic duty. They passed quickly through Illyricum and easily fought their way into the Po Valley. There, just outside Cremona, they

Map of Roman Italy in the first century

aggressively gave battle to the main Vitellian army under Caecina Aliens.
On that occasion Vitellius' forces were forced back towards the city,
thanks to the very high elan of Antonius Priscus' troops. Those troops
went immediately from the late afternoon's fight into an evening attack,
and relentlessly pushed the weaker Vitellian force from the battlefield
into Cremona itself – which was known as a pro-Vitellian city. Then
the situation became surreal, for despite a large-scale battle taking place
just outside the city, the Cremonans were holding their annual Autumn
Fair with much jollity and fun. The Flavian troops were incensed that
the townspeople were openly giving food and other aid to the Vitellian

soldiery during the hostilities. As a result, once the Vitellian troops were subdued, the city of Cremona was cruelly sacked and burned by the victorious Flavian soldiery. Murder, rape and looting went on for days. The news of this unprecedented sack by Roman troops of one of Italy's own cities horrified everyone and brought the leaders of the opposing factions to meet.

There followed confused negotiations in Rome. The unexpected outcome: Vitellius agreed to give up his imperial claims and to recognize Vespasian. Unfortunately, Vitellius' troops wouldn't agree to those practical terms – which would have meant the end of their opportunities to plunder and murder -- and they mutinied from their commander-in-chief. Later, confronted with the sudden arrival of contingents of Flavian soldiers from Priscus' army, Vitellian troops in the capital ran completely amok. Soon central Rome became a war zone and was partly sacked and partly burned. It was mid-December of AD 69, and the wild annual festival of Saturnalia was in full swing. Everyone was festive and almost everyone was drunk. City residents – the mob -- watched from side-streets and from rooftops as Flavian and Vitellian troops fought each other, spilling a good deal of blood. The crowds cheered for one side or the other, as if it were all some kind of entertainment. But then some over-enthusiastic young men went to rooftops and began raining heavy roof tiles down on "enemy" soldiers. That provoked more violence. There was widespread looting and killing, and chaos took over. Fires were started to burn out the civilian assailants, but then public buildings were fired, including the venerable old Temple of Jupiter Capitolinus. It had survived the fire of AD 64 but now burned to the ground. The City Prefect Titus Flavius Sabinus – Vespasian's elder brother -- was dragged to the Forum by out-of-control Vitellian troops and was publicly butchered in full view of the helpless emperor Vitellius and the crowd. All around, the merriment continued. Such an unreal situation was clearly beyond anyone's control. In this end-of-the-world chaos of late December 69, emperor Vitellius himself tried to flee Rome with his young son. They were both pursued and killed by Flavian soldiery. Vitellius' corpse was subjected to gross insults, carved up (in revenge for Flavius Sabinus' similar fate) and disposed of into the Tiber sewers. On mid-winter's day, the main Flavian army of Antonius Priscus arrived and occupied Rome, and most of the Vitellian troops fled north. Governor Mucianus and Vespasian's son Domitian were finally able to take up the reins of civil government and begin to restore order in the city.

At that time, General Vespasian had not even begun his long journey to Rome from Alexandria. It would be many months yet before he set foot in Rome. But the news of his accession raced around the empire, and the news of Vitellius' fall and death sped back to the new emperor. Domitian and the official regent Lucius Mucianus had been instructed to hold and govern Rome for Vespasian. And they did, despite the difficult situation, resolutely and at real risk of their lives, faithfully turning the empire over to Vespasian upon his tardy arrival at the City near the end of the year 70.

At the crisis point in December 69, Vespasian's teen-aged son Domitian survived rampage, fire and imminent slaughter in Rome by sheltering in the Temple of Jupiter. When that building caught fire, he disguised himself as a woman and escaped from the burning Temple by stealthily joining a passing procession of followers of the Egyptian goddess Isis. He took that procession's providential arrival as a divinely-wrought rescue and was ever afterwards thankful to the goddess. He afterwards gave his special fealty to her and to her Roman equivalent, Minerva the goddess of wisdom and learning.

It was a chastening season for Rome and its empire. The upheavals of the "Year of Four Emperors" had shaken everyone's confidence. A lot of brotherly blood had been shed. Fathers had battled with sons, neighbours with neighbours. Bloodshed in faraway Judaea was one thing, but carnage and slaughter of Roman against Roman at home in Italy was far more disturbing. The state was again nearly bankrupt; the capital had been majorly burned for the second time in a half-dozen years. The armies of all the contenders had become insubordinate and unreliable, and people of the time could not be sure that Vespasian would prove more than yet another transient ruler. In fact, he settled in for ten years of highly constructive peace. His successor sons Titus and Domitian provided the empire with a further eighteen years of internal peace and renewed prosperity.

The time of troubles was over. The Flavian family became the new imperial dynasty. Just as had happened exactly one hundred years earlier with Augustus, the civil wars were suddenly over with the accession of a strong leader, this time Vespasian. The general did not fail to note this comparison and understood the role into which it cast him as a "second Augustus". He filled that demanding role conscientiously and well. His political skills as emperor proved to be just as good as his well-proven military talents. He would reboot the empire.

CHRISTIANS WITHOUT THE APOSTLES

Although some newly-planted Jesus communities failed and had to be re-founded later, overall there was growth and a trend to consolidation and integration of beliefs and practices. The organizing instincts of people like Peter, of Jesus' brother James, and of Saul had produced, just in time, a standard form of organization which carried on after them. We recognize it in hindsight as the embryonic Church. In that organization were two kinds of leaders. Presbyters were the elders of a settled Christian community. They were neither priests (which did not exist in earliest Christianity) nor wandering prophets or teachers. In contrast to the many travelling prophets and teachers which went from community to community with some kind of "message", the presbyter was a resident of one community. He (rarely she) was considered to be a shepherd (**pastor**) of the local flock. Each community tended to be ruled and guided by a council of presbyters. Deacons (often she) assisted presbyters in subordinate roles. Usually these roles were administrative, but sometimes logistic, and sometimes organizational.

Before the great crises of the 60s, the strongest influence on emerging communities remained that of itinerant prophets who went from place to place evangelizing and teaching. Such "prophets and teachers" included familiar apostolic names: Saul, Peter, Luke, Mark, Philip and so forth. They would typically come, stay two or three days to preach and baptize, and then move on. Travelling prophets grew fewer as more and more communities established ongoing internal organizations around resident presbyters. After the first century, itinerant prophets and teachers faded away. Their successors in influence and decisional power were the resident presbyters, and later on the Bishops.

The elders of every community functioned as a council or management board – just as in Judaism. This office of "elder" was not necessarily filled only by older Christians, rather by those most committed and those with some discernible aptitude for the work involved. For example, St. Saul appointed a young man Timothy as presbyter for the large city of Ephesus and cautioned him not to take any guff concerning his relative youth. Primitive Christianity had no priests. A presbyter would counsel members of the community, would work to secure new converts, would lead in worship, baptize, bury and succour his little flock, assisted by one or more deacons. Deacons and deaconesses were appointed by the presbyters or by the congregation, as managers, assistants and administrators, and these individuals comprised a tiny team – often a volunteer staff of only one -- for each presbyter.

That pattern continued for centuries in some places. But at least in some big cities, by the latter decades of the first century a new development was occurring: the appearance of the office of Bishop. It happened almost by its own logic. A large centre would need and have several presbyters or Elders. They formed a Council and that Council oversaw the governing of the community. But as we know, in any peer group there are people whose talents, ambition and energy stand out from the general level. They become leaders. Among the presbyters, these became leaders who energized, managed and oversaw the others. The Greek word **Episkopos** – Bishop – simply means one who oversees; a person with oversight of an organization. A viable framework of church organization was slowly and erratically emerging across the whole realm of "Christendom", but in different communities it was in differing stages and styles of development.

Just as King Agrippa II had forecast, the great War with Rome was in every way a fateful catastrophe for the Jews of Judaea. Not only was Jerusalem wrecked, its Temple obliterated and the whole life of the region disrupted; the diversity of Judaism was physically destroyed. The Sadducees, the Essenes and the Zealot party simply disappeared, leaving only Pharisees and Jewish-Christians as the organized "posterity of Israel". Traditional Judaism found rescue through its great scholar-leader Yohanan Ben-Zakkai, who escaped from doomed Jerusalem sealed in a coffin and survived to pull the Pharasaic leadership remnants together at Jamnia on the coast, as successors to the Jerusalem hierarchy. The new Jamnia Council took over many of the functions of the Temple organization, yet much had to be jettisoned. The Temple itself was gone, with all its treasures, and it could not be restored in the foreseeable future. Its bloody sacrificial rites were abandoned forever, the Pharisees taking up an essentially Christian position on animal sacrifices. The Jamnia Council initially possessed no political power, but it quickly morphed into a governing council again dubbed the "Sanhedrin" (derived from the Greek "Synedrion" meaning "Council"). What was left, throughout the empire and beyond, were the synagogues. Those became the basis for Jewish religious life henceforth. Future centuries would bring successes and disasters to Judaism, but for the remainder of the first century Judaism was busy re-inventing and re-invigorating its religious life along new lines.

Christian leadership after 66 passed into the hands of local Christians who took great interest, and usually greater care, in unifying and ordering their local communities. Unity was their most evident concern; unity of belief and unity of procedures that would bring them the way of life necessary for the salvation of their souls. New writings began to appear, and centres began to correspond regularly and to work with one another, to compare and correct beliefs and to discuss problems. In community practices, the middle ground gained. Communities did strive to reach accommodations between themselves and their pagan and mainstream Jewish neighbours. It needed patience on both sides. The bad reputation of Christians up to the 60s slowly improved – but never disappeared -- as the pagan general public reached a truer appreciation of what Christianity was about. Some "high-class" pagan converts to Christianity also began to appear. At the same time, wildly aberrant forms of Christianity continued to flourish.

These aberrant forms varied from the quaint to the bizarre. There were groups here and there which believed that the awaited Kingdom of God had in fact already arrived, that it arrived within each individual as the intellectual "re-birth" of which Jesus had spoken. Very subtle and cerebral. Thus, some born-again Christians felt that they already lived in the promised Kingdom. This attitude has never entirely disappeared. There were death/resurrection-deniers who taught that Jesus had been a divine phantom rather than a real human being, had therefore not really suffered and died on the cross and, consequently, had experienced neither death nor resurrection. On the other side were those – including many Jewish-Christians -- who accepted Jesus as only a human being and great prophet who had been inspired and empowered by God. Their Jesus undoubtedly suffered on the cross and died. This too was a belief that demonstrated much staying power in antiquity.

More interesting -- or at least more titillating -- were groups which eschewed sex even within marriage, or practiced strict vegetarianism (as Jesus and his brother James had done), or which mistreated and punished the body in the belief that it was only a source of sinning. Such people appeared all through antiquity and the Middle Ages and are still around in modern times. More surprising, there were also a few late first-century groups – such as the Carpocratians -- which allowed rampant sexual promiscuity as a method of "mistreating" the body. There were communities much given to "speaking-in-tongues" raptures in which they ranted unintelligibly; and groups some of whose members sold themselves into slavery as "fund-raisers" for their communities. First-century Christianity was nothing if not diverse. A frequent first-century complaint, that church members got drunk on the communion wine, was matched by recurring censures of church officials who allegedly abused their offices, bullied their flocks, or had their hands in the communal till.

In large part the gentile-based Jesus-communities relied on Saul's teachings and followed his organizational instructions. In part they incorporated beliefs and practices from the apostolic "Jesus communities" founded from Jerusalem. And in part they muddled their way along with their own leaders, ideas and scriptural interpretations. There was, of course, plenty of debate and turbulence within communities. Some communities thrived on that. However, most communities did not; that seems to have been particularly true of Pauline foundations in Greece. Corinth was a site of instability and fractiousness all through the century.

Authority was what the circumstances of the early church required, for there was – especially in the latter decades of the first century – much anarchy in the Jesus-movement. The Apostles with their unquestioned authority had passed away before community practices and beliefs had really gelled, and the leaders who succeeded the Apostles seldom could exert much authority beyond their own localities. The successors to the Apostles leaned heavily upon the authority of the Apostles; upon the lustre of a direct apostolic connections; on the Hebrew scriptures; and upon the newly written Gospels (then termed "memoirs of the Apostles") and Apostolic Letters. Those resources were quickly supplemented by lore and legends about the founding fathers of each church community. The sixty or seventy years following 66 saw raw anarchy give way to recognized structures and processes which ultimately became The Christian Church.

Presbyters were not slow to take up the reins of authority. In the earliest phase of the Church, presbyters were usually appointed and taught by Apostles (for example, by Peter or Saul). The idea of "apostolic succession" germinated and became more important with time, when the Apostles themselves were no longer around. As the little communities grew in size and complexity, their presbyters increased in numbers and authority and, in the nature of things in the Roman empire, one particularly competent or assertive presbyter tended to emerge as the Bishop, a ruler figure.

Smaller and newer churches everywhere looked to larger, more experienced nearby ones for guidance and help. These guiding churches naturally were located in the large urban centres of the Empire. Rome, as the imperial capital and by far the largest city, in very short time achieved a pre-eminent position. Antioch in Syria, Corinth in Greece, Ephesus in Asia Minor, Alexandria in Egypt and Edessa and Adiabene in Mesopotamia were other foundations which from earliest days functioned as hubs for their regions. As for Jerusalem, despite all the realities of its decline, there was always lustre to the name of the Holy City.

Individual Christian communities interpreted their organizational heritages variously. On one hand were authoritarian communities in which the presbyters wielded authority autocratically over the congregation. If such a dominating presbytery was able and industrious for, say, ten or fifteen years, then the community could grow very large and unified. By then some presbyter would have been self-promoted to Bishop. However, if the presbyters proved incompetent or lazy or offensive to the flock, the remedies were unclear and rebellion was possible. Or, people just bailed out. That problem had to be faced in many communities. It persists today.

Authority from the top down was by no means the only model. Most early communities operated on a conciliar basis, their congregations being consulted on important matters by the leadership team of presbyter-Elders. Some communities took their cue from the communal or communistic life of the very earliest Jesus community. There were groups which believed that authority derived not by apostolic succession but by individual revelation, and in some instances such communities drew lots to revolve the duties of presbyter, deacon, preacher, prophet and cantor among congregation members at worship services. A member of such a congregation might serve as a deacon one week, as a presbyter the next, and as an ordinary member of the laity the week after that. More conservative Christians found this egalitarianism shocking.

The embryonic idea of the synod (in Greek, synedrion = "assembly") was present from the beginning; it matches the derived Judaic word Sanhedrin (= synedrion). The pre-eminence of Jesus' family in the Movement was long acknowledged, at least in the East.

—

In Rome, Peter and Saul's community was provided with at least three presbyters – Linus, Anenkletos and Clement -- to assist and then to succeed the apostles. Their joint presbytery lasted from 65 to 77 when Linus died. Anenkletos continued serving until his death in 88. Yet all through this time Clement – an educated Roman of the Flavian clan early converted by Peter – acted as a sort of "overseas liaison" secretary between the Roman church and churches elsewhere in the empire. The able and by-then experienced Clement took over Linus' post and eventually Cletus' as well, creating a unified church governance for all of Rome. Clement became the Bishop of Rome – the first pope. He was moreover related to the Flavian emperors.

Even before Mark of Cyrene (not the evangelist) died in Alexandria he had been smoothly succeeded as leader and presbyter of that important church community by Annianus, who served until AD 85. Alas, we know nothing whatsoever about Annianus or his successor Avilus. Annianus appears to be the Jewish name Ananias, but Avilus is an old Roman name.

What followed the storms of the late 60s certainly was a new and different age. From a time of "fiery trials" the empire entered calm seas. The new emperor, Vespasian, was the complete antithesis of his predecessor Nero: a big, bluff, tough-but-jovial military man with an earthy sense of humour and a commitment to restoring good, sensible government and the fiscal stability of the Roman state. Here was an emperor who went walking down the street without his Guard; who was on good terms with his family and friends, who had loved his one wife; who even was not above using his own novel pay2P public urinals and depositing his coin like everyone else. He was a decent man. He even managed to get along with the Roman Senate, quite a feat for any emperor. His ten years at the helm brought complete peace for Christians and recovery for the empire.

By far, the most important Christian development of the latter part of the first century was the emergence of writings which later entered the "New Testament". Even in Jesus' day his literate listeners were jotting down his sayings and noting down things that he had done. Among the Apostles, Matthew showed the greatest interest in note-taking, and in addition Matthew's circle was interested in comparing what he had heard from Jesus with the messianic prophecies of the Hebrew Bible (that is, the Old Testament). For Matthew wished to demonstrate that Jesus' teachings and deeds fulfilled the prophecies of the Hebrew Bible. After Jesus' departure, many of the Apostles wrote down or dictated orally their reminiscences of their Lord, and they discussed with one another some of his more memorable or difficult sayings and deeds. That knowledge then had to be imparted – usually orally -- to incoming new members of the Jesus communities. Matthew, Peter and John were leaders in this activity.

In these circumstances Matthew came to be known as a man with a full record of the Lord's Sayings. Others made selections and abridgements from his list, so that soon many records of sayings of Jesus were in circulation -- many different records. Some of the copies would have been used in teaching new converts, others may have been more useful for advanced study by literate believers. The traditions of the gospels being written by apostles are basically sensible. However, the putative apostle authors were not the only hands developing the scriptures from notes and memories. The multiplicity of notes and lists and stories eventually drove some interested scholarly individuals to write full narratives. While the Apostles had notes and source documents, it took wider knowledge and higher literary abilities to turn them into full works. Dozens of people with those qualifications wrote out brief gospel narratives, and at least a half-dozen of those works have survived the vicissitudes of two thousand years. Only four made it into the later collection of "inspired" writings which we call the New Testament.

Probably every Apostle possessed favorite sayings and information about Jesus. Just as Matthew and the unknown source for the "Gospel of Thomas" focused on collecting sayings of Jesus, we can suppose that some of Jesus' followers would individually have made brief records of memorable healings; of preaching to the crowds; of visits to the Temple in Jerusalem; and above all of the gripping events of Jesus' final arrest, trial and execution. "I remember when…" Stories also became embroidered with re-telling; they usually do. As chief among the Apostles, Simon-Peter may have collected or prepared written notes for his own teaching and baptismal use, giving context to the Sayings and providing a story of Jesus' mission. St. Saul had sets of notebooks.

Of course, every eyewitness remembers events differently, as witnesses always do. There were soon many stories and many documents, most of them just short "snapshots" of some event or other. Peter's son and amanuensis John Mark took on the job of sifting through his father's materials and trying to put the documents into some order useful for teaching new converts to the Movement. But as anyone will appreciate who has begun to research their family's history, we often begin too late – just as the key eyewitness generation is passing away. Even before Peter's execution in 67, Mark had to guess or suppose the order in which various events had occurred during Jesus' mission, for Peter could not remember with certainly, and Mark himself had not been part of that mission team. He knew much about what had happened but not when. After Mark himself passed on not much later than his father, the situation became still more problematic. Some of Mark's colleagues and inheritors were painfully aware that he had not been able to get everything in the right sequence. "The Good News According to Mark" was nearly thirty years in the making, before the final version. Even after 70, sporadic attempts at altering and adding to Mark's manuscript went on.

Mark's gospel never attained as wide a circulation as the gospels of Matthew and Luke which were soon also available. Ironically, both those other gospel documents had drawn heavily on material initially written for "Mark". Perhaps "Mark" was just too brief; more likely it was not "miraculous" enough and did not accord Jesus the divinity which later Gospel writers (especially John) conceded. For whatever reasons, Mark never became a favoured gospel until the 20th century.

In antiquity, **Matthew's gospel** account was thought to have been the earliest. That may be true of Matthew's "Sayings of Jesus", the precursor of the full gospel. Matthew's lists needed a biographical frame into which the sayings could be placed to establish a narrative "timeframe of sayings". The "Matthew" writers freely lifted 90% of "Mark" almost verbatim and fused it with Matthew's collected sayings of Jesus to produce a new gospel document combining sayings and prophecies with a mission story: "Matthew" more or less as we know it. It was a hit.

"Matthew" went into use in the Jerusalem Jewish-Christian community in the 50s, and it was in general circulation in Greek by the early 60s. Variants existed; one variant version of it – lacking the first two chapters of our familiar Matthew gospel – was called "The Gospel of the Hebrews". This variant "Matthew" remained the favoured gospel of the Jewish-Christian churches of Jerusalem and Judaea, especially after the Roman-Jewish War.

Two early church elders, Papias of Hierapolis in modern-day Turkey, and John of Ephesus, both writing at the very end of the first century, made interesting remarks on the origins of the gospel accounts of Matthew and Mark. The historian Eusebius reports:

> [Papias] used to say this: "Mark, being the recorder of Peter,
> wrote accurately but not in order whatever he [Peter] remembered
> of things either said or done by the Lord. For he [Mark] had
> neither heard the Lord nor followed him, but … Peter used to
> make teachings in the form of anecdotes] but without a systematic
> composition of the Lord's sayings. So Mark cannot be faulted for
> writing certain things just as [Peter] had recalled them. For Mark
> had but one intention: not to leave out anything he had heard,
> nor to falsify anything". That was related by Papias about Mark.
> But about Matthew`s gospel he said: "Matthew first composed

the Sayings in the Hebrew language [Aramaic]; and each person made sense of them as best he could".

The origin of **Luke's gospel** presents quite a different picture. Luke researched a number of writings about Jesus, and from that written information composed his gospel. Luke was the actual author, but his text was tampered with after it left his hands. When we encounter Luke in Saul's letters, he is in Saul's team in Asia Minor in 50. He may have even been a slave of Saul. He conceived the idea of writing a narrative "gospel" soon afterwards but did not get started until the close of the mission tour with Saul in 57 and their trip to Judaea then. For Judaea and the Apostles based there would have been rich sources of information for an account of Jesus and the active Apostles.

Both the Gospel of Luke and the Acts of the Apostles are dedicated to His Excellency Theophilus (meaning "lover of God"). The identity of Theophilus remains a mystery. Probably, Theophilus was the aristocrat Saul himself; or possibly a Roman official involved with his trial of AD 63 in Rome.

The polished Greek style of "Luke" and Acts is that of a highly literate writer, in marked contrast to the rudimentary Greek of "Matthew" and "Mark". Moreover, "Luke" is highly knowledgeable; the writer knows the correct technical names for officials, legal procedures and many other specialty terms. In Acts, the author at times changes from a third-person narrative to a first-person narrative ("we did such-and-such"). It is evident from a comparison of Saul's letters with the text of Acts that the first-person is Luke and no other.

John's gospel was the last of the four to arrive on the scene, the odd-man-out narrative. The traditional story told by Eusebius about the origin of this late gospel is this: several of the Apostles kept urging the Apostle John to write an account of Jesus' ministry to set right the order of events (apparently unsatisfactory in the other three gospels); to make clear the important links between Jesus and John the Baptizer; and to present a view of Jesus as a divine being. But, that traditional tale is naïve. "John" was written by a committee, using materials from Matthew, Mark and Luke (or their sources) along with some recollections of the old Apostle and brand-new material. "John" is a late production that had almost no impact in the first century.

—

But in the transmission of ideas things do go awry. The original gospel writers did not get everything right. In addition, constant re-copying of manuscripts introduced both accidental and deliberate alterations to received texts. Last but not least, the wide geographical spread of Christian communities meant that the young movement existed in local or regional forms which differed in languages, beliefs and traditions one from another. Each locality possessed its own cultural milieu. A document could be written in Aramaic, translated into Greek, and then the Greek translated into Latin. But would the meaning be faithfully preserved? It's an issue still with us in our many translations of the Bible.

IX
IMPERIAL REBOOT

A NEW IMPERIAL DYNASTY

Vespasian finally arrived in Rome near the end of the year 70. The long delay was in part due to the continuing Judaean War, but in larger part to Vespasian's apprehensions that his takeover would yet require lots of military action and that still other claimants to the throne would arise. So he tarried at Alexandria in Egypt, a place from which he could if necessary stop the grain ships from leaving for Rome. In short, he was positioning himself to starve the capital out to quell opposition. But he was lucky. That opposition never materialized. In fact, the people of Italy were tired and frightened of war in their midst, and there was neither serious opposition nor new claimants to contend with. Vespasian had well and truly won the throne.

Vespasian lacked many of the expected qualifications for imperial dignity. His family was respectable but certainly not illustrious; they came from Sabine country in Italy. His parents were not even particularly wealthy and had moved to Helvetia (= Switzerland) to pursue small-scale banking and related business opportunities there. Vespasian, his elder brother Sabinus and their younger sister Domitia were mostly brought up by their grandmother. Vespasian married Flavia Domitilla when he was 30, on the face of it a poor choice of partner, for Flavia was not even a full Roman citizen and had previously been the mistress of a Roman knight. But the marriage was a love match and remained so. Vespasian and Flavia produced three children: two sons, and a daughter who died in her 30s. Vespasian started his career in Thrace as a military tribune, then was briefly a Consul under Caligula. He commanded troops in the British campaign of 43-47 and was made a Consul again under Claudius for the year 51. In 63 Nero made him proconsul of Africa, his administration winning praise because Vespasian did not pursue the usual course of milking the province for his own financial gain. In consequence, he actually suffered private financial problems and avoided bankruptcy only by a loan from his brother Sabinus. Flavia Domitilla died before her husband came to the throne, but Vespasian remembered her with great affection. He never re-married but instead resumed living with his old mistress Caenis. They were both over fifty in AD 70, "seniors" by Roman standards.

Young Domitian married in 70, another love match. His bride was Domitia the younger daughter of the famous General Domitius Corbulo and his wife Cassia Longina. Domitia was an aristocrat, beautiful, wealthy and intelligent. Titus was twice wed in the 60s, the first time to Arrecina Tertulla, a Christian woman who died during the first year of the marriage, and then (AD 63) to Marcia Furnilla, of a senatorial family. When Titus later learned that the Furnilla family was anti-monarchist and indeed had been involved in conspiracies against Nero, he divorced Marcia. They had one daughter, Julia Flavia, well-spoken-of by everyone.

Vespasian initiated a brand-new dynasty, the Flavians, which ruled for the next quarter-century. It was a dynasty which was on the whole successful, and a big improvement on the Julio-Claudians. Internal peace was restored; the armed forces were brought back to obedience; the economy was stabilized and the treasury was slowly refilled; the frontiers were strategically rationalized; and the heavily damaged capital city was rebuilt. Vespasian managed to get along with the Senate. Although he and his late brother Sabinus were senators, they were the family's first members of that class. Vespasian himself, earlier in life, had known hard times, for the family only became wealthy in the 60s. As emperor Vespasian was approachable, earthy and not at all devious. Senators did not live in fear of him even though a couple of their number were executed for exceptionally stubborn and strident opposition. The military of course respected this glorious commander. And, remarkably, the Christian religion found the Flavian era decidedly congenial.

It was the Flavians' propaganda line that the gods had approved of and aided the Flavian takeover, but in fact Vespasian and his sons had planned their seizure of the empire very astutely. In the autumn of 69 AD Vespasian turned the Jewish war operations over to his son Titus and instructed his teen-aged son Domitian in Rome to act in a regency under Governor Mucianus of Syria, who was to be sent to Rome. Vespasian then set out for Alexandria where he would wait, able to cut off Rome's Egyptian grain supplies, while his various agents fulfilled his plans against Aulus Vitellius. Everything went off almost without a hitch.

Vespasian arrived in Rome a year later, and ruled until AD 79, successfully re-stabilizing the empire. He was keenly conscious of being a "second Augustus" with most of the challenges of the first Augustus who had taken over exactly one hundred years previously. Like that first emperor, Vespasian had much to do. First of all he restored order and discipline in the military. Vitellius' bloated Praetorian Guard was chopped back to its old size, and Titus was made the sole Praetorian Prefect. Vespasian vigorously squelched the tendency of legions to give their first loyalty to their field commanders. The emperor as commander-in-chief was again made the sole focus of loyalty. Not too surprisingly, some legions in the hinterlands continued to rebel and to put forward more candidates for empire. Most of these rebellions collapsed of their own accord. The most serious trouble erupted in Lower Germany (present-day Netherlands) where a foxy local chieftain named Julius Civilis led a populist rebellion which taxed the abilities of the nearby German legions to put down. The general who was acting as governor of Britain, Quintus Petillius Cerealis, was sent over to Germany where he systematically defeated Civilis and ended the rebellion. In addition to being a capable general,

Cerealis was a Christian and had been the husband of Vespasian's sister Domitilla, who died in 67 – Christian and probably martyred – at the age of just 22. The couple were the parents of yet another Christian, Flavia Domitilla. Julius Civilis and his tribesmen got off leniently; Cerealis took forgiveness seriously. Remarkably, Civilis remained alive and at liberty, and returned his tribe to good relations with the Romans. By the end of 71 the rebellion was all over.

Vespasian next reformed the wheezing financial administration system, being eager to ensure that taxes were efficiently collected and that state operations were carried out more honestly and fairly than in the recent past. The empire was not exactly broke, but it had an immediate cash crisis as a legacy from previous reigns. In the first century, if the state needed more money and it could not be extracted from the populace, it had to be extracted from the ground itself – by mining gold, silver and copper for new coinage. That's why the Flavian emperors took unusual interest in Spain – there were gold mines there. Vespasian and his successors developed those mines and others to replenish the empire's supplies of gold and silver coinage. The new emperor was rescued from immediate financial disaster by the Temple treasure looted from Jerusalem. That huge haul of booty kept the empire afloat during the crisis years.

Vespasian not only had to deal with the mess left by the civil war, in parallel he had to deal with deeper problems left by Nero. That he did by killing off Nero's big-ticket projects. Gone was the Corinth Canal project, gone was Nero's "Golden House", and after a respectable delay, gone was Greece's tax exemption. There was plenty of room for economies, and anyway most of the empire was still functioning and paying its taxes as usual. Right away the new emperor tackled the repair of Rome, which was still partly in ruins from the fires of AD 64 and 69.

Here was a different kind of emperor who was not given to killing his critics and who was not even very active in suppressing dissent. Vespasian's gruff sense of humour prevented him from being hated but he did acquire the reputation of a skinflint. He was keen on taxation – his grandfather had been that rare thing, an honest tax collector -- and the emperor taxed many items which had never before been subject to taxes. He even charged a small fee for Rome's public urinals to raise money from users, and then he made public jokes about the user-pee/user-pay arrangements – which he himself used and duly paid for. He astonished everyone by walking down the streets unguarded so that anyone might encounter the emperor face to face. He also abolished the frisk-searches of palace visitors that had been instituted by timorous old Claudius. By giving such trust, Vespasian got it in return. He never had to face serious assassination attempts although several plots were detected and defused. His watchwords were "peace" and "order" and he delivered on both, quickly and consistently. It may be difficult to square Vespasian as peaceable emperor with his record as the savage butcher of Judaea, but the historic record is clear on both issues.

Although he was parsimonious by nature, and despite the depleted Roman treasury which he inherited, Vespasian possessed large resources of windfall money from the Judaean war booty. That treasure exceeded the Romans' wildest imaginings; it was the largest haul of war booty ever taken by the empire. In the currency of the present day its value may have been around $50 billion. Thanks to this colossal haul of loot there was no financial collapse. Meanwhile, imperial expenses were falling fast and the regular sources of imperial income were still there, so that the finances of the state were more or less normalized by the mid-70s.

Vespasian with pleasure axed Nero's "Golden House" palace project in the middle of Rome. It was already the largest "house" on earth – a mile long. Begun in 64, it was only partially complete at the overthrow of Nero. It had features which would do credit to any modern luxury resort: indoor gardens; a revolving restaurant; swimming pools; theatre auditoriums; "luxury spa" facilities; an artificial lake; and much more. It was a work of amazing innovation and concept, but Vespasian wasn't interested. Neither was the colossal bronze statue of Nero on the grounds, standing nearly 30 meters high, to Vespasian's spartan tastes. The emperor terminated the whole project, took over the space, and commissioned instead the construction of an enormous new public amphitheatre there.

The colossal statue of Nero was however left in place[17] and gave this Amphitheatrum Flavium its more popular name: the Colosseum. The cost of this ambitious ten-year project was met using treasure taken from the Jerusalem Temple. Some of that loot is illustrated nearby on the still-standing Victory Arch of Titus.

This infamous Colosseum, when completed in 81, became the scene of hideous butchery of men and beasts, and of sadistic slaughter and tortures, all in the name of "entertainment" for the masses. Many Romans were revolted by the "shows", just as Nero had been in the old amphitheatre, and as we are today; but the 40,000 seats were usually filled with men and women baying for blood. Emperor Vespasian himself never got to see it in action, for it was not completed until the reign of his successor Titus. It might be remarked that under the Flavian emperors no Christians met their ends in the Colosseum as punishment for their faith; but tens of thousands of wild animals were cruelly done to death there.

Work to restore the burned-over parts of Rome continued all through Vespasian's ten-year reign. The Temple Tax for which Jews had always been liable continued to be collected under Vespasian, but with the Jerusalem Temple destroyed the money was now used to rebuild and repair a very different "Temple" – the Temple of Jupiter Capitolinus in Rome. This must have been a particularly bitter pill for Jews, especially as Christians were not subjected to the tax.

After a quiet decade of rule, Vespasian died peacefully at his ancestral farm in the spring of 79. The historians of Rome gave him an adoring press, and the Senate immediately voted to deify him as a god. His successor was his eldest son and long-time close colleague Titus, who took over without a hitch, the first biological son ever to succeed his father on the Roman throne.

Titus – officially named Titus Flavius Vespasianus Augustus like his father -- is hard to assess, for his reign of less than two years was too brief

17 The head was changed from time to time to show a current emperor's face. The colossus remained in place well into the Middle Ages, until finally demolished to recoup its tons of high-quality bronze. Only the stone base now remains.

to lay down any steady record of achievements, and in addition his basic character remains a puzzle. For Titus was not well-liked before his accession. He was a seasoned administrator and a famous army commander in his own right, who had held the major offices of the Roman State: consul, praetor, and aedile. He had proved himself a capable general in action first in southern Scotland and then in Judaea where he had taken over command of the Roman armies from his father at the height of the Roman-Jewish war. But most people didn't warm to him. After the war, Titus became the sole Praetorian Prefect and was given tribunician power; his father trusted him absolutely and he fulfilled that trust throughout Vespasian's entire reign.

Yet, before his time as emperor, Titus had been considered by the Roman populace as a tough and unsavoury character. There were at least three reasons for his unpopularity. First, he had the reputation of being ruthless; he was of course not alone among Romans in that kind of reputation, but somehow it clung to him. Second, unlike his father he gave plenty of evidence of being a spendthrift and ne'er-do-well. Finally, he carried on a long, scandalous and highly visible love affair with Queen Berenike from the Herodian royal family. Berenike was the sister (and consort) of King Agrippa II. The Roman people's long-standing irritation with Berenike – she reminded them of Cleopatra -- was only terminated when Titus abruptly sent her away in 79, just at the time of his accession.

Berenike was one of the most exotic and remarkable women of the century. She was born in AD 28, the year in which John the Baptizer began to preach in the desert. She was a daughter of King Herod Agrippa I and his queen Cypros III, and thus Berenike was a great-granddaughter of Herod the Great. Berenike had a tumultuous youth, being twice married and divorced as a mere youngster, then she again married, became Queen of Chalcis, and was widowed -- all before reaching age twenty. Next she went to live with her brother Julius Agrippa who had just succeeded to the Judaean throne in the early 50s as King Agrippa II. He was a great Herodian king who enjoyed a fifty-year reign, but he was the last of his line, for he remained unmarried and produced no children. Agrippa and Berenike lived together as King and Queen (he of Judaea and she of Chalcis) and it was believed by almost everyone in ancient times that they were incestuous lovers. To stanch those rumours Berenike married a young Cilician prince named Polemo but that marriage lasted only a few weeks, after which she renounced the Jewish religion and went back to her brother. It was before King Agrippa and Queen Berenike that St. Saul appeared in 60. Agrippa and Berenike were both second cousins of Saul.

She was beautiful, bright, bold and brave. And reckless, or maybe just wild. For her three marital adventures all ended in divorces which she herself initiated. In her twenties, when she began living at the court of her brother King Agrippa II, Berenike effectively shared royal power with her brother. She enjoyed the power and the glory of the court. Just as reported in the New Testament, they both interviewed their cousin Saul together in AD 60, as a royal couple. It went this way:

> *Agrippa and Berenike entered the audience chamber in full*
> *regalia and accompanied by a number of high officials. The*
> *Roman governor Festus introduced Saul as "a man you all know,*
> *whom the Jews of Jerusalem have called deserving of death. But I*
> *can find nothing wrong with him. He has appealed to Caesar, and*
> *I need to prepare a briefing note for the emperor. Perhaps you can*
> *advise me in that". Agrippa immediately invited Saul to speak.*

Saul didn't have to be asked twice and gave a half-hour speech recounting his history and his mission as a Jewish-Christian. He worked up to:

> *"I assert nothing beyond what Moses and the prophets have said*
> *– that the Messiah would rise from the dead and announce the*
> *Dawn to Jews and Gentiles alike".*

At that point the exasperated governor Festus interrupted Saul's long speech by yelling out,

"Saul, you're raving. Too much erudition is unhinging you."
Saul apologized to the King, who replied amiably, "You think
I'm almost a Christian already? Should I become like you?"

Saul: *"I do wish that all of you here would become as I am –
except for the chains."* The audience was bemused, for the "chains"
were only light ceremonial chains, not the heavy iron customary
for prisoners.

*Agrippa, Berenike and Festus left the room to talk privately. "This
man has done nothing wrong and should be released" insisted
Agrippa. "But he has already appealed to Nero," rejoined Festus,
"so we can't simply release him now."*

*"Well, Festus my friend, he is a relative of ours, so send him to
Rome in some dignity. As far as you can, look after him."*

Whatever her morals, Berenike was extraordinarily attractive. Nine
years later, during the Roman-Jewish War, when she was past forty,
Berenike met and fell in love with General Titus who was fully ten years
younger. (Remember that the Herodians sided with the Romans during
the conflict.) And Titus fell for her. Titus was visiting Agrippa's court at
Caesarea-Philippi in 68 and immediately fell in love with the Queen.
Berenike used her wealth and influence the very next year to support
Titus' father Vespasian in his campaign to become emperor. After the
conclusion of the main war in 71, when Titus finally returned to Rome
to assist his father in the government, Berenike stayed behind in Judaea
-- but not for long.

Berenike, Titus and her brother Agrippa II were all re-united in Rome
in 75. At that time Berenike advanced her relationship with Titus, living
with him at the imperial palace and acting to all appearances as his wife.
However, the Roman populace perceived the "Eastern Queen" as a sinister foreigner – a new Cleopatra -- and when she and the emperor-to-be

were publicly booed and denounced in the theatre in 78, Titus caved in and decided to send Berenike away.

But still she didn't stay away. Upon the accession of Titus as emperor the very next year, 79, the fifty-year-old queen hastened back to Rome, expecting to be wed to Titus and made empress. She was rebuffed yet again amidst a flurry of populist measures taken by Titus to rejuvenate his rather poor reputation. Their relationship was not mysterious at the time but is so today. After being pressured by all his counsellors, and under intense pressure from the Roman Senate, Titus steeled himself for a showdown with Berenike. Despite the age difference he would have liked to marry her; she knew that much. Politically it was impossible. The final scene was heart-breaking for both lovers. What happened to Berenike after her final dismissal from Rome? She simply disappeared.

Agrippa and Berenike – both Jews although Berenike had renounced her religion -- gave their relative Saul plenty of audience time and careful attention back in AD 60 because they were seriously interested in the New Way called Christianity. That interest continued and matured during the 60s. In the aftermath of the Jewish War, Christianity looked even more attractive as an alternative to a vanquished, broken mainstream Judaism. Indeed, after the War only two Jewish sects remained: the Pharisees and the Christians. Well before the war, Christianity was being openly discussed at Nero's court and some members of that court were converts. After AD 70 Christianity certainly flourished in peace under Vespasian and Titus, and for a further decade and more even under Titus' successor, the much-maligned Domitian.

After Titus ascended the throne in 79, he showed an entirely different side of his character, as if he had been born anew. Although he was still culpable of large-scale overspending, he was never in danger of bankrupting the state in his less than two years of power. His ruthlessness seemed to vanish. Here again he may have been showing the "good years" that most other emperors manifested – even Nero did – before moving on to hypothetical "bad years". But that seems superficial as an explanation. Titus may have been a closet monotheist, and certainly despite the

War he was sympathetic to both Judaism and Christianity. Significantly, Christians were right there in his family – his late uncle Flavius Sabinus, his first wife Arrecina Tertulla, and several of his cousins. Yet, try as he did, there was something about Titus which bothered the superstitious Romans – his stance was somehow bad, and the great trust that Vespasian had earned from the Romans was not earned anew by Titus. He remained acceptable yet somehow "not right". He came across as an Easterner, in a way an outsider, and his Berenike was intensely disliked by the Romans. Was Titus tinged with Judaism? Or Christianity?

Shortly after his accession Mount Vesuvius near Naples erupted spectacularly, burying the nearby resort cities of Pompeii and Herculaneum and damaging centres further away. Tens of thousands of lives were lost in this disaster, one of the most famous natural disasters to hit the world of antiquity. Among those killed was young Antonius Agrippa, the only child of the procurator Antonius Felix and his wife, King Agrippa's sister Drusilla. The disaster came unexpectedly, for Vesuvius was thought to be a dormant volcano. The region was (and still is) prone to earthquakes, and in fact a strong earthquake had severely damaged Pompeii and Herculaneum in 62. Small earthquakes occurred through July and early August of 79, then on 22 August smoke and steam began to issue copiously from the side of the mountain, apparently under high pressure. Many residents packed up and left the area.

Two days later Vesuvius erupted violently, spewing debris and ash twenty kilometers into the air. Lava began to flow and a rain of light ash began to fall. Many more people fled the cities. The eruption continued for two days and nights, then seemed to subside. More residents departed as the ash deepened and 24-hour darkness settled over the whole region, but those who still remained thought that the worst was over on 26 August. Not so; the eruption resumed the next day with even greater force, and lava flows along with fast-moving waves of superheated gas began racing down the mountain into the cities. The smell of sulfur was overpowering, and immense numbers of people were asphyxiated or roasted alive wherever they sheltered. After a full week the eruption ceased, the sky began to clear, and a lunar landscape was revealed to view. The two cities had entirely disappeared along with up to forty thousand of their inhabitants.

The elder Pliny, an eminent Roman naturalist, author, and the father of Pliny the later governor of Bithynia, was an Admiral of the Roman naval fleet at Misenum at the mouth of the bay opposite Pompeii. He lost his life by venturing too close to the disaster in a sailing boat. He had a keen – too keen – interest in the eruption, he had the use of naval ships and boats, and so he sailed straight into the danger zone. He and his crew never returned, killed by toxic fumes from Mount Vesuvius.

Titus organized relief and relocation efforts for the area, but there could be no question of bringing the dead back to life or of "repairing" cities which no longer existed. As if that were not enough, yet another serious fire burned sections of Rome in 80; but that cleanup was left to the next emperor, Titus' younger brother Domitian. Titus only had time to complete and inaugurate the new Colosseum in Rome and to finish a victory arch nearby. Then he died of natural causes at the beginning of the year 81 AD and was enrolled among the gods. Again the succession was smooth; younger brother Domitian took over, as Vespasian had promised and as Titus had announced. For twelve years Domitian had been waiting eagerly for his chance. He would greatly relish being emperor, and he would show the world how it really should be done!

CHRISTIANS WITHOUT THE APOSTLES

Despite the reticence of New Testament literature, we know from other sources about some of the post-apostolic local leaders and their successors, and about the earliest structures and processes of what would in time become "the Church". And about its many problems.

In **Ephesus**, where Saul had spent three whole years (53-56), he had designated his follower Timothy as the presbyter of the city and its district. Timothy was in his late twenties, the son of a mixed marriage of a God-fearer husband and a Jewish-Christian woman named Eunice. Young Timothy experienced many difficulties as a presbyter, including a term of imprisonment, and he was replaced after not very many years by a man named Boukolos. (It seems that presbyters and bishops were originally elective posts.) Boukolos' successor was a well-educated man named John (but not the Apostle John, with whom he has always been confused) who then held the post for a full generation, from around 75 through to the end of the century. This John claimed that in his youth he had seen and heard the living Jesus, and had been first instructed by the Apostle John; so he must have been from Palestine. Perhaps he was another of the refugees from the Roman-Jewish War. He was a masterful manager and leader, and in time he became known as "John the Elder" or "John the Presbyter". John the Elder was a leader not only of his Ephesian flock but also of other presbyters in his region, and thus he performed the essential supervisory and coordinating roles of a Bishop. This strong, skilful and fully literate leader was also a theologian much interested in getting the story of Jesus and the theology of the early gentile Church into writing. It was this John the Elder rather than the Apostle John who organized a group of leading Christians at Ephesus to expand oral and written memoirs of old John the Apostle into what we now call "The Gospel According to John". John the Elder's committee Including Aristion, Apollos, Luke and John the Elder himself. They assembled that awkward gospel document in the 70s and 80s. It went into circulation within a decade but throughout antiquity it was never favoured widely in the Church, except in the province of Asia where it originated. It did however find much use in Greece and Macedonia. By then – the 80s and 90s -- the Ephesian Church was strongly established and becoming noted for its theological debates.

The city of **Smyrna** (modern Izmir) lay close to Ephesus. Its first presbyter was an able man named Aristion. Through the influence of St. Saul, he was displaced by St. Timothy's brother Strataeas, but that presbyterial appointment was in due course followed by the return of Aristion who thereafter headed the Smyrnean community ably for twenty years or more, almost to the end of the century. Aristion the Elder and John the Elder worked well together; both were respected and of similar minds. Aristion was a member of John's gospel-writing committee. Smyrna continued strong in the faith and around 110 AD received Polycarp as its next, most illustrious second-century Bishop – and its great martyr.

In AD 65 Saul appointed his long-time gentile disciple Titus as presbyter of **Crete**. Again a disciple was cast into the potential role of a regional Bishop. But that sprawling island community was dispersed and long remained weakly knit organizationally. Only when it was divided into several bishoprics in the second century did it thrive.

The Church in **Corinth** claimed (and still claims) to have been founded by both Peter and Saul. The Corinthian Church proved notably faction-ridden from its beginning in the early 50s. It would have been a difficult community for anyone to govern. Saul's brilliant colleague Apollos couldn't govern it and in exasperation went to Crete for awhile to let Saul have free rein. Saul himself had a hard time with Corinth, complaining in the 50s that while some Corinthian Christians followed his line, others were of Peter's faction or of Apollos' faction – or even of "Christ's faction"(!). The problem was factionalism – petty politics and internal disunity of beliefs. Saul's designated successor Dionysius took over in 58 and had no better luck in achieving unity in the Corinthian church. Wrangling and internal sedition continued, leading to some kind of factional coup around 66 – either just before or just after Saul's last visit to the city in connection with the Herodian peace mission to Nero. After the civil war, in AD 70[18], the prestigious and much stabler Roman Church had to admonish Corinth, via a stern letter, to straighten itself out and to reverse the "coup". We don't know whether that letter had the desired effect and we remain in the dark about the last quarter-century in Corinth.

---

18 Most scholars date this letter – 1 Clement – to AD 96, but that seems impossible as the writer does not know of the fall of the Jerusalem Temple.

Rome itself escaped major religious strife due to three pieces of good fortune. First, the Jesus community there remained unified; the vast city had only a single Christian organization. Second, it was assisted in no small way by a few wealthy and socially illustrious new Christians. These included even members of the Flavian imperial family. Third, St Saul and St Peter had been reconciled during their last years together in Rome, and acting together they had made succession appointments of sterling quality. The three presbyters Linus, Anenkletos and Clement served together harmoniously – apparently the Roman presbytery involved permanent, lifelong appointments -- until in 88 Clement was left as the sole "Bishop of Rome". In 97 on Clement's death, a presbyter called Euarestus took over as Bishop.

To **Hierapolis** in Anatolia, not so very far from Ephesus and Smyrna, the Apostle Philip came to reside upon the outbreak of the Jewish-Roman War in 66. He may have headed the Church there, or not. In the next century we find Papias in the post of presbyter or bishop there. There were other church communities nearby: at Laodikea, Philadelphia, Colossae, Thyatira and Miletus. Of their officers no information has come down to us.

Of more easterly communities, **Antioch** stood next to Rome and Alexandria in size and influence. It was an old Jesus-community. In its infancy St Saul and St Barnabas had both worked there, in the early 40s. Barnabas had been the senior figure. Then Antioch had been overseen by St Peter during 48-56. Its Church in which both Jewish-Christians and gentile Christians participated amicably, retained a council of Elders (presbyters) and for most of the century governed itself on a conciliar basis. The post of Bishop was slow to emerge in the eastern churches. The historian Eusebius tells us that Ignatius was appointed as the "second successor" of Peter, but there must have been a lengthy period of conciliar governance before Ignatius became recognised as sole Bishop near the end of the first century.

Caesarea Maritima, the Roman administrative capital of Judaea where St. Saul was held in detention during 58-60, was the scene of St.

Peter's much earlier (ca AD 39) first gentile conversion and his subsequent first tangle with Simon the Magician. When Saul passed through Caesarea in 58, he paid a call on the Apostle Philip and his family who then resided there. They fled the Roman-Jewish War for Hierapolis seven years later, and the new presbyter of Caesarea became short-statured Zacchaeus of gospel fame.

Jerusalem, where it had all begun, was plunged into a leaderless condition upon the murder of Jesus' brother James in 62, along with certain of his associates. It may be that Peter re-assumed leadership in the years 63-66 just before the outbreak of the Roman-Jewish War. If so, he would have been an absentee leader for he spent most of that period in Rome where he was martyred in 67. Or, Jesus' and James' brother Jude perhaps became an interim leader during the years of the Roman-Jewish War. A council convened at the close of the War eventually elected as successor Jesus' and James' cousin Symeon, son of Clopas (St. Joseph's brother), who filled the post for decades and was martyred at a great age.

The earliest history of Christianity in **Alexandria** is impenetrably dark, though a Jesus community existed there as early as the 40s. The Christian Apollos came from Alexandria to Greece in the early 50s to work with Saul. The legendary Alexandrian presbytery of "Mark" supposedly ended in 62; he was then succeeded by Annianus who served until Avilius took over in 87. That "Mark" cannot be the John Mark of <u>Acts of the Apostles</u>. St. Jerome in the late fourth century asserted unequivocally that the Alexandrian Mark came from Cyrene and was not John-Mark the Evangelist. On the death of Avilius in 99, Cerdo became Bishop.

ALMOST A CHRISTIAN EMPIRE

We have seen how Christianity got started at Rome. Now it's time to look at how it grew there and elsewhere in the decades from the mid-60s to the mid-90s. St. Peter was the initial organizer in AD 43-46 of a Jesus community which had existed in Rome since the late 30s. It was then very small, and almost entirely Jewish. Before the end of the 40s, however, the community had grown impressively and included a cadre of gentile members who had come to Christ directly as enlightened "God-fearing" proselytes. The vast majority of this cadre comprised poor, lower-class Romans – including slaves. No record has survived of these people except among St. Saul's salutations in his letters. Alongside them were new Christians from the middle class and a very few adherents from the upper classes or from well-off social-professional groups. This tiny latter group of upper-class Christians played a disproportionately important role in Christianity under Nero and even more so under the Flavians.

St. Peter's crucial convert was Julia Pomponia Graecina, the wife of General Aulus Plautius the conqueror of Britain. She accepted the faith in 43 and maintained it for the remaining forty years of her life as one of the empire's high aristocrats. Her son and daughter were both Christians. The daughter Petronilla (named after her grandfather Petro) married another aristocratic new Christian named Titus Flavius Sabinus who became, in 57, the Prefect of Rome under Nero. As we have already seen, this man's younger brother was destined to become a Roman emperor: Vespasian.

There were other elite-class sympathizers. The Pudens family were early converts to Christ from the time of emperor Caligula, and they remained Christians ever after, even maintaining the main house-church of Rome. Saul as an aristocrat himself had access to the Roman elites; he began with the other Herodians at Nero's court and successfully made converts among the Praetorians. Nero's tutor and adviser Annaeus Seneca is best-remembered today as a philosopher and writer, and less as Nero's counsellor during the first decade of that Emperor's reign. Christians of the Middle Ages suspected, on the basis of what Seneca wrote, that he was a Christian. Some of his phrases and expressions seem just too similar to what appear in the gospels and in Saul's writings to be coincidence. Seneca was at least a Stoic, a school that in some principles hewed close to the Christian philosophy of the Good Life. There was in addition a mediaeval belief that Saul and Seneca had corresponded, and several letters still exist. Whether they are forged as most believe, or just possibly genuine, is uncertain. Some kind of linkage did exist. Interestingly, Seneca had a brother named Annaeus Gallio who served from mid-51 to mid-52 AD as Proconsul of Achaea (=Greece). This Gallio appears in the New Testament as a Roman magistrate supporting Saul and his missionary team against harassment by mainstream Jews in Corinth. Was Gallio too a sympathizer? Was the whole Annaeus family in some measure Christianized? They were certainly exposed to the ideas and were not opposed. In fact Seneca's writings set forth ideals of behaviour that accord very closely with Christian ideals.

Evidence of considerable early Christian presence at Rome is contained in St. Saul's letter of AD 57 to the Roman Christian community. Saul ends the letter with greetings:

> … *My greetings to Apelles, well-proved in Christ's service; to the household of Aristobulus; and to my kinsman Herodion; also to those of the household of Narcissus who are in the Lord's fellowship… Greet Asyncritus, Phlegon, Hermes, Patrobas, Hermas and all friends in their company… Greet Philologus and Julia, Nereus and his sister, Olympas, and God's people associated with them.*

People who had "households" were bigwigs and the "households" were sometimes substantial organizations. Narcissus – a common Greek name -- was likely not the "secretary of state" who served both Claudius and Nero. It's highly doubtful that the "Epaphroditus" of Saul's letters was Nero's Treasurer, but he was someone transmitting money to Saul. Officials maintained "households" whose slave members at least would have been obliged to follow their master's religion. Aristobulus was certainly the Herodian prince of that name who was visiting Nero's court until his appointment as King of tiny Chalcis at the very time of Saul's letter. The very name "Herodion" signals a young Herodian family member. Saul calls Herodion his "relative" and "the littlest Herod". That was in 57. By 62 when Saul wrote from Rome to the Jesus community at Philippi in Macedonia, he could say even more:

The brethren who are now with me here send their greetings to you, as do all God's people here [in Rome], particularly those who belong to the emperor's household. [Philippians 4: 21-22]

The "emperor's household" was Nero's court. The arson trials and mass punishment of Christians which occurred after the Fire of Rome were still a few years in the future. After that disaster, for a decade Roman Christians of note took great care to remain secret followers. At least some of these first plantings of Christianity in the imperial establishment and the upper echelons of society continued to flourish into the time of Vespasian, Titus and Domitian.

By the time of the Flavian dynasty, the evidence for Christians at the imperial court becomes unambiguous. Vespasian's Christian brother Titus Flavius Sabinus was murdered by Vitellius' troops at the very end of the strife of 69, but his children passed on the Christian tradition in the family. And this was not just any family – in that same year 69 it became the new imperial family.

As emperor, Vespasian made no trouble for any Jewish or Christian groups. Neither did Titus, whose timely change of character carried him buoyantly through his twenty-month reign (79-81). Because of his unexpectedly benign behaviour as emperor, the Senate voted to declare him a god. Titus on his accession had become quite a different man, perhaps in part from absorption of Christian ideas which were circulating at the court and in his family. Several of Titus' relatives went as far as to be baptized. Titus died after only twenty months at the helm of the Empire. He left a daughter Julia but no male children and was succeeded in 81 by his twenty-nine-year-old brother Titus Flavius Domitianus, just as Vespasian had directed.

Domitian was twelve years younger than Titus. His fifteen-year reign as emperor has not had a good press – neither in his own time nor since. Only now is his reputation being rehabilitated. He proved a strict ruler and a martinet for efficiency and obedience. He was a loner, a strategist of great ability, but a perfectionist who held himself and others to the letter of the law. In general he had the mind of a demanding but principled administrator. He could be an annoying micro-manager and was from start to finish always an indefatigable workaholic. Not surprisingly, Domitian tended to be a solitary soul; of his court officials we hear little for he overshadowed them all and used them as obedient assistants. Domitian suffered from bouts of depression and may have been a manic-depressive type. His black sense of humour was not well received in his time. On one occasion, a group of senators known to be ambivalent about the emperor were invited to dinner by him. They had to go, of course. Arriving at the palace in the evening, they were taken in black coaches to an underground banquet room similarly painted black and set at black tables. Black was for the Romans as for us, the colour of death. The emperor had his guests served a supper of foods normally associated with death, funerals and the gods of the underworld. Domitian then gave a short after-dinner talk on funeral customs. At every stage the guests were terrified that the death being implied would be their own. But then, after the meal, they were taken to their homes in ordinary coaches and given fine gifts from the emperor, thanking them for indulging his practical joke. Practical joke, or subtle warning?

Most of the emperor's bad reputation was undeserved. Domitian was very intelligent, and his reforms of the imperial administration improved it significantly, and he like the other Flavians enjoyed the military record that the old Romans considered so important in their leaders. He was clear-minded, logical and principled to a fault in his decisions. His religious beliefs were somewhat ideosyncratic. While he conformed punctiliously to the state religion, his own patron deity was the goddess of wisdom, Minerva. He also venerated the goddess Isis for her rescue of him in 69.

Physically, Domitian was of medium height, muscular and handsome. In 70 when he was not quite twenty, he fell head over heels in love with

Domitia Longina and married her. The marriage lasted through good times and bad. They experienced both, including the infant death of their only child and an affair by Domitia, but they stayed together.

As emperor, Domitian waged a successful war on corruption in the bureaucracy, and he was for long popular with the common people, the military and even with a section of the Senate notwithstanding his ongoing power struggle with that institution. Earlier emperors had wielded the broom against corruption, but Domitian was the first to build checks into the system and to personally enforce those checks energetically and consistently – indeed forcefully. His officials, used to making illicit money out of their appointments, did not appreciate the emperor's probity. But the taxpayers did. The first part of Domitian's reign was quiet and little troubled; it seemed a continuation of the preceding two reigns. The administrative tightening that was taking place behind the scenes was creating – for the first time – a highly efficient and reasonably fair taxation system. Domitian undid the Neronian currency devaluation but was unable to maintain the fully restored level, so that a slightly devalued level returned and remained the long-term norm all through the second century.

Domitian provided well for the defence of the empire. For sound strategic reasons, he decided to adjust and secure the northern boundary of the empire on a defensible line following the Rhine and Danube rivers. That "adjustment" involved some military activity and a great deal of fort-building. The Rhine portion was strengthened with a thickened line of frontier forts without provoking a major war or revolt. However, it was no sooner done than trouble broke out along the Danube River which constituted the other half of the Empire's northern boundary in Europe. Tribes there began making incursions into the Roman territories. The Dacians led by their capable king Decebulus were the main problem. At the end of 85 they were able to annihilate a whole Roman legion, which drew Domitian's immediate attention. Being a cold-hearted strategist, he immediately moved a replacement legion from Britain where it was busily occupying the north of Scotland – not a priority area. In 86 the counterattack on the Danube began in which Domitian personally commanded -- though not without setbacks. Hard fighting continued until 88 when a treaty was finally signed. The Dacians however had been defeated only by the Romans' resort to military overkill, and Domitian was dissatisfied with the outcome. The old magic of invincibility seemed to have deserted the Roman legions.

Immediately afterwards, in 89, provoked by ongoing senatorial opposition and an attempted coup d'etat by a rash German-front general named Antoninianus, Domitian got tougher with all opposition and deliberately undertook a showdown with the Senate. First, the emperor personally went to Germany and there dealt swiftly with Antoninianus, whom he suspected of being in league with dissident senators. It may have been true, but by 89 Domitian's growing paranoia was scenting opposition everywhere. The Roman Senate had never taken kindly to its increasingly subservient role under the emperors. Domitian rubbed salt into old wounds by setting policy and taking actions without even consulting the senators. During Domitian's absence at the Dacian War, the senators decided to make their weight felt against the emperor's stringent policies. Autocrats never like challenges of that sort, and Domitian was an autocrat through and through. By 90 he had more or less written off the Senate as a useful part of the state. He wanted instead to emphasize the role of the emperor as the supreme head of the Roman state. A twin concern of Domitian was loyalty to the Roman state and respect for the emperor as the symbol of the state. The old issue of the emperor's "divinity" – which had been slumbering since Caligula's reign -- re-surfaced at this inauspicious time. By the year 91, emperor and Senate were overtly fighting. It rapidly got worse. After 93 the emperor did not hesitate to imprison, banish and even execute his most recalcitrant opponents.

Neither side would back off. Mostly, the emperor dealt out banishment as a punishment; no other emperor resorted so frequently to banishment as a sentence. At the same time Domitian launched an empire-wide propaganda campaign aiming at a personality cult for himself. He decreed new laws on public and private morals and attempted to regulate matters which had never before been regulated. He kept all Jews subject to payment of the "Temple tax" (which in the absence of the Jerusalem Temple was still used perversely to support the Temple of Jupiter in Rome) and he extended that tax to "people who live like Jews" – presumably God-fearers and Christians. He next made the castration of free males illegal. Domitian then made homosexuality illegal, a decree which triggered derision in most quarters, many local revolts and another failed coup d'etat. He was, of course, unable to enforce any of these morals decrees, yet he tried. Domitian began using the title "Lord and God" (**Dominus et Deus**) and requiring it from others. He gradually stopped discussing policy matters with even his own advisers.

The 90s brought ominous changes in Domitian himself. His niece Julia (emperor Titus' daughter), one of his very few real friends, died while he was away fighting on the Danube. The emperor became ever more aloof and withdrawn, and exceedingly demanding. Stress and depression were taking their toll. To be an emperor always required a huge work effort and a punishing time commitment. Augustus had known that. The post had destroyed some men – Tiberius, Caligula and Nero. Domitian, who wanted to run the empire himself and was not a delegater, eventually found himself crushed beneath a burden that no man could bear. Though just over forty years old, he was living an ongoing nervous breakdown. He became enveloped by constant suspicion, was quick to take offense, and was obsessed with respect and obedience. His mind slowly became unhinged.

Always given to introspection and frequent hours of seclusion, Domitian tried to fight the challenges of rulership simultaneously on all fronts. Being a loner, he never acquired, as most earlier emperors did, a set of ministerial associates. Tiberius had Seianus, Caligula had Macro, Claudius had Pallas and Narcissus, and Nero had Seneca, Burrus, Epaphroditus and Tigellinus. Domitian chose to forge ahead alone, even though he kept up the pretense of ministerial help. Ruinously overworked, wracked by anxiety and stress, he needlessly generated opposition. The harder he tried, the worse it got. By 94 Domitian had entered a dark period of severe stress and mental illness, and he responded to every problem by becoming ever stricter and less tolerant, striking down anyone who resisted his plans or orders.

It was a common story with the emperors. They started well and got worse with time. Yet Domitian accomplished a great deal: he rationalized and cleansed the imperial administration; he created a stable and beautiful coinage; he greatly strengthened the border defenses of the empire; and he systematically – and magnificently -- repaired the damaged city of Rome. In fact, by any measure, Domitian was one of the Empire's all-time greatest builders. He had a clearer understanding of economics and imperial finances than any of his predecessors or successors. Militarily, he was frustrated when his general Julius Agricola attempted with limited success to conquer Scotland in the mid-80s; he boldly brought that endeavour to a close. In Dacia Domitian himself took the field forcefully and competently but was unable to score many resounding victories. In the 90s he began to consider why, after centuries of successes, victories should now be denied to the Romans. Why?

It is certain that in Domitian's mind religious issues ultimately underlay the failures in military ventures. The traditional gods protected and empowered the Roman armies. Domitian sincerely believed that. The gods of Rome had always done so in the past. Not to acknowledge and propitiate those gods was "atheism" in the view of the state and of the emperor. Atheism made the gods angry. And now it made Domitian angry.

Christianity in particular was becoming all too clearly an issue in state security. Domitian was well aware that several of his relatives were Christians, and he knew a good deal about the faith which his own uncle and sister-in-law had espoused and which his brother had admired. He himself had no objection to Christianity, in fact was sympathetic in some degree. But Domitian was not a Christian. The recent Roman-Jewish War, not yet 20 years past in the year 90, showed what disasters could flow from worship of the Jewish God. That war must have demonstrated to most Romans that their gods were in fact more powerful than the God of the Jews and Christians. The Flavians readily accepted that idea, for it had been their war, and had been won by the gods of Rome. Those same gods had brought the Flavians to the throne of the Caesars. Especially since the reign of Titus, Judaism and Christianity had made inroads in Rome at the court and in the imperial family itself. But even that was the believers' own business, until Domitian was told that some Christians refused to make the patriotic token sacrifice to the state gods and showed a distinct lack of respect for the emperor's divine nature. Disrespect; sedition.

In 94 the emperor began to take a hard line directed explicitly against Jews and Christians, having by then identified "seditious" converts to Christ in his own court and in his own family. The emperor's cousin Titus Flavius Sabinus III and his wife Flavia Domatilla were closet Christians and Domitian knew that well enough, yet he had designated their two young boys Vespasian Jr and Domitian Jr as his successors. On Domitian's death, the imperial throne was to go to one or other of those young Christians.

Until the Flavian era, most Christians had somehow been able to come to terms with respecting the state gods. At the marketplace, one threw a few grains of incense on the tiny flame representing the genius of the emperor and the gods of the state. Most people, Christian or not, did this almost unthinkingly as a patriotic act. Only Jews were formally excused the act. But increasingly with time, Christians began denying the validity and power of the traditional gods of the empire. Some Christians did acknowledge the reality of the state gods but held that those gods were in subjection to the One God. Other Christians denied the very existence of the state gods; there was no Jupiter at all. In pagan eyes, that was atheism. It was also sedition. That was why the gods of Rome were offended and were now withholding their support from Rome's armies. These were not matters to be taken lightly, and Domitian did not treat them lightly.

The emperor personally investigated Jewish and Christian activities at his court and didn't like what he found. When court Christians were confronted with the order to make the customary offering to the state gods, most complied -- but not all. Worse, some of the most recalcitrant

Christians were Domitian's own relatives, who were high officials of the state. Domitian decided to apply the acid tests of loyalty to all his high-ranking officials – consuls, prefects, legates, procurators, praetors and his household officers: a token offering of incense to the Roman gods and verbal acknowledgement of his own supreme authority and divinity. He demanded a straight answer to the straight question of whether they accepted the emperor's divinity as the basis for their state duties. Not surprisingly (to us), some court Christians – even two Consuls -- failed both these tests. That was treason. A few close relatives of Domitian who were Christians and in the "August Family" declined to recognize the divinity of the emperor or to sacrifice to the state gods. Disrespect, sedition, atheism, treason and ingratitude. Domitian replied coldly, "There will be consequences."

He moved violently against those high Christian officials of his own family who refused to acknowledge him as a living god and to honour the traditional state gods. A man driven obsessively by principle, and a man now becoming mentally ill, Domitian was implacable. Even Consuls were arraigned and condemned: Acilius Glabrio, Marcus Clemens, Titus Flavius Sabinus III and the emperor's own nephew Titus Flavius Clemens were all executed between 93 and 95. They were all Christians, all top-level representatives of the state, and all relatives of the emperor. Wives and children were banished to distant places.

Most significant for history, Domitian's nephew Titus Flavius Clemens' two young sons Vespasian Jr and Domitian Jr had been designated as the emperor's successors. This family was now revealed as tainted with recalcitrant, seditious, "atheistic" disloyal Christians. When the senior Domitian turned against the Christians in his court, the boys and their mother were sent into exile (AD 95) and struck out of the imperial succession. Their Consul father was executed for treason. Christians would not after all ascend the throne of the empire. Only months later, Domitian himself died.

Thus, Rome almost got a Christian emperor before the end of the first century, but that was not to happen for another 220 years. In all

of Domitian's prosecutions the precise charges which were specified --
"novelties", "atheism", "Jewish practices" and "disrespect towards Roman
institutions" – make it abundantly clear that all these notables were
Christians -- as indeed they were. Christianity in just sixty years from
the crucifixion of Jesus had penetrated the highest circles of the imperial
rulership, and Jesus had very nearly conquered the Roman empire.

—

Domitian was assassinated in September 96. The plot was hatched by a
group of desperately terrified senators and others who felt – rightly or
wrongly – that their names were on one of the emperor's "death lists". The
conspirators included both Praetorian Prefects. Astoundingly, Domitian's
wife Domitia knew that her husband was going to be killed. For Domitia it
seemed a mercy killing of a suffering, dying man. The assassin Stephanus
was a young Christian ex-slave of that Christian consul Flavius Clemens
who had been put to death the year before. Feigning injury, Stephanus
came for an audience with Domitian with a bandaged arm that concealed
a dagger. After the first blow the wounded emperor reached for the dagger
which he kept under his seat cushion, but he found only a hilt. The blade
had been removed earlier by the conspirators. There was a fierce struggle
in which both Domitian and Stephanus died. Immediately there was a
huge sigh of relief in many quarters. Domitian was dead! The tyrant was
dead. The Senate promptly voted to damn his memory, and as Domitian
had no designated successor at the time, his successor was a doddering
66-year-old bureaucrat and lawyer of the Senate's own choice: Cocceius
Nerva. The Flavian dynasty was at an end.

   Yet Domitian had manifested some admirable qualities. He married
only once, to Domitia Longina. The imperial couple produced no surviving children, just a soon-dead infant "Divus Flavius", and possibly the
marriage was not always happy. Midway in the reign, when Longina
had an affair with the actor Paris, Domitian divorced her; but then he
forgave her and they resumed their marriage. The only other woman

Domitian ever loved was his probably-Christian niece Julia Domatilla, Titus' daughter. Possibly these two women were the only human beings for which he felt deep affection. Domitian showed many streaks of common sense and realism, right up to the end. After getting himself all worked up over the possibility of Davidic sedition in Palestine, and over Jewish-Christian sedition in general, he laughed off his personal audience with two members of the Royal House of David -- none other than peasant grandsons of Jesus' brother Jude. Domitian realized that these great-nephews of "the Messiah" were just poor harmless rustics and he waved them off home.

Domitian's reign was the longest since that of Tiberius sixty years earlier, and Domitian himself was by far the hardest-working emperor of the first century. Still, it ended badly. By 96 a reign of terror was beginning, directed mostly against the senatorial aristocracy. The emperor's behaviour became more and more abnormal. He had highly-polished stones installed as "mirrors" in the palace corridors so that no one could sneak up on him unobserved. Everyone around him was wondering "Will I be next? Is my name on a death list?" Even his wife was afraid. Finally, in the autumn of AD 96, the inevitable happened. Domitian was not assassinated in a vast senatorial uprising or by some would-be military successor to his throne, but by an ordinary young man, a former servant of the dead Christian consul, with a personal grievance and a concealed knife. Domitian's own wife made no move to stop events from taking their course.

Yet, as with Nero a generation before, certain parts of society lamented the passing of Domitian. He was always popular with the military and with people outside Italy, for his concept of empire was very much about partnership of all the parts of the realm, not just about Italy lording it over others. Though Domitian could be terrifying, he was intelligent, upright, an honest dealer and an outstandingly hard worker for the empire. Even a section of the Senate respected Domitian for his probity and his achievements.

At long last the Senate found its moment of opportunity. It was the first time the Senate had ever picked an emperor, and as Marcus Cocceius Nerva – himself a senator -- had no children and possessed a very long service record as bureaucrat and lawyer, he seemed a safe choice. Old Nerva had made his reputation as governor of Africa a half century back in the reign of Claudius. After that, he had laboured as a prosecutor on Nero's more difficult cases, and as a security and intelligence chief. He was an imposing figure, very tall and lean, with a long face. He was 66 years old when he became emperor.

Alas, his reign as emperor lasted less than twenty months (AD 96-98) during which he proved himself senile and incompetent in almost everything he undertook. During those months he tried to undo the stringent tyranny of Domitian but the result was chaos and anarchy as long-pent-up forces were let loose. Nerva was quick to reduce taxes but found that the empire's income then plummeted faster than economies could be made. Finally, though Nerva was the Senate's golden boy, he was much disliked by the military which was bearing the brunt of the expenditure reductions. The military had adored Domitian. To placate the army, a few months before his demise Nerva formally adopted a popular young general as his successor and heir. The man's name was Aelius Ulpius Trajan, who duly became the next emperor and ruled for twenty years (AD 98-117) over the empire at its peak.

CENTURY'S END

The first century was over, though the people of the time perceived no such milestone. For them the emperor Nerva's scant year and a half on the imperial throne ended in the eight hundred and fifty-first year since the founding of the city of Rome. For them our change of century was just Year 3 of Trajan. Few Romans could remember the celebration of Year 800 under Claudius, and fewer still would be alive to mark the Romans' Year 900 under Antoninus.

—

Yosef Ben-Mattityahu was born in AD 38 in Jerusalem, the son of illustrious and wealthy Pharisee parents. His father Matthias was from the highest order of Jewish priests and his mother was a direct descendent of the Hasmonean kings of Israel. Given the time and place, it is quite possible that Josephus' father had seen and heard Jesus a few years before Josephus' birth. It is even barely possible that he was the "Matthias" who replaced Judas Iscariot among the Apostles.

Never overcome by modesty, Josephus himself informs us in his books that he had a brilliant mind and received a first-class education. He was academically precocious and excelled in his studies of Judaic religion, law and history. We can only agree. In his twenties, Josephus was sent on a delicate mission to Rome to negotiate with emperor Nero for the release of several detained Jewish priests. That was just at the time (63 AD) that Saul was undergoing his first trial in Rome. Josephus' mission was successful. Among the ten illustrious men who had gone to plead a case with Nero were Alexas Helcias (a Temple Treasurer) and the just-retired High Priest Ishmael. When the group left Rome, successful in their own plea, Nero detained four of the delegation. The impetus for Josephus' mission was that the priests from Judaea were men of sufficient importance to warrant sending an envoy from Jerusalem to Rome in an effort to redeem them. Josephus was not acting for the Temple's prosecution in Saul's case before Nero. However, the remanded priests' presence in Rome had some connection with Saul's trial, as we have seen.

A year after Josephus' return to Jerusalem, the Roman-Jewish War started, and he was appointed as commander of the Jewish Galilean forces. After initial Jewish successes the Jewish garrison of Jotapata fell as the Romans assaulted in force. The survivors holed up in a cave and decided to commit mass suicide. According to Josephus, he was trapped in the cave with forty companions in the summer of 67. The Romans under General Vespasian demanded that the group surrender, but they refused. Instead, they drew lots and killed each other, one by one. The sole survivors of this process were Josephus and one companion, who thereupon surrendered to the Roman forces rather than commit suicide. Josephus may well have jiggered the lots. And maybe he jiggered the story too.

Josephus next claimed to have experienced a revelation from God that Vespasian would shortly become emperor. (In Jewish lore, it was Rabbi Yohanan Ben-Zakkai who had this revelation at this time.) After the prediction came true twenty months later, Josephus was released by Vespasian, who considered Josephus' gift of prophecy to be divine. He was not only released but became a client of the new Flavian emperors. According to his account, he even acted as the Romans' negotiator with the defenders of Jerusalem during the great siege of AD 70, in which his parents and his first wife perished.

The war over, Josephus went off to Rome in the entourage of the new emperor's son Titus, and became a Roman citizen, taking the Roman name Titus Flavius Josephus. Re-naming was standard practice for new Roman citizens. In addition to citizenship, he was granted property in conquered Judaea and a life pension. But Rome looked sweeter, so there he stayed. And there, under Flavian patronage, Josephus eventually wrote his works. **The Jewish War** published in AD 75 is ostensibly a definitive history but is factually unreliable since Josephus doctored his account to show a heavily pro-Roman and pro-Josephus bias. In AD 94 Josephus wrote **Jewish Antiquities**, a massive book recounting and explaining – for Greco-Roman readers – the history, culture and religion of the Jews. In Rome Josephus married a captured Jewish woman who soon left him. In his middle years he married a third time, to an Alexandrian Jewish woman by whom he had three sons, two dying young. However, Josephus divorced this third wife, and at 60 years of age married yet again, this time to an ethnic Jewish woman from Crete, a member of a distinguished family. They had a happy married life and produced two sons Flavius Justus and Flavius Simonides Agrippa. Josephus died at about age 65 in the opening years of the second century.

In Josephus' **Jewish Antiquities** we encounter political tales as seen by an insider who had access to imperial court records and to records of the Herodian royal court. The book provides the main non-Christian reports of the founders of Christianity which have survived from Antiquity. Josephus, in the course of his immense memoir, mentioned John the Baptizer, Jesus, James the brother of Jesus, and other prominent first-century figures. This remarkable passage appears in Josephus' Antiquities :

> Now there was about this time Jesus, a wise man, if it be permissible to call him a man; for he was a doer of wonderful works, a teacher of such men as receive the truth with pleasure. He drew over to him both many of the Jews and many Gentiles. He was [the] Christ. And when Pilate, at the suggestion of the principal men amongst us, had condemned him to the cross, those that loved him at the first did not forsake him; for he appeared to them alive again the third day; as the divine prophets had foretold these and myriad other wonderful things concerning him. And the sect of Christians, so named from him, is not extinct at this day. [Antiquities XX: 10]

This passage has been the object of vast research and controversy. Is it from Josephus' own hand? A Christian copyist's addition? The reluctant consensus of scholars is that Josephus did write something about Jesus but that "improving" Christian amendments to the text were made in Antiquity. There is no hard evidence one way or the other. Later in his text Josephus mentions James the brother of Jesus and alludes to "the aforementioned Jesus" – the paragraph above. Finally, Josephus in the same history describes the ministry and death of John the Baptizer, and the judicial murder in 62 of Jesus' brother James. These mentions in the 90s provide powerful confirmation of all those individuals' historical existence. Josephus had two special friends who provided information for his books and who allegedly vetted them for accuracy. One was St.

Saul's nephew Julius Archelaus in Rome; the other was none other than King Agrippa II in Palestine.

As our first century ends, the elderly Josephus is reminiscing at his writing-table. He's old and ill; he knows that his time is short. Josephus has a great deal to remember: standing trembling before Nero in the Great Palace, to plead for the lives of four Temple priests. He well recalls his grim years in the Roman-Jewish War, and his sordid surrender to the Romans. Soon after came his own unforeseen transformation from bearded priestly Jew to clean-shaven Roman citizen – he still recalls the feel of that first razor, and he has submitted to a razor ever since. His books. His histories. His friends at the court – especially Titus and Clemens. His Christian affiliations, much like those of his own patron Titus -- but neither of them was ever baptized. His long-time friend King Agrippa. His four wives – three passed on now, the other divorced. Now he himself is passing on; he can feel it day by day. Cataracts ended his reading and writing years ago. His own people, the Jews, revile him as a traitor and turncoat, but he still has friends among the Christians and the pagans. Nice people, the Christians; well, some of them. His court friends too have mostly passed on. His day is done. It's time to die. And anyway, who will remember him in years to come? Who will read his books?

—

"The Emperor is dead." In the hills above Ephesus in Asia Minor, a lean, tired old man hears the news and is perplexed. Which emperor? Domitian or Nerva? Time passes so quickly now… Old **John Bar-Zebediah** still meets regularly with a few students and friends, but it is more a social time than the sharp intellectual give-and-take of long ago. They accompany him to the services where he takes the bread and wine with long, long memories of that meal with his Lord so long ago. The Apostle John is the last survivor of the Twelve. He remains strong in the faith, happy with its spread through the world, conscious of much yet to be done. He is no longer clear-minded but weary, weary of the world, and in certain respects puzzled. The Lord's promised return still has not occurred. Much of contemporary Christianity (about which John knows a good deal) has diverged greatly from the teachings which as a young man he received at Jesus' feet; but he is convinced that God will guide the Church into right ways as it grows. And it is growing! Tens of thousands now confess the faith all across the empire and far beyond. John has done his part, in thought, in action, in teachings and writings. Very soon his body will die, he knows, and his soul will be taken up into heaven into the Presence of God, to see again his master and friend Jesus, and to find eternal repose with the other saints in Paradise.

His are the last apostolic memories. They have been gently extracted from him by his younger associates. That now means all his associates, for he himself has reached his 83rd year. Together they wrote a memoir of the Lord's doings. On a "good day" John can recall the day of his Call, seventy years before: how he leapt out of the boat right behind his brother and was welcomed into the tiny band. He was the youngest. As they walked away down the road, the hired men were cleaning up the gear for tomorrow's fishing. But John never went back, never even looked back. John can remember some of his Lord's miraculous healings; but he himself had never been much of a healer. He trained as a priest. He recalled the great Temple in its glory days, and the great City. The priests, the sacrificial animals. Crowds everywhere. All gone now. John also recalled those crisis days, leaning over on the dinner couch to whisper to Jesus, "Who?" after his Lord had said that one of the inner group would betray him. And burned into his memory were the twenty-four hours that followed: the arrest, trial, crucifixion. Bringing his sorrowing Aunt Mary home. Then the incredible excitement of Easter morning. He remembers all those glorious years growing the Movement, travelling the mission trails with Peter and gathering in the great Harvest. Then came the killing of his brother James and his period in hiding. Twenty years later, Jesus' brother James was killed, signalling the coming of the war that sent John off to Anatolia. After the war when the Temple was no more he stayed on in Ephesus, teaching a few students and seeing his memoir written... Bishop John had been most kind to him and treated him with that love which the bishop had received from him when the younger John first arrived in the Jesus Movement. He had spent two years on Patmos, banished there by Domitian, but finally he came back to Ephesus.

Yes, isn't it amazing? -- His own cousin Jesus was the Messiah of Israel, the divine Son of God, maybe even possessing the Wisdom of God itself, wrapped for a while in flesh to teach us of the divine love that young John had so strongly felt when travelling with Jesus. Now "Young John" –become old John -- is breaking out of his own failing wrap of flesh to join his Lord again.

"Nerva is dead, blessed father, and General Trajan is the new emperor", repeats his attendant. It is the news of today. Who is this new fellow? So many emperors had come and gone. So many years. "Come, O Lord, come quickly."

—

The widow **Domitia Longina** is also preparing for her end, her health in decline from some unknown affliction. She is only fifty. The doctors don't know what to do. But no matter, for she will recover and live for a further thirty years. Meanwhile, Domitia is no idler. Of course, she doesn't live in the Palace any longer. She continues to live well, and to manage her family's brickmaking business. It has many customers, some because of her illustrious past and her connections, some out of respect for her famous father General Corbulo, and some because her factory manufactures bricks of excellent quality. Each brick carries a stamp which proudly proclaims "Made in the factory of Domitia Longina, wife of the emperor Domitian". She still loves him when all the world reviles his memory, and she honours his memory in this way. Domitia leads a quiet life now, occasionally seeing her relatives and her many friends, but staying out of the limelight. In private moments she remembers her childhood and the father she adored. How like him her Domitian was. Both gone now.

In his royal city of Caesarea-Philippi in Palestine, **King Agrippa II** has just celebrated fifty years on the throne. His celebration is somewhat muted, for he has no close family, no children, few bosom friends. The Herodian family, mostly through its reckless in-breeding, has imploded and will soon disappear and pass from the world's stage into history. His sister Benenike passed away in AD 93, still full of energy and verve but ill from some unfathomable disease. "She", he thinks to himself, "and not me was the real end of Herod's line, for she possessed to the end the old King's decisiveness and verve and ambition." Agrippa cannot lay claim to those qualities, but he has been a great survivor and not a bad man. Now he senses that his time too has arrived; the pains, the attacks of dizziness, his unsteady legs, the feeling of death closing in. After that, the Romans will annex his kingdom; they have gently told him so.

A very few young Herodians attended Agrippa's celebration. Saul's sixty-year-old nephew Julius Archelaus was there with his beautiful daughter, "little Berenike" – now herself a widow. The name Berenike stirs old memories in the King. He falls silent. Agrippa's only nephew, Antonius Felix' "little Agrippa", perished long ago in the disaster at Pompeii. Most others are gone too. The family is vanishing and cannot be renewed. "Who's left? Let me see… not many…" The party is over. Then he says his evening prayers and retires, alone, to his bed.

Though none could know it, the empire is entering its best years – the second century AD. The new century would see capable, energetic and intelligent emperors exercise power, one after another: Trajan, Hadrian, Antoninus Pius, Marcus Aurelius. Each emperor would choose another man of merit and adopt him – just as Augustus had done at the beginning. Through their long and generally successful reigns, the empire would evolve and develop in internal peace. Its borders would be extended into Rumania and Ukraine, into Scotland (again) and down to the Persian Gulf in Iraq; horizons for trade would include India, China, Scandinavia and East Africa. In religion, paganism would become more complex and exotic as new cults spread across the Imperium Romanum (or "Romania" as people were already calling the empire). The Greeks would start calling themselves and all people of the empire, no matter what their ethnic origin, "Romans". Christianity would grow in popularity and intensity in the second century, and would find its organizational form, the Church. It would become, over the century, mainly a non-Jewish religion and it would begin to manifest an intellectual culture of its own. Christians would take to writing about their religion, and to engaging in complex verbal battles about it and in defence of it. Rival streams of belief contended as always, but now battles were fought through writings about the disputes and the areas of accord.

Christians would become very prickly about any acts that smacked of worshipping pagan gods and pagan emperors. The age of the martyrs was dawning. By the end of the second century, the new faith would have a rather long history of growth and would have acquired its own saints and heroes, its own scriptures, myths and legends.

Judaism, after the storms of the first century, would in the second suffer more great reverses through two more destructive Roman-Jewish Wars. Thereafter the Jews, defeated though not broken, would cease to be a major and pro-active force in the Empire. But the solidity of the Jewish faith was unimpaired and it entered a long period of scholarship and self-examination. The political place of Judaism would be taken – not yet by Christianity – by a clutch of "salvationist" pagan religions from the East. The old state cults were slowly weakening, failing to engage people's deeper emotions, but for the most part they carried along through the calm second century within any great upheaval. For almost everyone, the late 60s of the first century were a remembered nadir of fortunes, from which all aspects of life were still recovering to reach – for some -- a new zenith in the second century.

When the last Apostle – John Bar-Zebediah -- passed away in 100, his successors could look back upon a century whose great events and great personalities were already taking on heroic, legendary qualities. The oldest of those successors had some memories of the fantastic reign of Nero and of the ill-fated years that immediately followed; but no one alive had any personal memories of Caesar Augustus or Tiberius – or of John the Baptizer or Jesus. The whole early part of the first century had become the province of story and legend, and Roman historians were just beginning to narrate and interpret its exciting course.

—

On the first day of January in our year AD 101, the emperor Aelius Ulpius Trajan Augustus came with his Praetorians, his twelve lictors, members of the Senate and the priestly colleges, and the new Consuls, to ceremonially close the great bronze doors of the Temple of Janus in Rome. For the whole empire was at peace. The turbulent, amazing and indelible first century was over.

X
Notes

SOURCES

CENTURY is a "documentary novel" which rests on ancient writings that have survived the ages. Only a few written historical documents have survived, along with some works of art, buildings, monuments and assorted other objects. They are <u>our only primary sources of knowledge about that time.</u> Legends and fables have come down too, changed over time and in general unreliable as to whatever facts may underlie them. Many are best described as fiction. Written stories, histories, letters and the like may seem more solid fare, but they too may not have originally told the whole truth and in addition they have often been altered by copyists over the ages. That is particularly true of Christian writings originating in that far-off century.

Secular histories mostly promise greater confidence. A handful of great Roman histories for the period – by **Publius Cornelius Tacitus**, **Lucius Suetonius Tranquillus** and **Lucius Cassius Dio** – are all that has survived of that genre, and even then large parts of Tacitus' "Annals" and "Histories" have been lost. The history of **Velleius Paterculus** extends only up to AD 30 and thus is of limited value for the first century, but Velleius is one of only three history writers who were mature eye-witnesses to their times (the others were St Luke and Flavius Josephus).

Tacitus, Suetonius and Dio all wrote in the second century, long after the events they describe. All three were men of the wealthy senatorial class which was notably anti-monarchy, and thus all three writers had similar axes to grind. And they did grind them. Yet all three had been promoted to high positions in the empire – Tacitus ended up as a provincial governor, Suetonius as an official of the imperial court, and Cassius Dio as a tribune. Their accounts, sometimes more suspect biography than history, are focused on the emperors and their actions, and each narrative is heavily biased to the authors' common aristocratic/professional social viewpoint. The scandal-filled work of Suetonius was so resented at the imperial Court that the author's use of court records was curtailed after his "Augustus" and "Tiberius" chapters appeared.

Cornelius Tacitus offers, by general consensus, the most detailed, most balanced and most convincing account. His first work, "Histories", is mostly lost, but its detailed narrative for the civil wars of AD 68-70 has been preserved nearly complete. His later "Annals" of the reigns of the emperors Tiberius through Nero was not so highly prized in ancient times. If his namesake (and possible descendent) the third-century emperor Tacitus had not ordered the Annals re-copied and distributed, the work would certainly have joined the vanished 95% of ancient writings. Even so, only two partial copies survived to the Renaissance – one copy with its first two-thirds and its ending missing, and the other with its last two thirds missing. And that is all we have. How precarious has been the survival of ancient works! The "Annals" originally covered the reigns from Tiberius to Nero. The middle third of Tacitus' history, covering the whole reign of Gaius Caligula and the early years of Claudius, still remains lost to us, along with the concluding part of Nero.

Tacitus stuffs his historical writing with facts and details; he names names and often provides valuable context and details for the events he describes. Yet we must be on guard, for Tacitus is full of anti-emperor bias. His deplorable picture of Tiberius is not supported by the history of Velleius Paterculus who worked with that emperor and was very much his fan. Whom should we believe?

Suetonius Tranquillus' Lives of the Twelve Caesars, apart from the long section on Augustus, is little more than a tissue of gossip and racy rumour about the men who held the throne. Suetonius' work is closer to scurrilous biography than to reliable history. With the exception of Augustus and Vespasian, all twelve "Caesars" through to Domitian mostly come across as monsters of evil and depravity, and even factual accuracy and balance are sometimes sadly wanting in Suetonius.

Cassius Dio, the latest of the writers, presents a picture more favourable to the rulers, and often at variance with the stories of Tacitus and Suetonius who were nonetheless among his principal sources. The three historians by no means agree on the facts and circumstances of great events they mention. Yet behind it all lie real events, things that undoubtedly happened even if the historians sometimes mis-inform us -- or were themselves mis-informed -- about the causes, details and consequences of those events. For the first century, Tacitus remains the best source overall, despite his bias and other shortcomings.

Scholarly contention about the value and accuracy of New Testament writings from the first century will probably never abate. Yet some of these writings, especially **St. Luke's** Acts of the Apostles, have unique historical value on the first-century rise of Christianity, a topic unaddressed by other authors. Moreover, when Luke provides checkable details, he generally has them right.

Flavius Josephus (a.k.a. Yehosef Ben-Mattityahu) stands in a class by himself. A priestly Pharisaic scholar who became a Roman notable later in life, he has left several historical writings of which Jewish Antiquities and The Jewish Wars are best known. Both have survived the ages in complete form because they touch upon Christianity – earning them the privilege of being diligently re-copied over 1900 years. Much of the narrative is tendentious or irrelevant to modern interests, when not outright mendacious, but we learn a great deal about the first century only from Josephus, an eyewitness. He had access to Flavian court records and was a close friend of the Herodian King Agrippa II. He is our only worthwhile source for the fascinating family of Herod the Great and his kin.

The **rabbinical scholars** of the 200s and 300s wrote a great deal of commentary (Mishnah) on the Jewish scriptures, helping to clarify what issues existed in Judaism then. (The Talmuds had not yet been written.) Unfortunately, there was – apart from Justus of Antioch -- no adequate Jewish counter-blast to Flavius Josephus concerning the Roman-Judaean War. Josephus' account is often questionable but held the field in his time. Last and least, **Philo of Alexandria** wrote on the Jewish religion and on philosophy at mid-century. He was not a true historian but was a first-hand Jewish "Hellenist" witness to important historical events of the times of emperors Caligula and Claudius, as seen from the vantage point of the Empire's second city Alexandria in Egypt.

—

Facts often morph into tales and legends. The ancient writers present us with mixtures of these. We can accept as fact that a great fire broke out in Rome in July 64 AD, for all authors agree on it. In two historical accounts, the emperor Nero, who was at Antium (modern Anzio) at the time, rushed back to the city and energetically led fire-fighting and relief efforts. But popular legend has put him on his palace roof fiddling while Rome burns. What should we believe? Did Nero himself torch Rome? Our historians are of very different opinions. The conflagration was likely accidental. Nero's own palace and adjoining administrative buildings burned to the ground. There was some reason to suspect that the fire may have been arson by Christians; Tacitus reports that. That was certainly the government's conclusion at the time, and horrific mass punishments followed. But even then, rumours continued to be rife that the emperor himself had fired the city to clear space for his Golden House construction project. In an ancient world without "media", rumours always ran wild. Our historians didn't know the truth because no one at the time knew "the truth".

The same unreliability found in the secular Roman histories manifests itself even more strongly in religious writings. First-century Christians penned many narratives about the life and work of Jesus of Nazareth; many letters passed between Christian communities; and many other documents were authored, edited, altered and circulated. Where they agree, we think we possess facts. But where they disagree or are silent, legends quickly sprout. Some of these although manifestly false are still with us. The early Christian writings were never meant as historical records, nor as "holy scripture"; rather they were essays, letters, advice, memoirs, instructions and opinions about what followers of Jesus should believe and do. They are full of the credulous superstition, supposition and fervour of the age. Of the gospel writers, Luke was by far the most scrupulous historically, but even he has shortcomings. Copyists, revisers and later Christian theologians had no qualms about adding to or "correcting" manuscripts. Therefore, what we have received is certainly not exactly what was written by the original authors, and those authors themselves did not possess all the "facts". Similar remarks apply to first-century Jewish writings.

Although 90+% of all ancient writings have been lost, some ghosts of them have survived as quotations by later writers who still had access to them. These snippets, assuming they have been accurately quoted, give a glimpse of passages of lost or later-altered works. Later writers often commented on the works of their predecessors or gave information on the origins of those works – such as when, where and by whom they were written. Extensive exact quotations were frequently provided for reference. Mining for such information is tedious but it is often the only means of retrieving ancient writings and of glimpsing – maybe – something close to original versions. Of "later writers" three deserve mention in the context of Christian documents. **Clement of Alexandria** authored a big meandering work called <u>Miscellanies</u> near the end of the second century. It's an interesting pot-pourri of information and views on first-century and second-century events in the Church. **Eusebius of Caesarea** wrote his huge <u>History of the Church</u> in Greek in the early 300s, just as Christianity was triumphing in the empire. It quotes earlier authors very extensively and is full of "facts" along with much comment and mis-interpretation. Finally, **Saint Jerome** – the great scholar who created the Latin Vulgate Bible by his exacting translation from Hebrew and Greek source versions -- wrote a biographical anthology called De Viris Illustribis (Famous Men) in Latin at the end of the 300s, giving information about many first-century figures. Jerome's content is interesting for its frequent differences from Eusebius and other writers. Jerome was a mighty Latin scholar who worked from Bethlehem in Palestine and could fluently read Hebrew and Aramaic as well as Greek. A strange man of vast intellect, he has been undervalued.

A great many others, from the close of Antiquity right up to our present time, have written about aspects of the first century. The authors of the Middle Ages still had access to many works now lost, and especially the Byzantine commentators quoted extensively from such earlier works. From the Renaissance in the 1400s until the present, there have been re-discoveries of ancient writings long believed lost, and these discoveries continue. The first-century Didache was recovered in the 1870s, the Dead Sea Scrolls were discovered in the 1940s, and the Egyptian Nag Hammadi cache of books was a sensation of the 1950s and 1960s.

Those are the main primary written sources. Archaeology has filled in many gaps in knowledge through recovery of inscriptions, datable monuments, infrastructure and first-century letters, artifacts, technologies and cultural relics. The city of Pompeii near Naples, suddenly buried in AD 79 by the eruption of Mount Vesuvius, has preserved in death a detailed picture of life in that time and place. Excavations at hundreds of other sites have provided similar pictures of personal, civic and religious life in the early Roman Empire. Many monuments – from public notices to gravestones to building inscriptions –provide bits of useful information.

A great many writers and recorders who lived between the second century and our present century have tried to interpret the first century. While the Roman empire remained in being, these students of its history had many more resources than remain to us. We can only sigh with envy as Eusebius of Caesarea (ca AD 300) writes of browsing through old government archives and finding letters of famous people. He allegedly found even letters between Jesus Christ and Prince Abgar V, a ruler of Edessa. The Library at Alexandria with its hundreds of thousands of works must have been a heaven-on-earth for historical and literary researchers. Drawing from those institutions, later writers have recorded information which otherwise would be lost to us. The archives and the Library have vanished completely through fires and pillage, and finally in the seventh century from the deliberate and complete destruction wrought by the Muslim Arabs in Alexandria. Yet copies often did exist, so that bibliographically-based writing – criticisms, histories and essays – continued all through the thousand-year Byzantine Empire (to AD 1453) and through the Middle Ages and Renaissance in Europe, right into modern times.

NAMES AND PLACES

In the first century as today, everyone and every place had names. Moreover, like today again, people used "diminutives" and nicknames as simplified or abbreviated forms. In our day, Richard may be called Rich or Dick; James may be called Jim or Jimmy; Elizabeth may be called Liz or Beth or Betty or Betsey; and so on. Much the same thing went on in the first century. For example, in the New Testament we meet a Jewish-Christian couple Aquila and Prisca, but the latter – a woman -- is sometimes called Priscilla ("little Prisca"). St Saul's friend Silvanus appears sometimes as Silanus and maybe as Silas. Apollos may or may not be short for Apollonius, but Ariston is definitely the same name as Aristion. Cletus is certainly short for Anencletus (and also for Anacletus). Paul – formerly Saul -- himself remains a great enigma. This novel accepts Robert Eisenman's inspired idea that Paul/Saul was a known historical Herodian aristocrat, one of Herod the Great's grandsons no less.

Some ethnic names were very common then. Popular Jewish male names included Hananiah (=Annas or Ananias or Ananus), Eleazar (=Lazarus), Jesus (=Joshua, Yeshua), Joseph (=Joses, Yehosef), James

(=Jacob, Yakob), Jude (=Judas, Yehuda), John (Yohanan), Matthias, Saul, Simon (=Shimyon) and Zechariah. Judith, Martha, Mary (=Mariam, Mariamme), Anna (=Hannah), Salome and Susannah were common names for women. Somewhat surprisingly, in the first century none of Abraham, David, Moses or Ruth was a particularly common Judaean name. Many Jews bore Greek names, but this in itself carried no suggestion of foreignness. The most popular ethnic Greek male names in the eastern half of the empire probably included Alexandros, Antigonus, Antipater, Apollonios, Archelaus, Aristobulus, Demetrios, Epaphroditos*, Eumenides, Hermes, Hermas*, Narkissos* (=Narcissus), Nikanor, Philippos, Ptolemaios, Stephanos*, Sophokles, Stachys*, Simonides and Timaeus. The Greeks employed a very wide repertory of names. The asterisked names above somehow came to be considered as stereotypical slave names by Romans.

Ethnic Roman names were compounds, usually specifying first the **praenomen** – seldom used as a personal name -- and second the **nomen** or family name. From the first century BC an adjectival third name (the **cognomen**) was sometimes added, qualifying the other names. There were few praenomens to choose from: Aulus, Gaius, Titus, Lucius, Marcus, Servius and Publius were the commonest and accounted for more than half of all praenomens. What then were people actually called? The emperor Servius Sulpicius Galba was normally identified as Galba. The emperor whom we know as Nero was, at birth, Domitius Ahenobarbus. Only when their complete names are viewed do we realize that the Neronian-era characters whom we know as Seneca and Gallio were in fact brothers: Lucius Annaeus Seneca and Lucius Annaeus Gallio. And there was a third brother, Lucius Annaeus Serenus. Most male cognomens were just descriptive adjectives: Flaccus ("mild"), Florus ("exuberant"), Rufus ("red-haired"), Ahenobarbus ("auburn-beard"), Verus ("true"), Clemens ("merciful"), Felix ("fortunate"), Gemellus ("the twin"), Sabinus ("of Sabine origin") and so forth. Females also used cognomens, for example Blandina ("alluring"), Graecina ("of Greece") and Pulchrae ("beautiful"). There were hundreds and hundreds of cognomens in use.

A practical quirk of families, familiar also in modern times, was to give the father's name to a son and again to a grandson, and so on. This can make some identifications tricky. The Flavian imperial family was awash with Titus Flavius Sabinus males and Flavia Domitilla females.

In contrast to the Greeks, the Romans were quite protective of their name-forms as elements of their persona, yet they sometimes changed or added to their names. Emperor Gaius' name was never Caligula – that was a nickname – his name was Gaius Claudius Drusus Germanicus. His father had added "Germanicus" to his own name Nero Claudius Drusus after achieving military victories in Germany, and the Roman Senate allowed all his descendants to use it too. Adoption always involved a change of name; thus Domitius Ahenobarbus became Tiberius Nero Claudius when Claudius adopted him. He's our "Nero". Augustus' deceased wife Livia Drusilla was posthumously adopted into the Julian clan and became Julia Augusta. Especially, freed slaves would always add their former master's name to their own upon manumission. That could produce cross-cultural whoppers such as Julius Tiberius Abdes Panthera or Claudius Atroverix.

Ethnic names persisted everywhere in the empire, often partly Graecized or Romanized. A man called Piabi or Sebennos was sure to be Egyptian; the names Lug, Britomar, Cunorix and Isarn were common Gaulish tags. Germans used names which are still current: Hermann (romanized as Arminius), Alberich (=Albericus), Adelwolf (=Adolfus), Adelbert, Richard (=Ricardus) and so forth. North Africans might sport old Punic names such as Hanno or Mago, or they might have indigenous African names such as Bdennu or Yuba. Punic-derived names were also found in Spain: the name Annaeus mentioned above reflects an original Punic form Hanni as in "Hannibal". To the east of the empire were the Parthians with their own large storehouse of oriental names, some Graecized (for example Monobazes, Tiridates, Mithradates, Vologaeses) and others not (Farsi, Mani, Gundapur, Shapur).

It was all rendered even more untidy by rather permissive spelling practices. Even among fully literate Romans, the letters C and G sounded almost identical so that Caius=Gaius and Cnaeus=Gnaeus could often be interchanged acceptably. The emperor Vespasian's name was rendered "Ouespasianos" in Greek, reflecting its Latin pronunciation "Wespasianus". The Roman sounds "u" and "v" shared the same written letter V – something that riled emperor Claudius.

First-century **place names** were mostly different from modern names, although many modern ones have been derived from ancient tags. Some equivalents are shown in the maps.

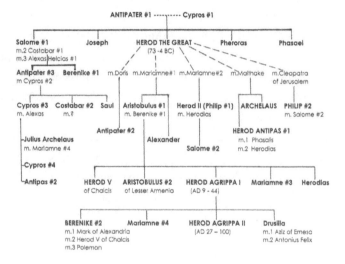

SIMPLIFIED CHART OF THE HERODIAN FAMILY
Rulers in boldface capitals, e.g. ANTIPAS
Wives and husbands in plain type, e.g. Polemon

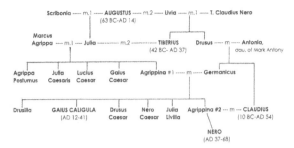

Scribonia ---- m.1 ---- **AUGUSTUS** ---- m.2 ---- Livia ---- m.1 ---- T. Claudius Nero
(63 BC-AD 14)

Marcus
Agrippa ---- m.1 ---- Julia ---------- m.2 ---------- **TIBERIUS**   Drusus ---- m ---- Antonia,
(42 BC- AD 37)   dau. of Mark Antony

Agrippa   Julia   Lucius   Gaius   Agrippina #1 ---- m ---- Germanicus
Postumus   Caesaris Caesar   Caesar

Drusilla   **GAIUS CALIGULA**   Drusus   Nero   Julia   Agrippina #2 --- m --- **CLAUDIUS**
(AD 12-41)   Caesar   Caesar Livilla   (10 BC-AD 54)

NERO
(AD 37-68)

SIMPLIFIED CHART OF THE JULIO-CLAUDIAN FAMILY
Emperors in bold capitals e.g. CLAUDIUS

Titus Flavius ------- m ------ Vespasia Polla
Sabinus #1

Julia Petronilla --- m --- Titus Flavius   **VESPASIAN** --- m --- Domitilla #1   Flavia
Sabinus #2   (AD 9-79)
(AD 7-69)

Domitilla #2   **TITUS** --m.2 -- Marcia   **DOMITIAN** -- m -- Domitia
(AD 39-81)   Furnilla   (AD 50-96)   Longina

Flavius Clemens   Titus Flavius
m. Flavia Domitilla   Sabinus #3 ------------- m ---------- Julia Flavia
(AD 57-95)

Vespasian #2   Domitian #2
(fate unknown)   (fate unknown)

SIMPLIFIED CHART OF THE FLAVIAN FAMILY
Emperors in boldface capitals e.g. DOMITIAN

The Great Families

Bibliography

Readers who want to learn more about the first century are directed to the following books, articles and URLs which deal with the whole spectrum of topics touched on in CENTURY.

AUTHOR	TITLE	PUBLISHER	YEAR	ISBN
Akenson, D. H.	Saint Saul	McGill-Queen's U Press, X+346 pp	2000	0-7735-2090-2
Alston, Richard	Aspects of Roman History (2nd Ed)	Routledge, XV + 455 pp	2014	978-1-315-87166-0
Ando, Clifford (Ed.)	Roman Religion	Edinburgh Univ. Press, XVII+393 pp	2003	0-7486-1565-2
Aries, Philippe & Georges Duby	A History of Private Life; From Pagan Rome to Byzantium	Harvard Press. IX + 670 pp	1992	0-674-39974-9
Balsdon, J. P. V. D.	The Emperor Gaius (Caligula)	Oxford Univ. Press, XIX+243 pp	1934	
Barnes, Arthur S	Christianity at Rome in the Apostolic Age	Greenwood Press, 222 pp	1938	
Barnstone, Willis	The Other Bible	Harper & Row, 742 pp	1984	0-06=250030-9

AUTHOR	TITLE	PUBLISHER	YEAR	ISBN
Barrett, Anthony	Caligula [2nd edition]	Routledge. XXIII + 384 pp	2015	978-0-415-65844-7
Barrett, Anthony, E. Fantham, J. Yardley	The Emperor Nero	Princeton University Press. XV+300 pp	2016	978-0-691-15651-4
Beard, Mary	SPQR: A History of Ancient Rome	Liveright Publishing. 606 pp	2015	978-0-87140-423-7
Boardman, John; Jasper Griffin & Oswyn Murray	Oxford History of the Classical World	Oxford Univ. Press, VII + 882 pp	1986	0-19-872112-9
Boatwright, Mary T.	Peoples of the Roman World	Cambridge Univ. Press, XVIII + 241 pp	2012	978-0-521-54994-3
Bond, Helen K.	Caiaphas	Westminster John Knox Press, 220 pp	2004	0-664-22332-X
Boyle, A.J. & Dominik W.J.	Flavian Rome	Brill, 754 pp	2003	90-04-11188-3
Bruce, F.F.	The Canon of Scripture	InterVarsity Press, vvv pp	1988	
Buckley, E. & Dinter, M.T.	A Companion to the Neronian Age	Wiley-Blackwell, XVII + 486 pp	2013	978-1-4443-3272-8
Carcopino, Jerome	Daily Life in Ancient Rome	Penguin Books, 365 pp	1941	
Champlin, Edward	Nero	Belknap Press/ Harvard U P, 346 pp	2003	0-674-01822-2
Conzelmann, Hans	History of Primitive Christianity	Abingdon Press, 190 pp	1973	0-687-17251-9
Crossan, John Dominic	The Historical Jesus	HarperSanFrancisco, XXXIV + 505 pp	1991	0-06-061607-5

AUTHOR	TITLE	PUBLISHER	YEAR	ISBN
Dunn, James	Beginning from Jerusalem	William B. Eerdmans, 1347 pp	2009	978-0-8028-3932-9
Dunn, James D.	Christianity in the Making I: Jesus Remembered	Wm. B. Eerdmans, XVII + 1019 pp	2003	0-8028-3931-2
Var. Editors	Fathers of the Church, Volume 1	Catholic University of America Press	1947	
Var. Editors	Early Christian Writings	Penguin Books, 199 pp	1968	0-14-044475-0
Edmundson, George	The Church in Rome in the First Century	http://www.ccel.org/edmundson/church	1913	
Eisenman, Robert	Dead Sea Scrolls and the First Christians	Castle Books Ltd, 449 pp	2004	0-7858-1885-5
Eisenman, Robert	James the Brother of Jesus	Penguin Books, XXXVI + 1074 pp	1997	0-14-02.5773-X
Esler, Philip F. (editor)	The Early Christian World (Volume 1)	Routledge. XXVI + 689 pp	2000	0-415-16496-6
Eusebius Pamphyli	History of the Church	Penguin Books, 435 pp	1965	
Ferguson, John	The Religions of the Roman Empire	Cornell University Press, 296 pp	1970	0-297-78325-4
Filson, Floyd V.	A New Testament History	SCM Press, XI + 428 pp	1965	
Flavius Josephus	Complete Works (tr. Wm. Whiston)	Kregel Publications, XXI + 770 pp	1963	no ISBN
Foster, Herbert Baldwin	Dio's Rome (Books 61-67)	Pafraets Book Co. (Troy, NY)	1905	

AUTHOR	TITLE	PUBLISHER	YEAR	ISBN
Foster, John	After the Apostles	SCM Press, 128 pp	1951	no ISBN
Freeman, Charles	A New History of Early Christianity	Yale University Press, XX + 377 pp	2009	978-0-300-12581-8
Frend, W. H. C.	The Rise of Christianity	Darton, Longman, Todd, XVII+1022pp	1984	0-232-51314-7
Gardner, Jane F.	Being a Roman Citizen	Routledge. 244 pp	1993	0-415-00154-4
Goodman, Martin	The Roman World 44 BC-AD 180 [2nd Edition]	Routledge, XVIII + 413 pp	2012	978-0-415-55979-9
Grabbe, Lester	Second Temple Judaism	T & T Clark, 150 pp	2010	978-0-567-55248-8
Grant, Michael	Jesus	Weidenfeld & Nicolson, 261 pp	1977	0-297-77134-5
Grant, Michael	Nero	Weidenfeld & Nicolson, 272 pp	1970	SBN 297-00101-9
Grant, Michael	History of Rome	Charles Scribner's Sons, XXI + 537 pp	1979	0-684-15986-4
Grant, Michael	The Army of the Caesars	Weidenfeld & Nicolson, XXXIV + 365 pp	1974	0-297-76711-9
Grant, Michael	The Jews in the Roman World	Dorset Press, XI + 347 pp	1984	0-88029-025-0
Grant, Michael	The Twelve Caesars	Weidenfeld & Nicolson, XI+282 pp	1996	0-297-81724-8
Grant, Michael	Greeks & Romans	Weidenfeld & Nicolson, IX+197 pp	1992	0-297-82071-0

AUTHOR	TITLE	PUBLISHER	YEAR	ISBN
Green, Bernard	Christianity in Ancient Rome	T & T Clark, 258 pp	2010	978-0-567-03250-8
Gruen, Erich S.	Diaspora	Harvard Univ. Press, 386 pp	2002	0-674-00750-6
Hengel, Martin	The Zealots	T & T Clark, XXIV + 487 pp	1989	0-567-29372-6
Hoehner, Harold	Herod Antipas	Cambridge Univ. Press, XVI + 437 pp	1972	0-521-08132-7
Holland, Tom	Dynasty	Doubleday, XXVI + 482 pp	2015	978-0-385-53784-1
Horsley, Richard	Bandits, Prophets & Messiahs	Trinity Press Internat., 272 pp	1999	1-56338-273-3
Jackson-McCabe, M. (ed)	Jewish Christianity Reconsidered	Fortress Press, X + 389 pp	2007	978--0-8006-3865-8
Jewett, Robert	A Chronology of Paul's Life	Fortress Press, VIII + 160 pp	1979	0-8006-0522-5
Jones, A. H M.	The Herods of Judaea	Oxford, XIV + 261 pp	1967	
Jordan, Ruth	Berenice	Barnes & Noble, XX + 248 pp	1974	06-493402-0
Keay, S. J.	Roman Spain	Univ. of California Press, 240 pp	1988	0-520-06380-5
Kelly,Christopher	The Roman Empire: A Very Short Introd'n	Oxford Univ. Press, 153 pp	2006	978-0-19-280391-7
Kirschenbaum, Aaron	Sons Slaves & Freedmen in Roman Commerce	Magnes Press (The Hebrew University), XIII + 227 pp	1987	0-8132-0644-8

AUTHOR	TITLE	PUBLISHER	YEAR	ISBN
Koester, Helmut	Ancient Christian Gospels	Trinity Press Internat., 448 pp	1990	0-334-02459-5
Laes, Christian	Children in the Roman Empire	Cambridge Univ. Press, XV + 334 pp	2011	978-0-521-89746-4
Lampe, Peter	Christians in Rome in the First 2 Centuries	T&T Clark International	2003	0-567-08050-1
Levick, Barbara	Vespasian	Routledge, XXXII+ 310 pp	1999	0-415-16618-7
Levick, Barbara	Claudius	B.T. Batsford Ltd, XVI + 256 pp	1990	0-7134-5209-9
Levick, Barbara	Vespasian (2nd Edition)	Routledge	2017	978-0-415-70889-0
Madsen, Jasper Majborn	Eager to be Roman	Duckworth & Co, IX + 166 pp	2009	978-0-7156-37531
Maier, Paul	The Flames of Rome	Doubleday & Comp., 443 pp	1981	
Maier, Paul	The First Christians	Harper & Row, 160 pp	1976	0-06-065399-X
Matyszak, P & Berry, J	Lives of the Romans	Thames & Hudson, 304 pp	2008	978-0-500-25144-7
Millett, Martin	Roman Britain	B T Batsford, 144 pp	2005	0-7134-8951-0
M. Mitchell & F. Young, eds	Cambridge History of Christianity Vol. 1 Origins to Constantine	Cambridge Univ. Press, XLVII + 740 pp	2006	978-0-521-81239-9
Morgan, Gwyn	69 A.D.	Oxford Univ. Press, XIII + 322 pp	2006	0-19-512468-5

AUTHOR	TITLE	PUBLISHER	YEAR	ISBN
O'Connor, Daniel	Peter in Rome	Columbia University Press, 242pp	1969	
Osgood, Josiah	Claudius Caesar	Cambridge Univ. Press, 357 pp	2011	978-0-521-70825-8
Pagels, Elaine	The Gnostic Gospels	Vintage Books, 214 pp	1981	0-394-74043-3
Perowne, Stewart	The Later Herods	Hodder & Stoughton, XVI + 216 pp	1958	
Potter, D.S. & Mattingly, D.J.	Life, Death and Entertainment in the Roman Empire	Univ. Michigan Press, XIV+353 pp	1999	0-472-10924-3
Raven, Susan	Rome in Africa	Evans Brothers Ltd, XVI + 191 pp	1969	0-237-44357-0
Reader's Digest	Jesus and his Times	Reader's Digest Assoc, 336 pp	1987	0-89577-257-4
Alexander Roberts & Jas. Donaldson (eds.)	Anti-Nicene Fathers (Vol. VIII)	T&T Clark / Wm B Eerdmans [reprint]	1995	0-8028-8094-0
Roberts, Alexander & Jas. Donaldson (eds.)	The Ante-Nicene Fathers (Vol. 1)	T&T Clark,VIII + 602 pp	1885	0-567-09374-3
Ruepke, Joerg	Religion of the Romans	Polity Press, XV + 350 pp	2007	978-07456-3015-1
Scullard, H. H.	From the Gracchi to Nero	University Paperbacks, XII + 460 pp	1963	
Sevenster, J. N.	Paul and Seneca	E. J. Brill, 251 pp	1961	
Shotter, David	Rome and her Empire	Longman, X + 453 pp	2003	0-582-32816-0

AUTHOR	TITLE	PUBLISHER	YEAR	ISBN
Skarsaune, Oskar	In the Shadow of the Temple	InterVarsity Press, 455 pp	2002	0-8308-2670-X
Smith, Vincent A.	The Early History of India	Atlantic Publishers,	1999	81-7156-618-9
Sorensen, Villy	Seneca	Canongate, 352 pp	1984	0-96241-030-4
Southern, P.	Domitian : Tragic Tyrant	Routledge, VIII + 164 pp	1997	978-0-415-16525-7
Staniforth & Louth	Early Christian Writings	Penguin Books, 199 pp	1987	0-14-044475-0
Streeter, Burnett	The Primitive Church	Macmillan Co., XIII + 323 pp	1929	
Suetonius, Gaius	Lives of the Twelve Caesars	Wordsworth Editions, 364 pp	1997	1-85326-475-X
Sutherland, C. H.	Roman History and Coinage 44BC - AD69	Clarendon Press, XIII + 131 pp	1987	0-19-872124-2
Tabor, James D.	The Jesus Dynasty	Simon & Schuster, XIII+363 pp	2006	0-7432-8723-1
Tacitus, Cornelius	The Histories	Penguin Books. 316 pp.	1964	
Tucker, T. G.	Life in the Roman World	Macmillan Co., XIX + 453 pp	1929	
Turcan, Robert	The Cults of the Roman Empire	Blackwell, XIII + 399 pp	1996	0-631-20046-0
Velleius Paturculus	The Roman History (Yardley/Barrett)	Hackett Publishing	2011	978-1-60384-591-5

AUTHOR	TITLE	PUBLISHER	YEAR	ISBN
Vermes, Geza	Christian Beginnings	Penguin Books, XVI + 273 pp	2012	978-0-141-03799-8
Wacher, John	The Roman Empire	J.M. Dent & Sons Ltd, XI + 314 pp	1987	0-460-04331-5
Walter, Gerard	Nero	George Allen & Unwin, 334 pp	1957	0-8371-9302-8
Wellesley, Kenneth	The Long Year AD 69 [2nd edition]	Bristol Classical Press,	1989	1-85399-049-3
Wilken, Robert L.	The Christians as the Romans Saw Them	Yale Univ. Press, XIX + 214 pp	1984	0-300-03066-5
Wilson, Ian	Jesus : The Evidence	Weidenfeld & Nicolson, 208 pp	1984	8014-0567-x
Wiseman, F. J.	Roman Spain	G. Bell and Sons Ltd, VI + 232 pp	1956	
Wright, Esmond (gen editor)	The Ancient World	Hamlyn, 319 pp	1979	0-600-30323-3
Zissos, Andrew (editor)	A Companion to the Flavian Age of Imperial Rome	Wiley-Blackwell, XXII + 602 pp	2016	978-1-44436-009

CPSIA information can be obtained
at www.ICGtesting.com
Printed in the USA
LVHW09s1930300918
591948LV00001B/2/P